TECHNIQUES AN

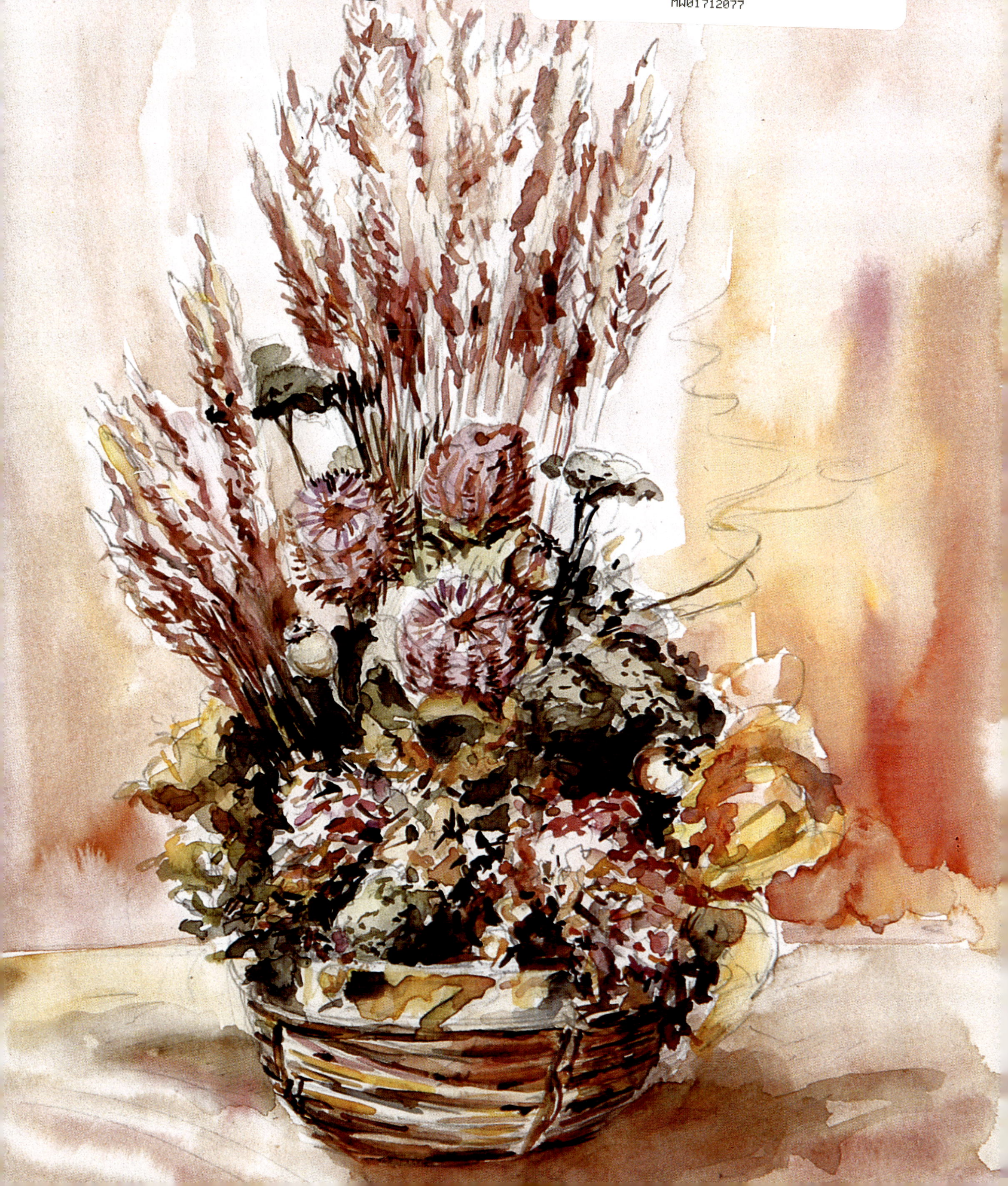

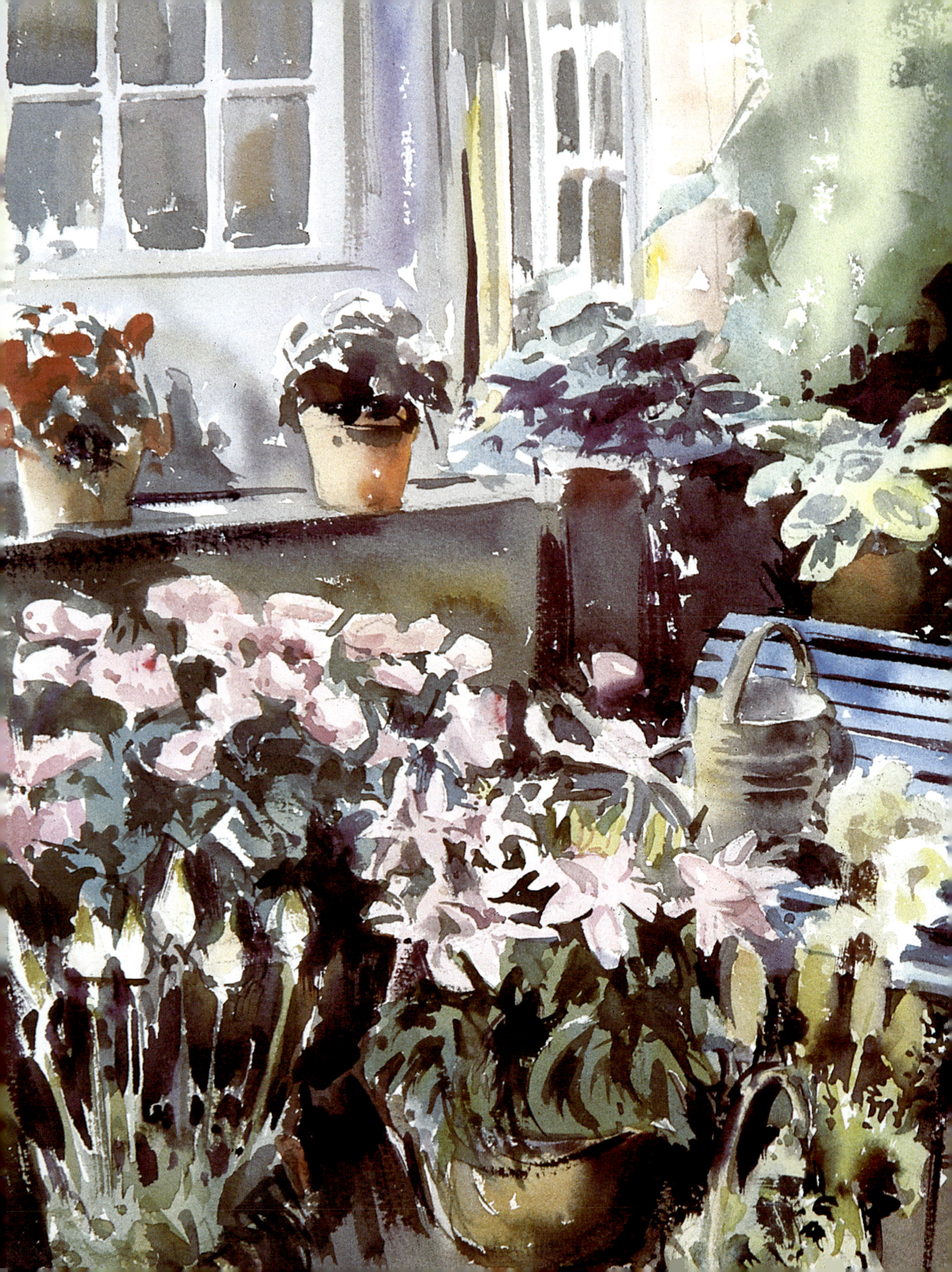

TECHNIQUES AND EXERCISES

Watercolor PAINTING

FLOWERS

JOSÉ M. PARRAMÓN

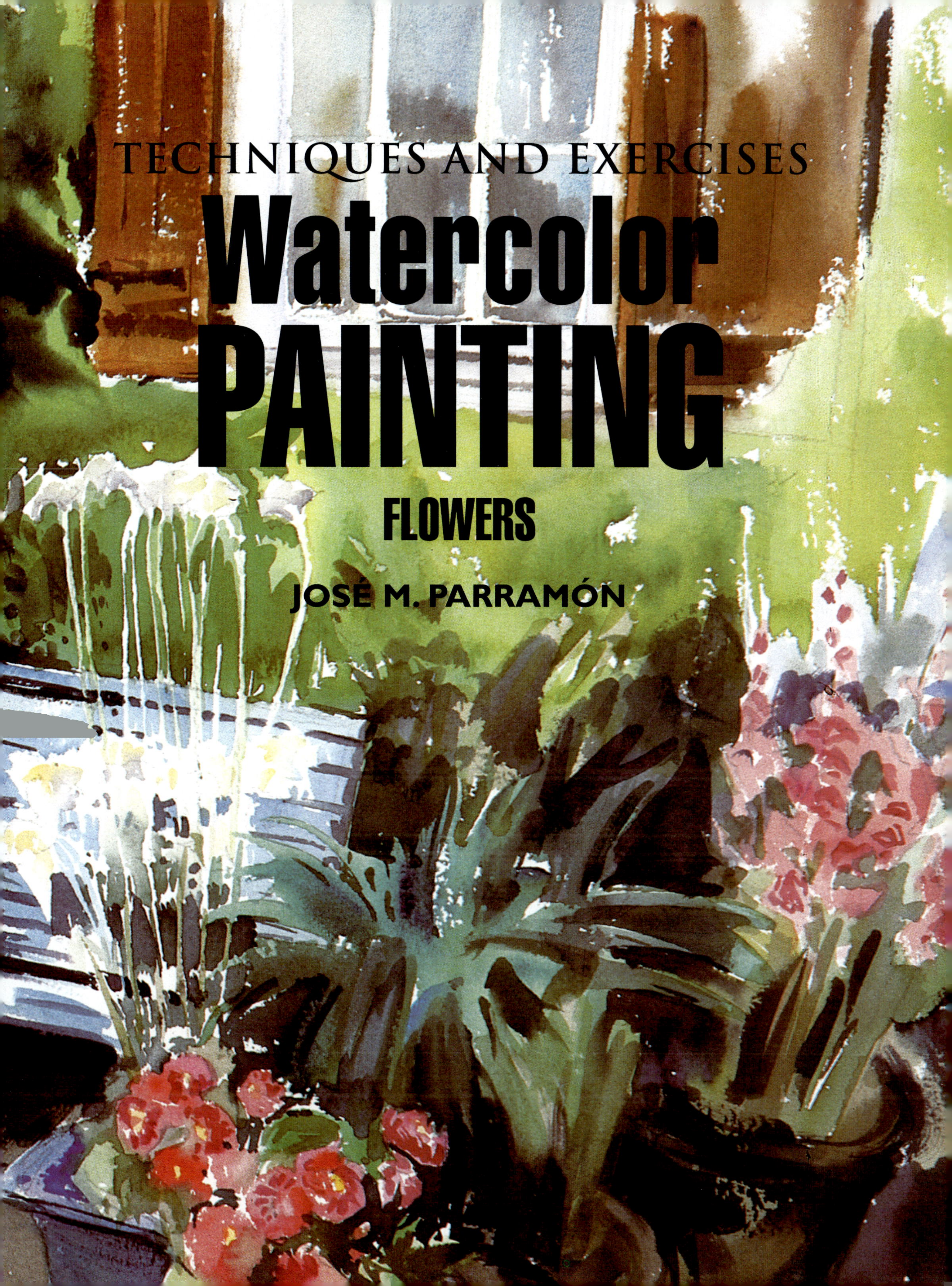

The guide sheets at the back of the book are numbered in the margin and designed to be cut with paper cutter.

Project director: José M. Parramón Vilasaló
Texts: José M. Parramón and Gabriel Martín
Publishing, layout and design: Lema Editions, S.L.
Cover: Award
Publishing director: José M. Parramón Homs
Editor: Victoria Sánchez
Coordination: Eduardo Hernández
Original title: "Pintando Flores a la Acuarela"
Translated by: Mike Roberts and Brian Menzies

Photographics and photosetting: Novasis, S.A.L.

First edition: September 1999

Published and distributed by Ediciones Lema, S.L.
Gran Via de les Corts Catalanes, 8-10, 1° 5ª,
08902 Hospitalet de Llobregat (Barcelona)

ISBN 84-89730-97-0
Printed in Spain

Index

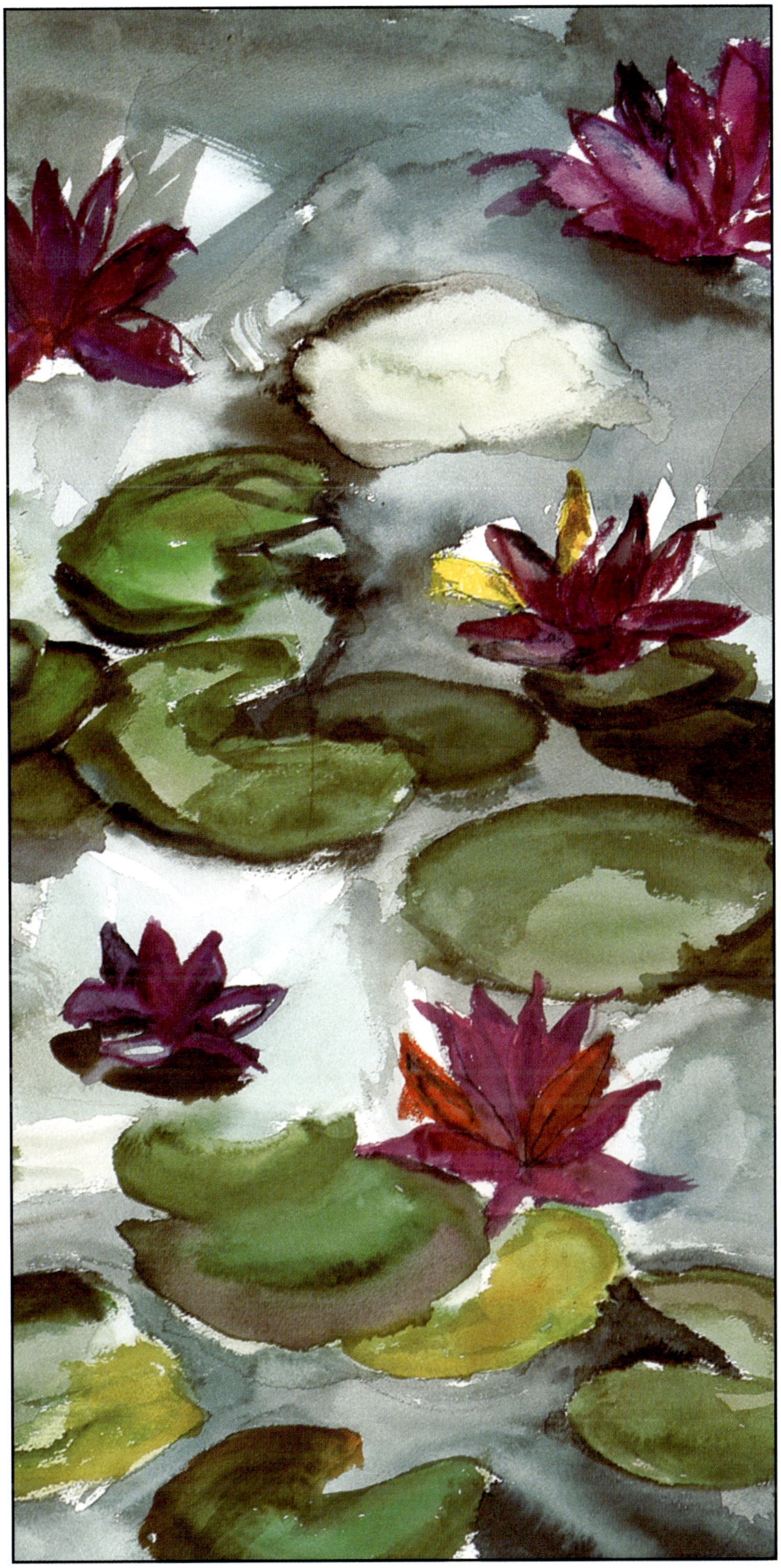

1

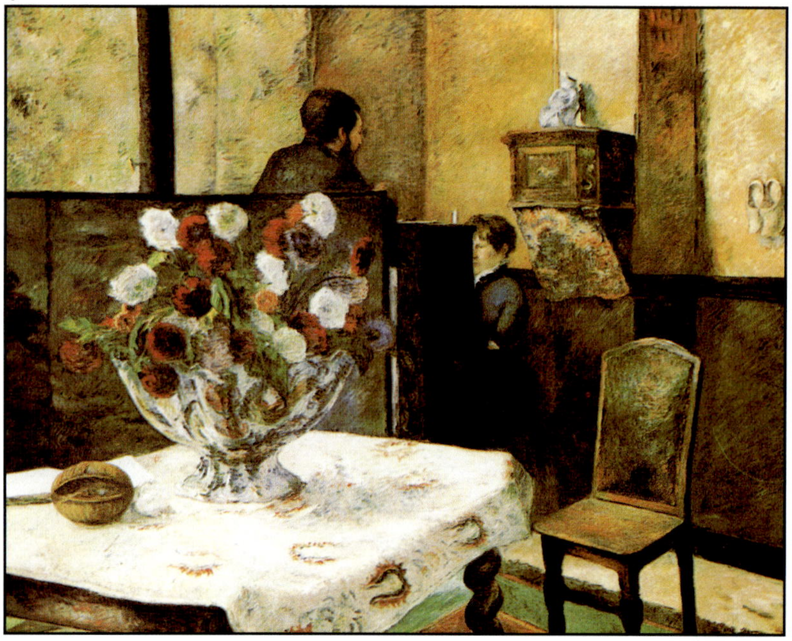

Fig. 1. **Interior** *by the painter Paul Gaughin (Nasjonalgalleriet, Oslo). A floral subject does not have to appear on its own, but can be placed in a context (i.e. forming part of an interior scene). Although they appear along with other elements, there is no doubt that the flowers are the centre of attention in this picture.*

Fig. 2. **Flowerpot** *by Ignacio Zuloaga (private collection). Flowers are a versatile theme that can be adapted to any technique, from tenuous washes to thick layers of color.*

2

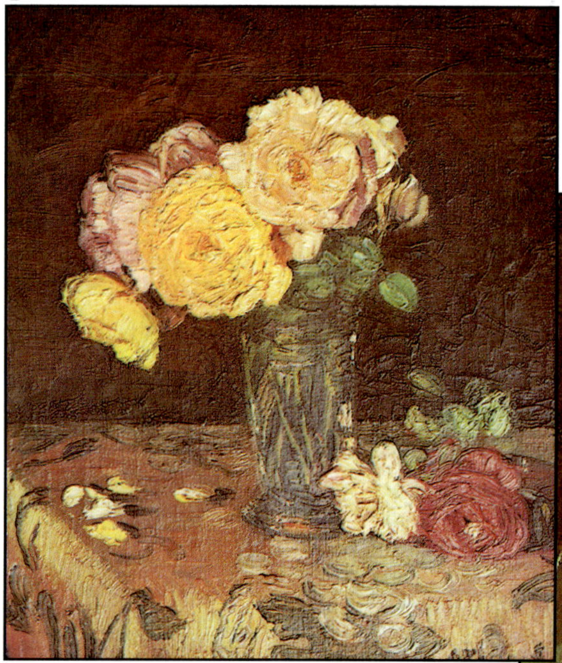

3

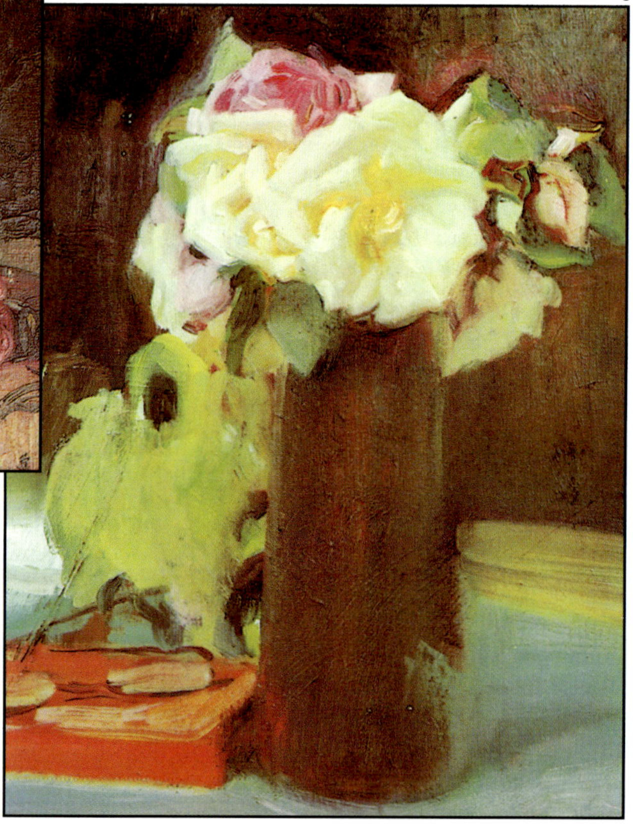

Fig. 3. **Flowerpot** *by Joaquín Sorrolla (Museo Sorrolla de Madrid). By mastering painting techniques, an artist can expertly recreate the texture of materials. Compare the velvety appearance of the petals of the flowers with the uneven ruggedness of the ceramic vase.*

Introduction

Of all the objects that man is surrounded by, flowers have always had an important role to play. Small objects that man has stolen from nature and manipulated for his own pleasure. We are seduced by their fragrance and by their beautiful shapes, colors and textures. They are able to inspire poetry, bring out our most passionate feelings, and free the artistic world from the ambiguities of academic knowledge. Because the greatest attraction of flowers, apart from their enchanting forms, is how they create such a veritable explosion of color that can transform the greyness of a winter landscape into the brilliant festival of color that celebrates the arrival of spring. Just as Henri Matisse expressed when he wrote that "*the dominant tendency of color should serve as the greatest method of expression. The expressive side of color prevails over me like an impulse*".
That expressive generosity is why flowers are such a popular theme with beginner artists. And neither is it a theme that necessarily requires any special artistic skills.
Artists have always wanted to reproduce nature and find that flowers are the greatest manifestation of its splendor. Emil Nolde, during his frustrated struggle to recreate the vibrant colors of flowers, wrote that "*as I painted, I wanted the colors, through myself as the painter, to appear on the canvas with the same kind of intensity that nature herself has created her figures, like minerals and crystals are formed, as algae and moss grow, like flowers should be brought forth to bloom beneath the rays of the sun*".
But it is not only nature that is flooded with flowers. They also appear in more human surroundings, forming an integral part of our cities in beautiful flower beds that cover the lawns of parks, in florists' lavish shop windows, in colorful flowerpots that adorn balconies and as beautiful centrepieces on the tables of thousands of homes.
Arranging flowers, having grown and cut them in one's own garden, is a highly satisfying and enriching experience. Because flowers, apart from bringing beauty and decoration into any household, are also, without a shadow of a doubt, one of the most painted still life themes there are. Floral still lives are as important a theme as any other and are also an excellent subject for introducing oneself to the use of color and composition. The artist selects the flowers and arranges them as he likes, and has as much time as he needs at his disposal and does not have to compete with changing weather conditions. Everything works in the artist's favor.
Floral painting, just like any other genre, demands a fair amount of natural ability coupled with the right practical and technical expertise. It is the latter two that you shall be able to learn as you read this book, and then you can use your newfound knowledge along with your own natural talent to put each of the exercises into practice. When I refer to natural talent, I am not only speaking about skill and dexterity, which are undoubtedly important traits for painting successful pictures, but more importantly about patience and constancy. Some of the exercises are accompanied by guide sheets that have been specially designed so that you can practice the exercises along the same lines as the original artist without too many complications. From the uncountable number of possibilities offered by floral painting, I have chosen a considerable variety of practical examples and styles used by a selection of professional artists. This book also includes several suggestions and hints that will help you to achieve more satisfactory results. However, in order to paint this genre, you will need an unconditional love for nature and should spend every moment admiring its every beauty. Never forget that flowers are one of the most beautiful things that we shall ever set our eyes upon, and by painting them, we are doing no more than prolonging the time that we have them before us, in the hope that, no matter how beautiful they might be, they shall never die.
All that is left is for me to hope that you enjoy using this book, and that your work is nothing less than a pleasure.

Gabriel Martín

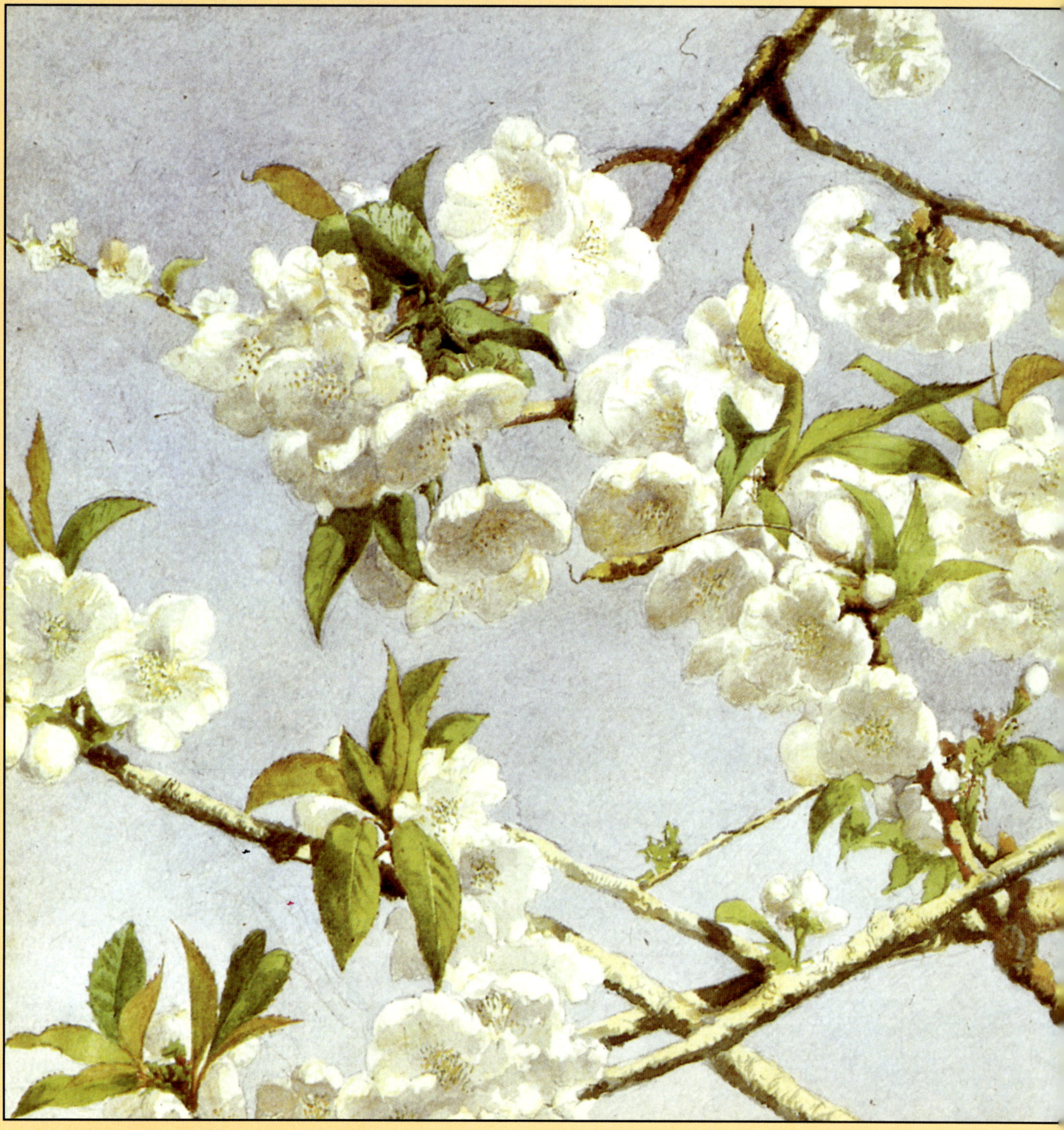

Fig. 4. ***Apple blossom*** **by John William Hill (Brooklyn Museum). Here is a beautiful floral composition, in which the clearly oriental influence brings the beautiful Japanese Ukiyo-e engravings to mind.**

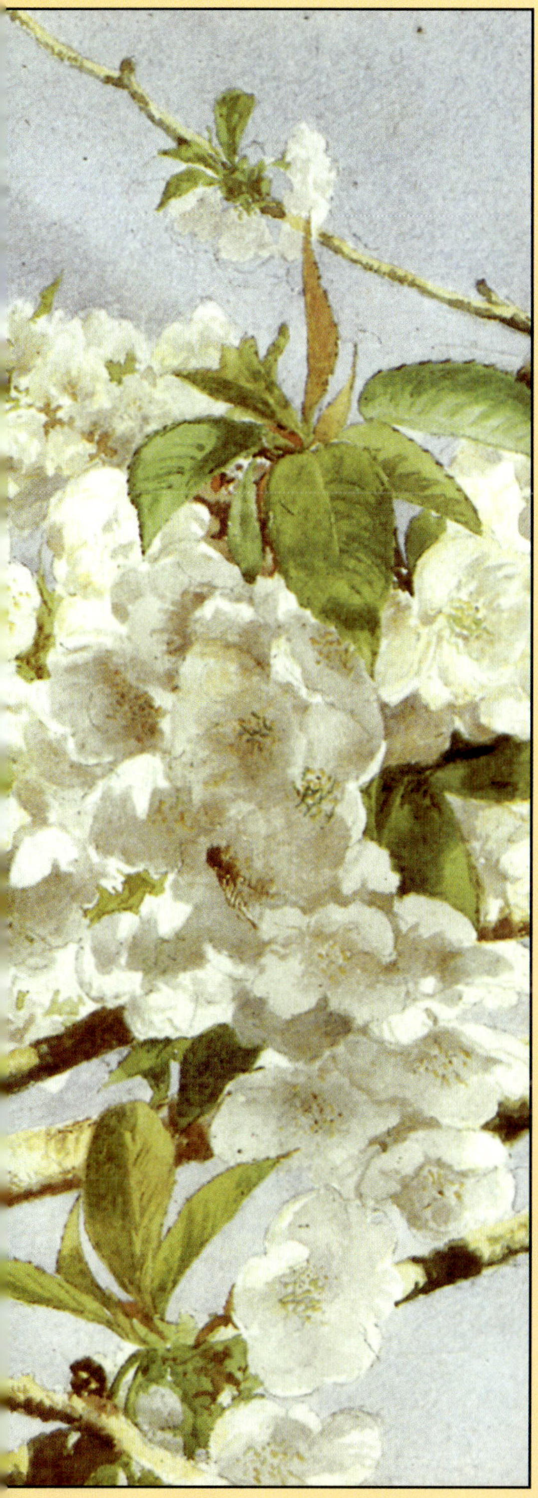

FLOWER PAINTING AND THE GRAND MASTERS

John Ruskin, the English artist and critic, once said that "few artists are capable of recapturing the fragile nature of flowers". He was quite right. Although flowers provide the artist with a never-ending source of inspiration, history has provided us with very few people who have been able to do justice to a genre that has so often been considered a minor category. The artists that are discussed on the following pages are a selection of those who have made the most outstanding contributions to floral art. You will find a definitive gallery of some of the greatest masterpieces, along with comments on the composition, interpretation and colors used by these grand masters in their works of floral art.

Flowers in Oriental Art

The painting of flowers, birds and animals reached its heyday in China in the so-called Song period between the 11th and 13th centuries, when the social status of the artist was transformed from one of a simple artisan to that of a cultured painter.

Chinese floral art was first used to illustrate poetry, but those illustrations gradually became an artform in their own right, an aesthetic exercise in recapturing the true spirit and essence of flowers and plants. The idea of flower painting as an expression of cultural spirit had been born.

To satisfy this spiritual need, a large amount of training was necessary to learn the correct brush movements, vital for bringing the right sensations of life, growth and movement to the paintings. Chinese artists had an extraordinary talent for putting elegance, simplicity, freshness and delicacy into their floral paintings.

Oriental floral art tends to show flowers accompanied by insects or birds, and it is quite rare for flowers to appear on their own. Calligraphy and shading tend to dominate in these paintings, providing a decorative and analytical treatment of the subject, a far cry from more naturalistic European paintings. They are characterised by the simplicity of their composition, the absence of artifices and superfluous effects and an extensive knowledge of the possibilities of color and the effects that the brush can produce.

However, the ability of Chinese painters to suggest color and form is most evident in their monochrome paintings made using Chinese ink. The art of painting with ink (called Sumi in Japan), entirely depends on tonal effects and on calligraphic precision with the brush.

5

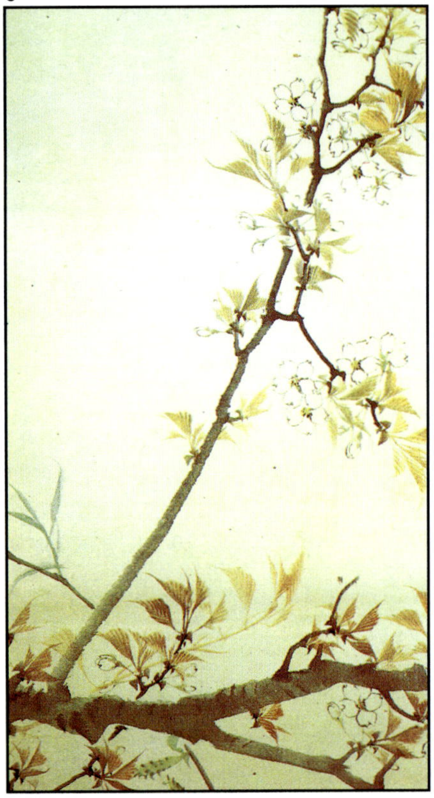

6

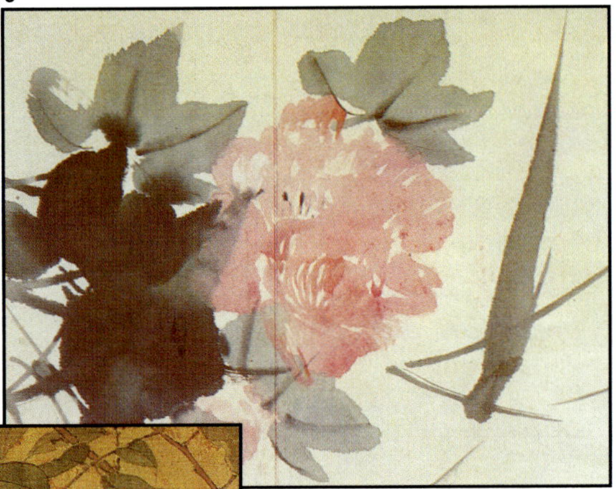

Fig. 5. Part of a floral scroll painted by Matsumura Keibun (British Museum, London). This work, clearly outlined with soft washes and exquisite details, has a style that is closely related to oriental mystique and the Japanese temperament.

Fig. 6. **Hibiscus** *by Tani Buncho (British Museum, London). Not only should the painting capture the physical appearance of the flower, but should also breathe life into its very spirit and essence.*

7

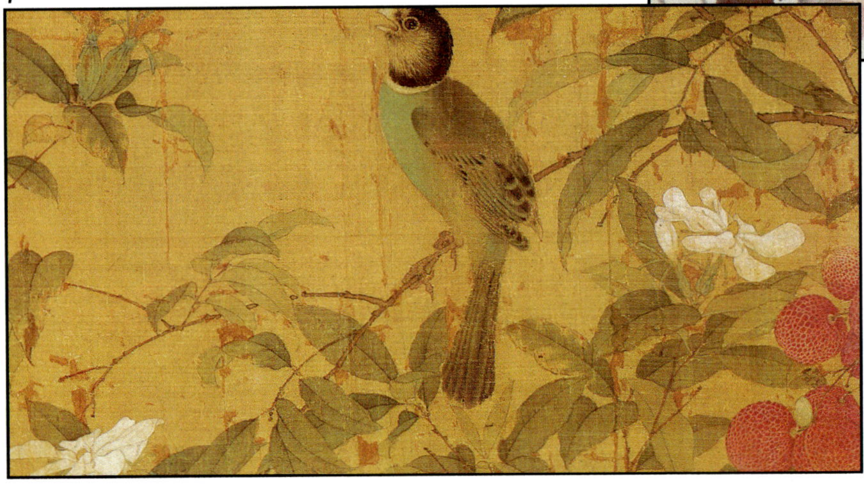

Fig. 7. **Bird and flowers** *by Chao Chi (British Library, London). Flowers were often accompanied by brightly colored birds that brought more life to the paintings.*

Albrecht Dürer and Floral Painting

Albrecht Dürer, the German artist, printer and theorist was responsible for introducing the aesthetic ideas of the Italian Renaissance into Northern Europe. This allowed him to provide his floral watercolors with a combination of the technical refinement and expressiveness of traditional Gothic German art and the careful execution, naturalness and craftsmanship of classic art. His watercolors of animals and flowers that survive today prove the artist's curiosity for the natural world that surrounded him. According to researcher and art critic Heinrich Wölfflin, "even in the most modest of Dürer's flowers, we can see how much care he put into his work, how his stalks stretch high and proudly, and how his leaves follow their own paths and lavishly reveal their jagged or ear-shaped endings".

For Dürer, each shape is clearly seen and conceived, so that the flower is made to stand out by its accurate outline. His flowers are created using a color-based painting system, delicate techniques and a contemplative attitude. Consequently, his work reflects a true love for the details of everyday things, that can make grass seem like a microcosm in front of the spectator's eyes.

A neutral background, normally white, provides a feel of distance in the work despite its apparent bareness and lack of concretion. This background, which we could say adopts the quality of light, makes the painting of the contours of the plant clearer.

There is no artist alive today who is as demanding as Dürer was when it came to detail and form.

8

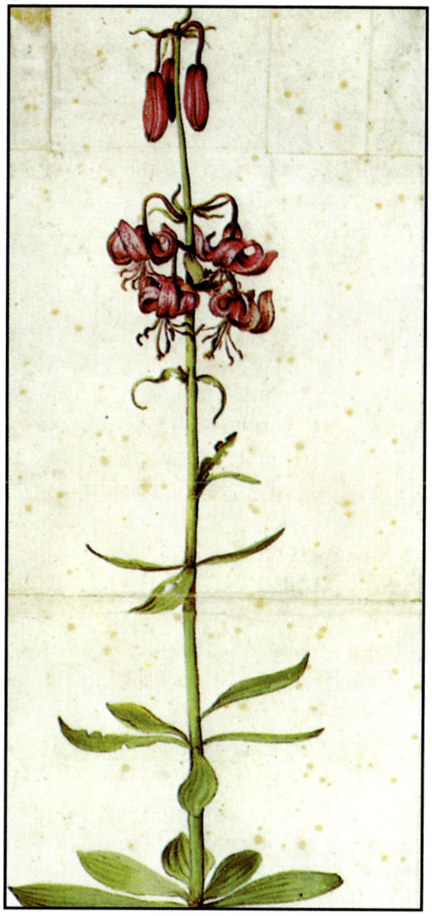

Fig. 8. **Lis Martagon** *by Albrecht Dürer (Graphische Sammlung Albertina, Vienna). Dürer's interest for botany led him to paint extremely detailed paintings of flower structures.*

9

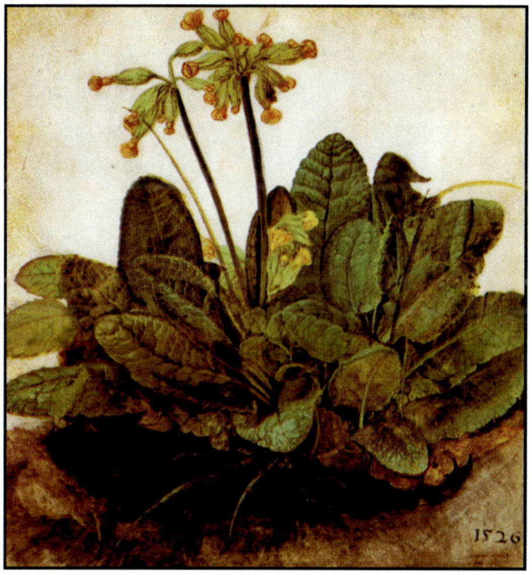

10

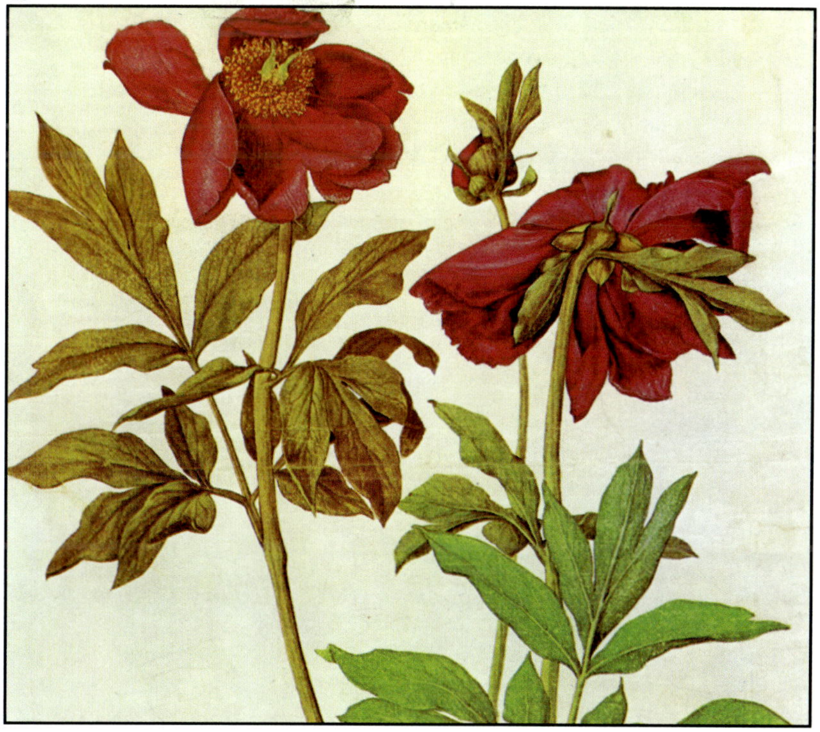

Fig. 9. **Primroses** *by Albrecht Dürer (Graphische Sammlung Albertina, Vienna). Sometimes Dürer added a first appraisal to the ground, but left the background white so that the form and outline of the plant could stand out more.*
Fig. 10. **Two wild peony stalks** *by Albrecht Dürer (Graphische Sammlung Albertina, Vienna). Here you can appreciate Dürer's meticulous style of painting.*

Floral Still Lives of the Baroque Period

As you probably know, still lives were one of the principal themes of the Baroque period. Baroque still lives gave very little importance to depth, and the background was usually smothered by a dark gradation. This chiaroscuro effect meant that floral still lives, with their radial layout, included outstandingly tactile qualities, sensual patterns and a disconcerting appearance. Most of the flowers that were painted in the still lives of the period were home grown rather than wild. This fact has led researchers to establish a relationship between the meticulous and surprisingly accurate work of the artist with the concern of gardeners and botanists specialised in the reproduction and development of plants. The abundance of herbalists and gardens with collections of exotic plants created an enormous demand for paintings of flowers. Flowers were often painted with the same kind of interest, sophistication and luxury of detail that was expected of the portraits of the most important people of the time.
Dutch artists, renowned landscape painters, were also famed for their floral paintings, and reached levels of perfection that have rarely been surpassed. Their paintings evoke images of permanently flowering nature, eternal springtimes and earthly paradises, all with a certain allegoric mood. The flowers generally appeared in generous bunches along with elaborately decorated baskets, vases or jugs that acted like pedestals, intensifying the monumental treatment of the subject. Occasionally, different animals and insects would appear in amongst the petals of the flowers, bringing more life to the image and more credibility to the composition, and creating a level of pictorial harmony that gave even more artistic credit to the genre.
Some of the most important painters of the era included the Dutchmen Jan Brueghel de Velours, Balthasar van der Ast and Ambrosius Bosschaert *the Old*, and the Spaniard Juan de Arellano.

11

12

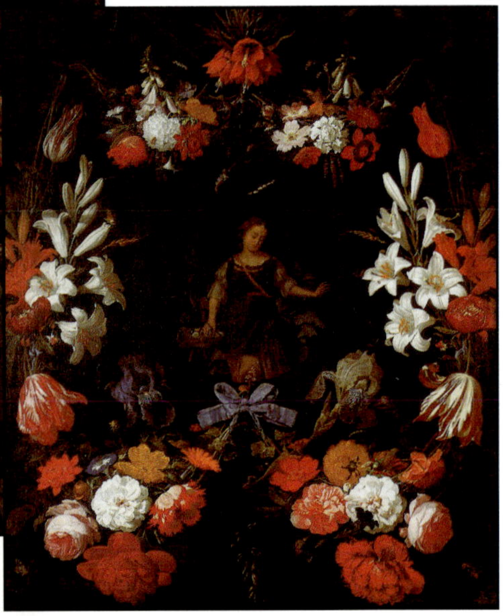

13

Fig. 11.* Basket of flowers *by Ambrosius Bosschaert* the Old *(private collection). The interest for herbalism and the discovery of new species of flower led baroque artists to paint splendid still lives.
Fig. 12.* Floral wreath *by Jacob Marrel (Museo Lázaro Galdiano, Madrid). The highly suggestive layout of this painting and its meticulous style lend it an extraordinary artistic value.
Fig. 13.* Garland of flowers *by Abraham Mignon (Museo de Bellas Artes, Bilbao).

Botanical Studies

In the 17th and 18th centuries, flower paintings played an important role in the growing interest in natural science, and most of all, in the appearance of botany, the science of studying, describing and classifying plantlife. Specialised artists were needed to produce detailed pictures of every known species of plant or animal. This liaison between art and botany meant that much more scientifically accurate floral paintings came into fashion.

Throughout the 18th century, once commercial relations had been set up between Europe and newly discovered overseas territories, scientific expeditions often took specialised watercolor painters along with them to produce exact reproductions of any species they found that up until then had been unknown to the western world. Some of the most important artists in this new field of botanical art included Pierre-Joseph Redouté, the 18th century watercolor painter and engraver, Claude Aubriet, the French botanist who spent a good part of his life in the Parisian Plant Garden carrying out an exhaustive study of exotic flowers, and Samuel Dixon, who worked from his native Ireland on watercolors of plants, animals and fruit that he painted in such three dimensional pictures that they almost looked real. These artists usually worked with thin watercolor washes that were superimposed onto a careful and meticulous drawing, normally drawn with a lead pencil. Their pictorial studies of flowers needed to be extremely precise, and every minor detail needed to be perfectly distinguishable.

They worked with a simple style, with limited colors and, just like Dürer, they used white backgrounds that highlighted the details better. Several prints were made of each picture, and they became extremely popular amongst the wealthier classes of the time, and also as part of "curiosity boxes", the predecessors of what we now know as natural history museums.

14

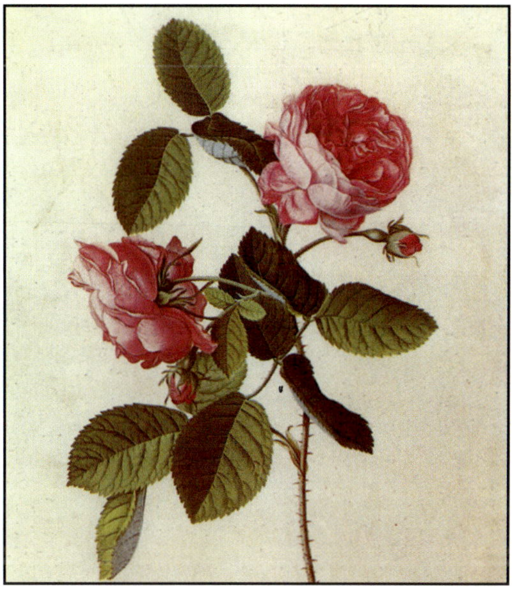

15

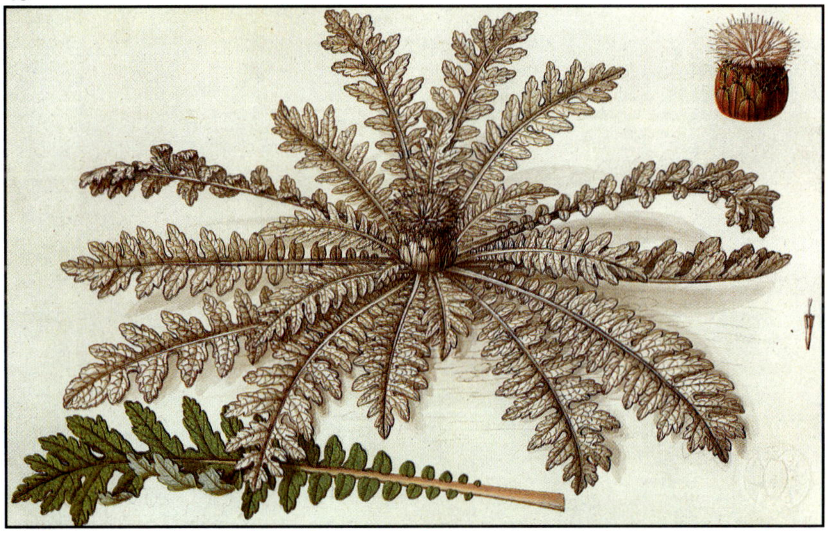

16

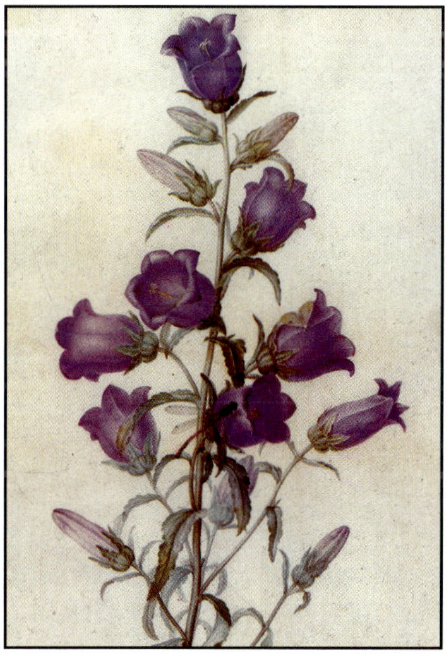

Fig. 14.* Common Provence rose *by G. D. Ehret (Victoria and Albert Museum, London). The interest for botany led to the commercialisation of complete albums full of floral prints like this.

Fig. 15.* African Cinara *by Claude Aubriet (Museum Library of Natural History, Paris). In these floral paintings the artists were given no scope for artistic interpretation. The picture simply had to be as realistic as possible.

Fig. 16.* Canterbury bellflower *by Pierre Joseph Redouté (Victoria and Albert Museum). Botanical studies demanded that the artist worked hard on detailing each of the components that made up the plant with almost scientific resolution.

Monet's Gardens

In 1893, Claude Monet transformed his small estate in Giverny into an aquatic garden. This inspired him to grow exotic water lilies imported from Japan. It was not long before they became one of the artist's greatest obsessions and he used them as subjects in many of his later creations. Monet worked in two phases; he started outdoors, where he could observe the subject, light and colors naturally, and went on to a second phase, the finishing, which took place in his studio.

If you look at his paintings of water lilies, you will notice how the forms of the leaves and flowers seem to float on an open space without any kind of positional reference: groups of flowers float between other plants whose vibrant colors are reflected on the water, whilst neither the sky nor the horizon appear in the picture.

Monet designed the arrangement of flowers and plants in his Giverny garden with his own artistic criteria in mind. In doing this, he had transformed the space into a compendium of colors and shapes that could transmit the artist's internal space, which considered the garden to be the perfect image of nature. The water lily flower constitutes the symbol of what Monet defines as "invisibility of being", which we relate to melancholy and the void that was left by the death of his wife, Alice. His paintings of lilies should be interpreted as portrayals of his most intimate feelings.

If you look closely at his aquatic landscapes, you will see how his shapes gradually lose more and more of their contours until they eventually become little more than a mass of colors that merges into the background and the reflections on the water. There is no doubt that, with this type of painting, Monet established himself as one of the pioneers of modern abstract art. During his later years, Monet suffered from an eye disease that affected his ability to perceive color. Consequently, his work included even more intense colors that were subjected to a dominant range of blues.

The theme of flowers, water lilies, water and reflections carried on inspiring Monet right up until 1926, the year that he died.

17

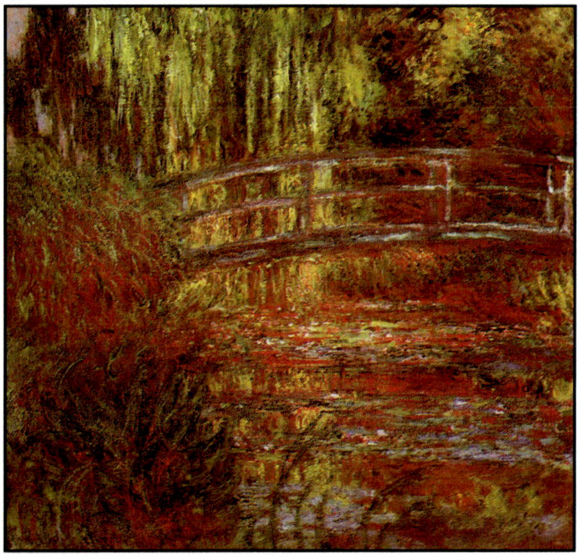

18

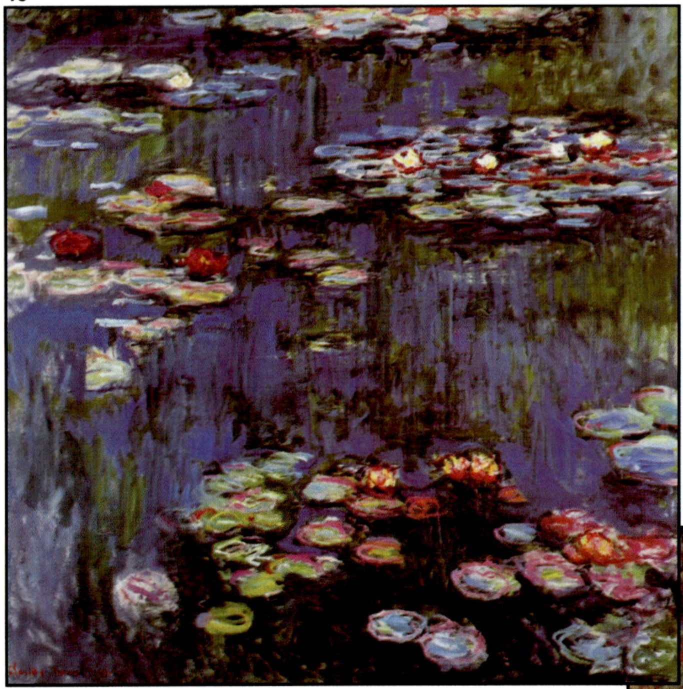

19

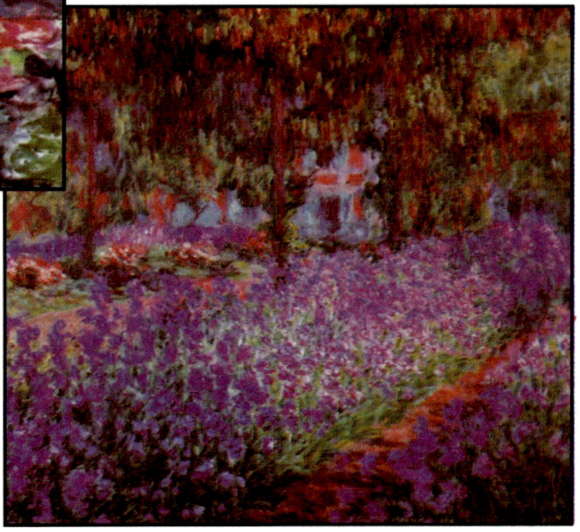

Fig. 17.* Pond of water lilies *by Claude Monet (Museum of Fine Arts, Boston).
Fig. 18.* Water lily flowers *by Claude Monet (National Museum of Western Art, Tokyo).
Fig. 19.* Irises of the garden *by Claude Monet (Musée d'Orsay, Paris).

Fig. 20.* The arch of flowers at Giverny *by Claude Monet (Phoenix Art Museum).
Fig. 21.* The water lily pond without willows: In the morning *by Claude Monet (Musée de l'Orangerie, Paris).

20

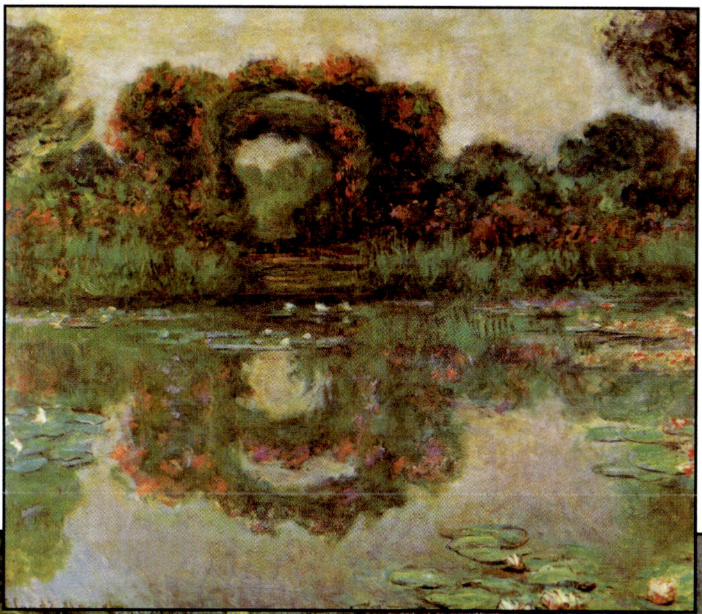

21

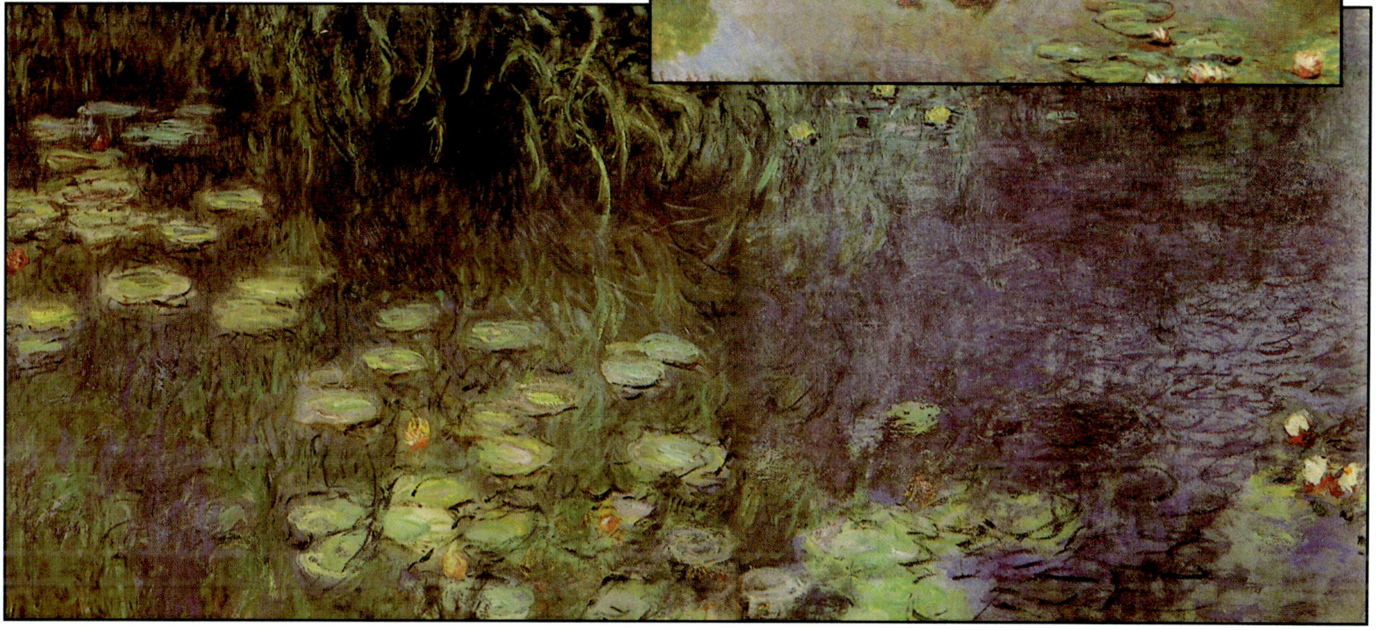

22

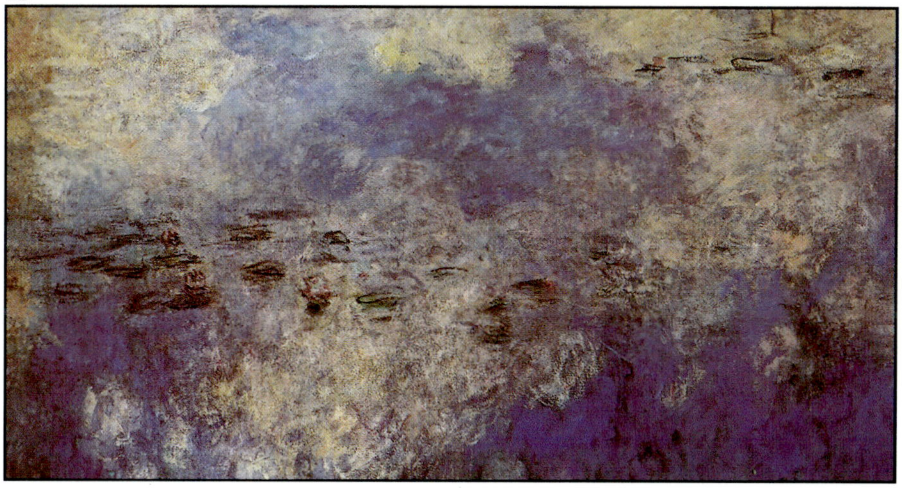

Fig. 22.* The water lily pond without willows: The clouds *by Claude Monet (Musée de l'Orangerie, Paris).

Van Gogh's Sunflowers

The personal drama that tormented Van Gogh's life, his social insecurity, madness and misery, led him to paint floral compositions as a simple reflection of the psychological problems that he was suffering. He was particularly interested in the expressive and emotional value of sunflowers, and used them to manifest his changing moods. Consequently, his sunflowers are shown in deformed, ragged shapes that convey a continual feeling of tension.

Van Gogh put a new expressive and symbolic meaning into his floral compositions that is shown by brightly contrasting colors and the use of short, broken brush strokes, more common in divisionist paintings than impressionist ones. By doing this, he portrayed the insecurities and worries that shadowed his life.

He wrote the following to his brother Theo. "I do not wish to reproduce what I see before my eyes, rather that I arbitrarily use color to express myself more strongly". One example of this is his painting *Four Sunflowers*, which shows four withered flowers that appear overlapping one another in the foreground as if they wanted to rebel against their inevitable desiccation. They symbolise the growing pains that would eventually take Van Gogh's life.

This vigorous representation of sunflowers reached its expressive peak with *Vase with twelve sunflowers*. The reason that this painting causes such impact is, undoubtedly, the characteristic use that the artist makes of contrasting complementary colors. The color derives towards orange and the shades are multiplied until they almost take on a green hue, in such a way that the yellow of the picture acquires every possible effect as a result of the contrast. It is clear that, in this painting, Van Gogh is conveying more optimism than in the aforementioned work, a result of the breath of fresh air that he felt when he moved house to sunny Provence in France. Remember that, for Van Gogh, the sunflower symbolised the burning sun of the Mediterranean coast.

23

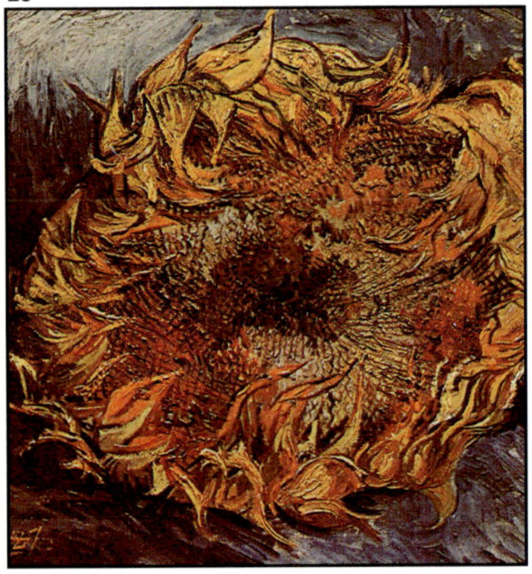

24

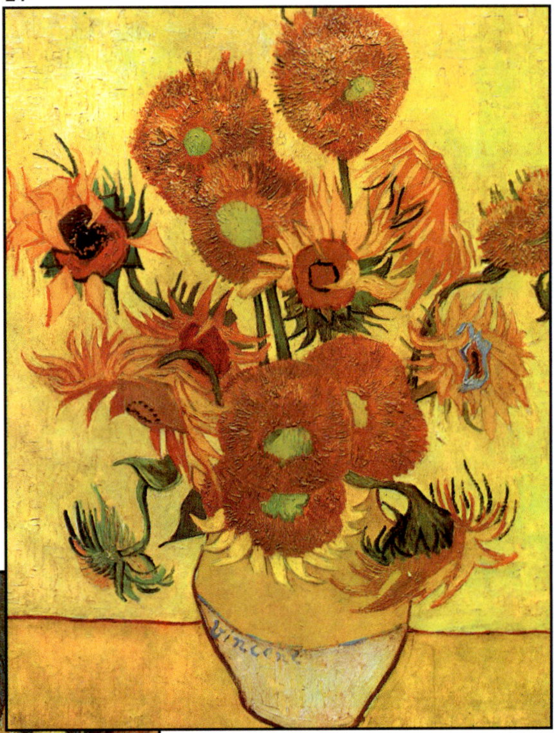

Fig. 23. **Dead nature** *by Vincent van Gogh (Metropolitan Art Museum, New York).*

25

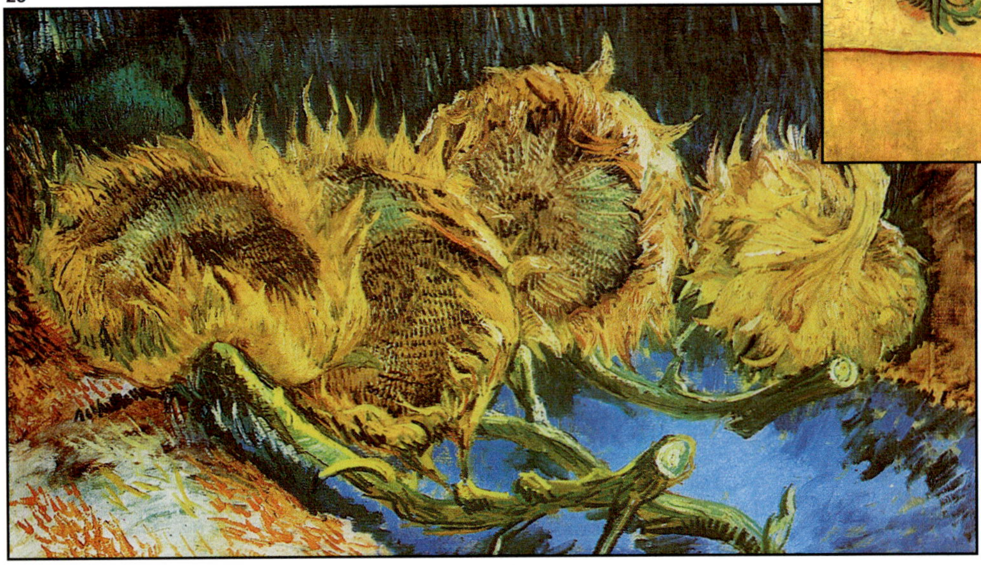

Fig. 24. **Sunflowers** *by Vincent van Gogh (Rijksmuseum Vincent van Gogh, Amsterdam).*
Fig. 25. **Four sunflowers** *by Vincent van Gogh (Rijksmuseum Kröller-Müller, Otterlo).*
Fig. 26 (next page). **Vase with twelve sunflowers** *by Vincent van Gogh (Neue Pinakothek, Munich).*

26

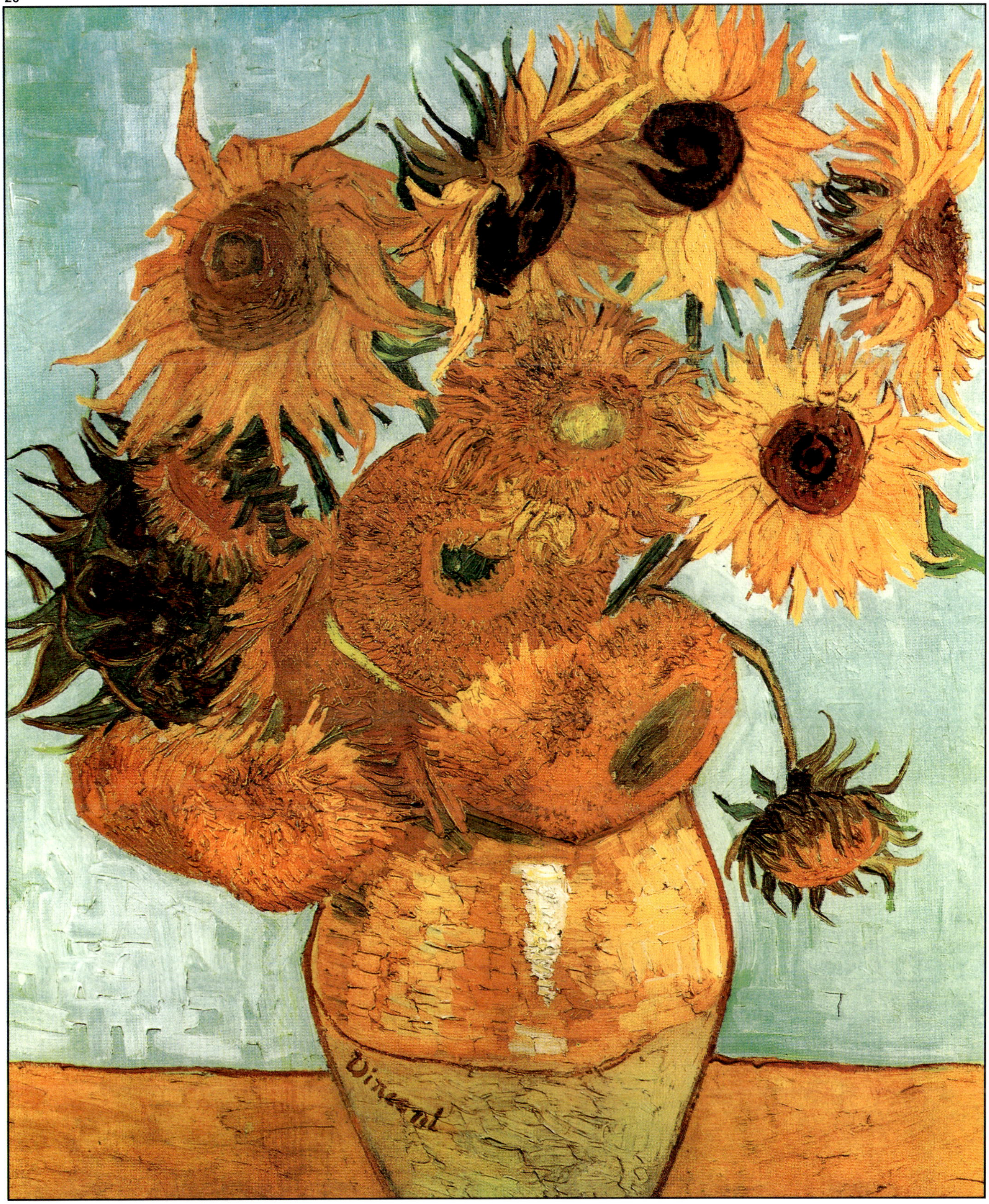

Expressionism: Schiele and Nolde

The expressionists showed a direct opposition to the emphasis that impressionism put on imitating nature. The main aim of expressionism was to recreate nature by exaggerating its lines, colors and forms.

For Egon Schiele, the line was a fundamental aspect of his work, as can be seen from his paintings of plants and flowers. Curiously, in these paintings, his plants adopt anthropomorphic characteristics. It was not in vain that he said: "Now I mainly observe the body movements of mountains, water, trees and flowers. Everywhere they remind one of the movements of the human body, similar feelings of joy and sorrow, but in plants". We can see this in his painting *Sunflower*, an isolated and abandoned flower whose branches and leaves resemble an outstretched human body, and the flower becomes a reflection of the melancholic state of the artist. If we study this painting, we understand what Schiele meant when he wrote "(...) of the joy and sorrow in plants". His other work portrayed similar ideas, with flowers and plants being his main subjects.

Just like Claude Monet, the German artist Emil Nolde used plants as the central theme for most of his work. His wash technique was particularly interesting. He used a highly absorbent rice paper canvass that he soaked in water so that his colors, when applied, would saturate the paper and blend into each other. The paper was saturated in such a way that the painting could often be turned over and viewed in reverse.

It produces pleasing results: flowers with dense washes that, with the contrasting effect of pure colors, intensify the expressiveness and portray the explosion of vibrant colors that sweeps over the German Baltic coast, where Nolde lived in a small, isolated village for nearly all of his life.

27

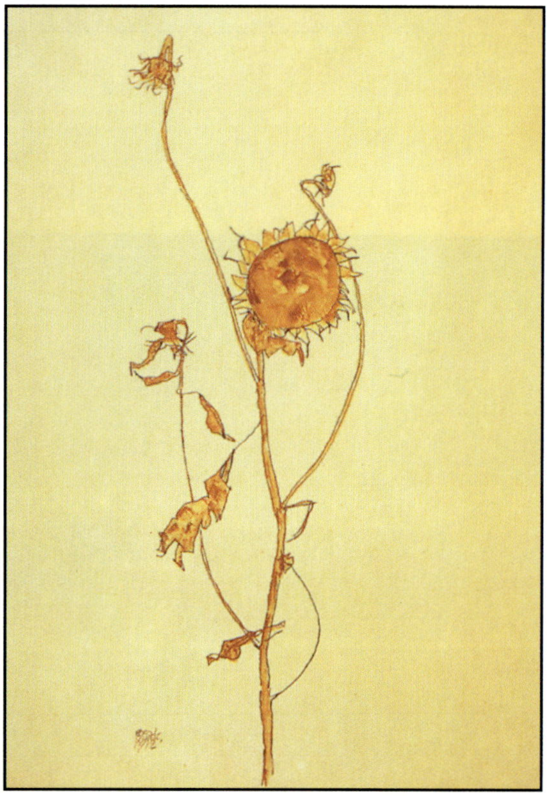

28

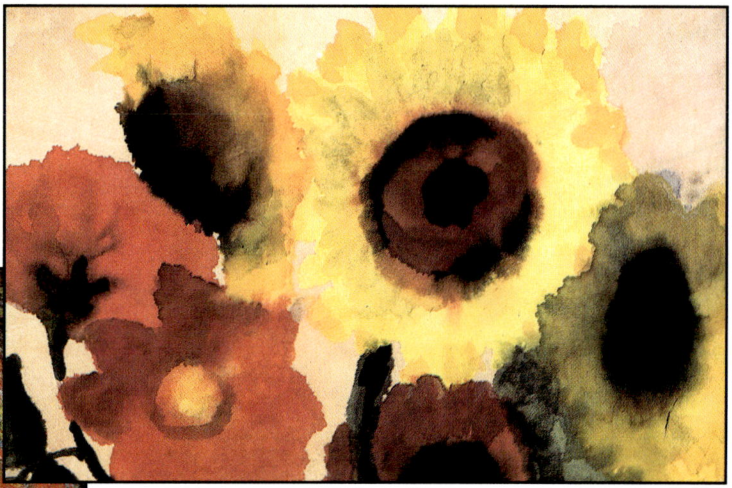

29

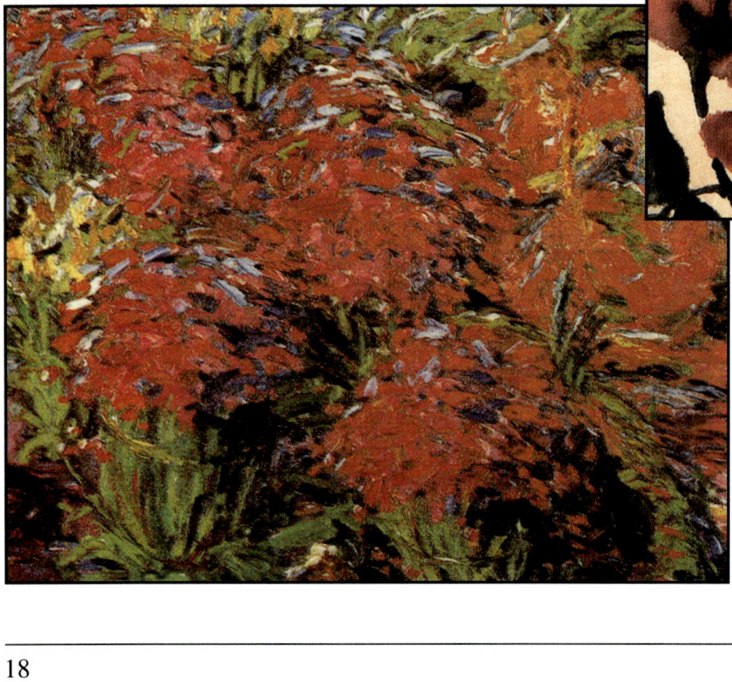

Fig. 27. **Withered sunflower** *by Egon Schiele (private collection).*
Fig. 28. **Summer flowers** *by Emil Nolde (Sprengel Museum, Hanover).*
Fig. 29. **Garden path** *by Emil Nolde (Museo Thyssen-Bornemisza, Madrid).*
Fig. 30. (next page). **Sunflowers** *by Emil Nolde (Sprengel Museum, Hanover).*

30

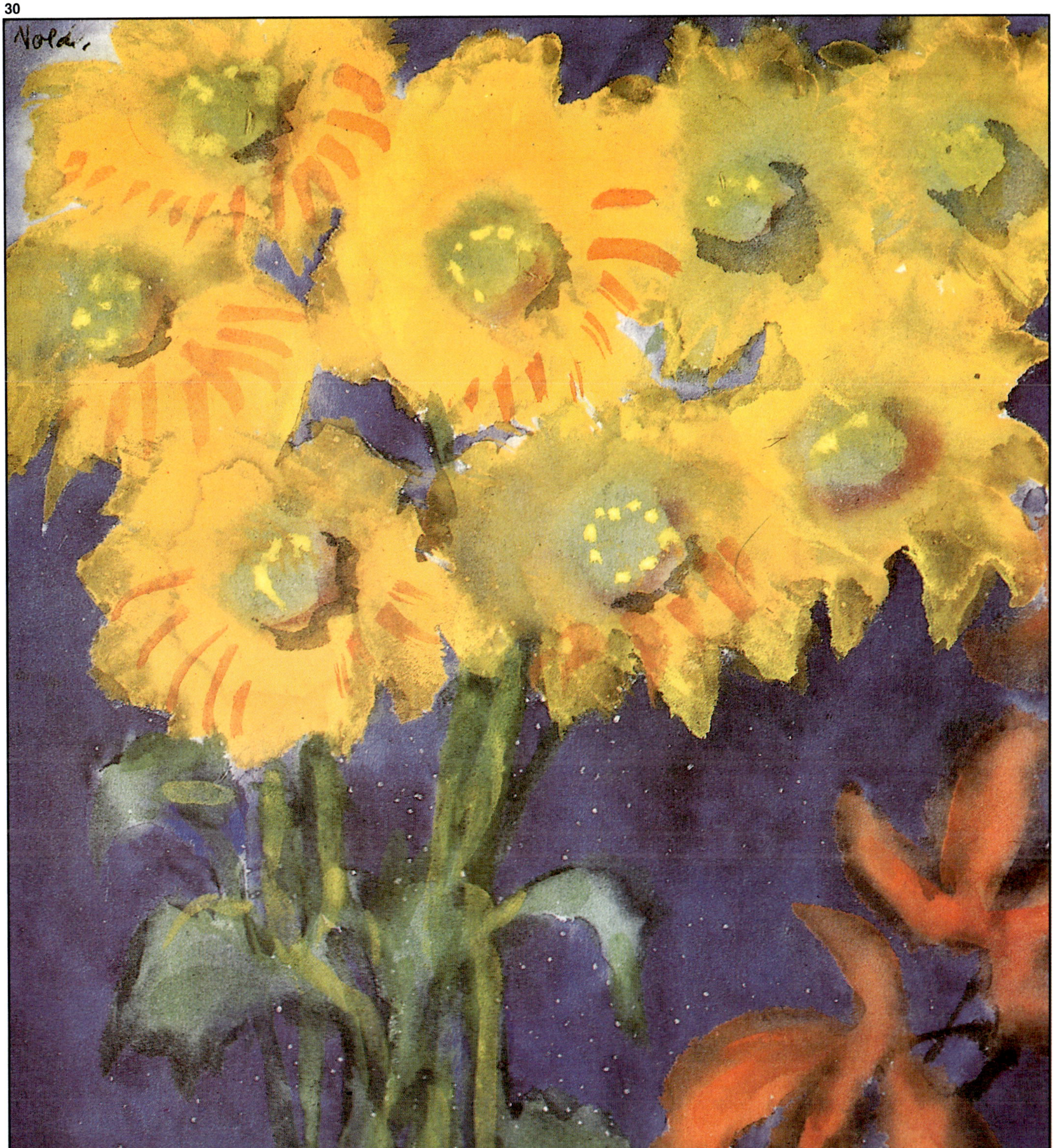

Flowers in Modern Art: Warhol and O'Keefe

Flower painting is still important in the modern era. Many contemporary artists that still use traditional methods, as well as more abstract painters, have adopted the genre as a way of exploring color and texture. For many of the most important artists of the 20th century, the form that flowers suggest to them is ideal for exploring new methods of expression.

Therefore, Andy Warhol, for example, transforms flowers into a multicolored image that reminds us of the typical colors that are often used in comic strips and advertising. He creates a lively contrast between areas of vibrant and fluorescent colors. Warhol produced a series of identical pictures of flowers, where the only difference between each one was the changing variety, intensity and density of color that was applied to them. Warhol's flowers had to look like small consumer products, as if they were mass-produced without any kind of manual intervention, in keeping with the ideology behind pop art.

From early on in her life, Georgia O'Keefe was inspired by the vision of garden flowers like roses, poppies, camellias, orchids and irises. The iris was one of her preferred subjects, a flower that came to be something of a trademark for this American painter. Her flowers are painted in close up, the ends of the petals often being cut off by the edge of the frame. As she said herself, it was necessary "to reach the most basic by simplifying form". When her flowers are painted on large canvasses, they appear oversized and allow the spectator to clearly visualise their internal structure. This interest for reproducing the solitary flower on such a large scale corresponds to the romantic idea of giving human characteristics to painted flowers.

"A flower is relatively small. Everybody makes associations with flowers and the idea of flowers. (...) So, I said to myself, I am going to paint what I see, what a flower means to me. But I'm going to paint it big to persuade people to take the right amount of time over contemplating it".

31

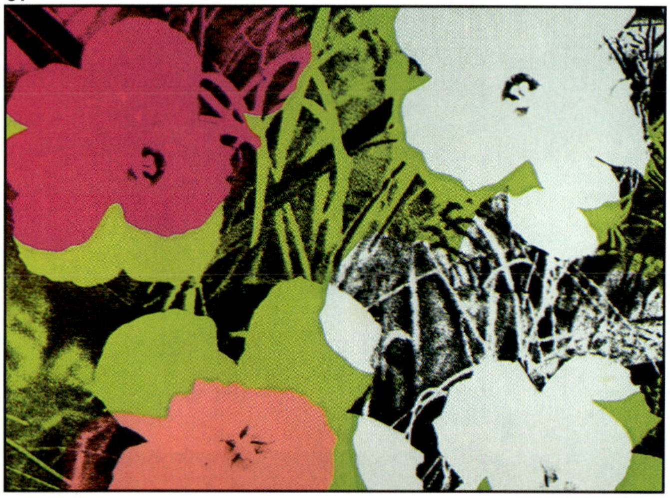

32

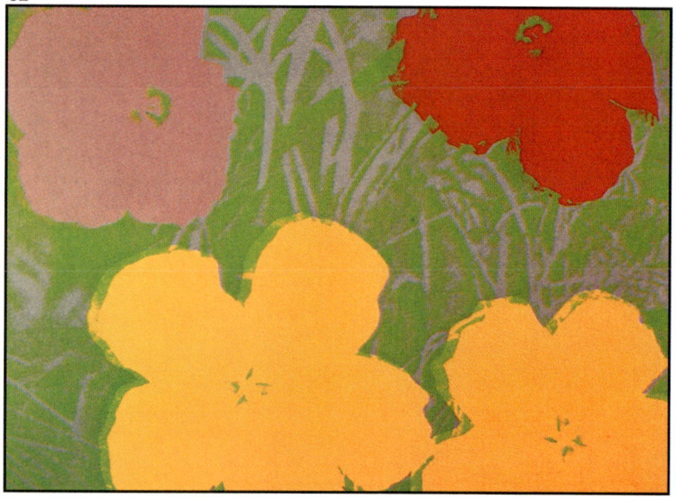

33

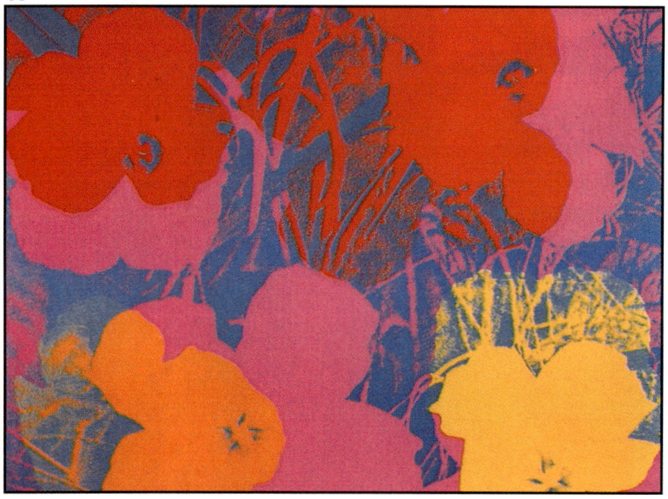

34

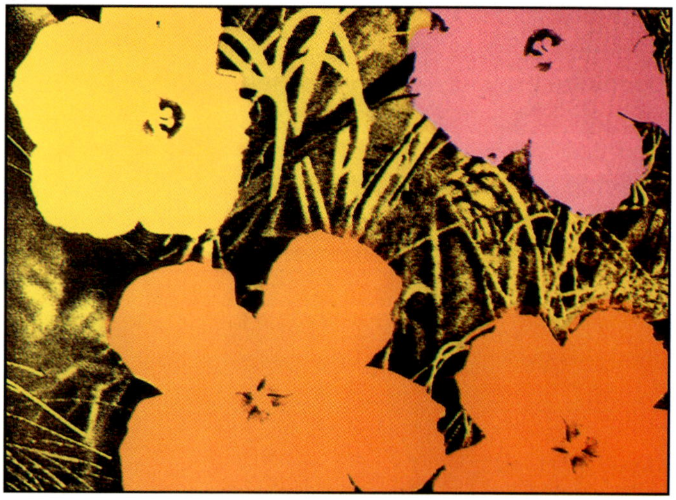

35

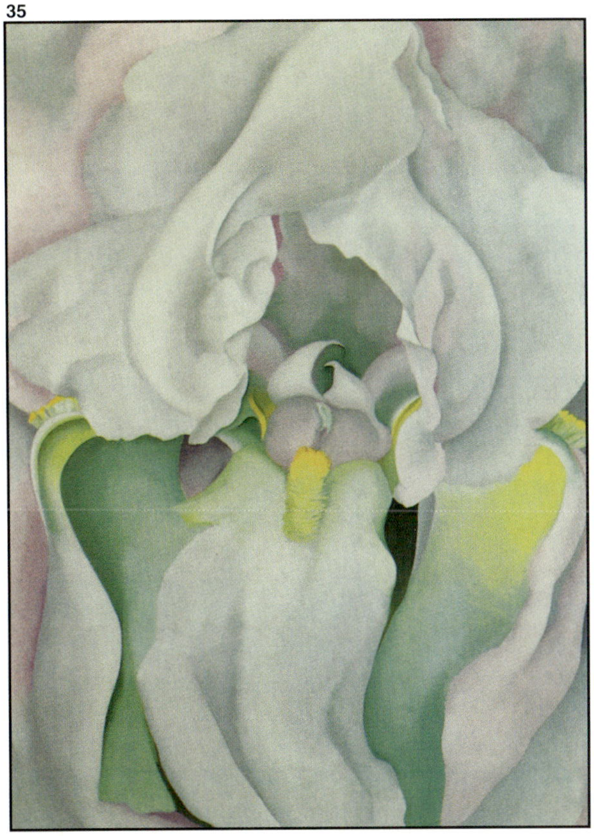

36

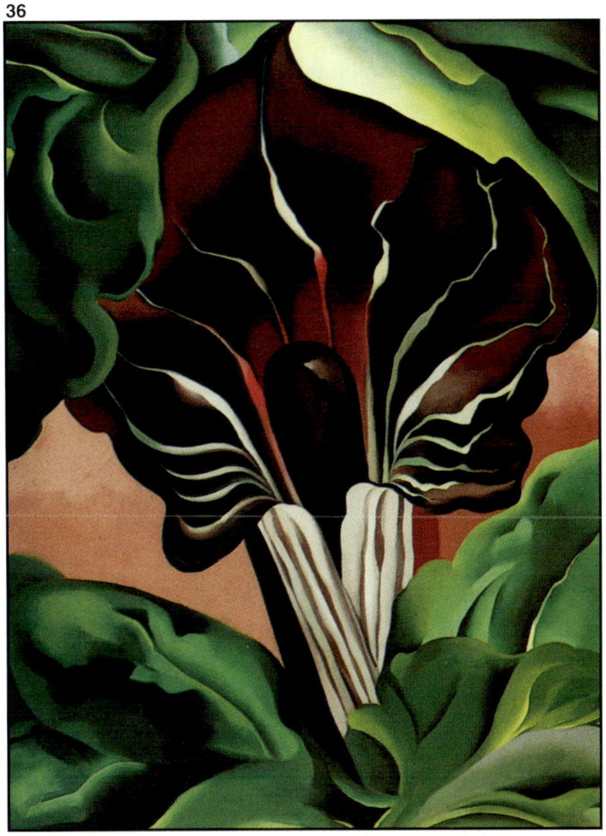

37

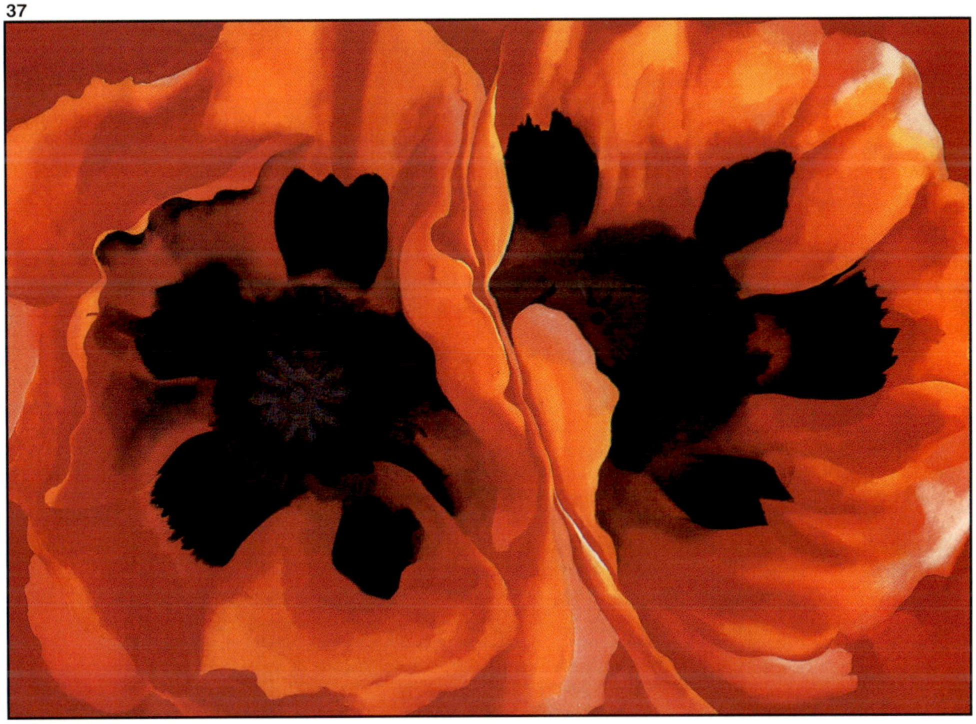

Figs. 31, 32, 33 and 34 (previous page). **Flowers, 1970** *by Andy Warhol. A folio with ten silkscreen prints. 250 copies with a numbered stamp on the back (Neue Galerie Ludwig, Aachen).*
Fig. 35. **Light iris** *by Georgia O'Keefe (Virginia Museum of Arts).*
Fig. 36. **Aracea no.2** *by Georgia O'Keefe (Alfred Stieglitz Collection, Washington).*
Fig. 37. **Wild poppies** *by Georgia O'Keefe (Weisman Art Museum, Minneapolis).*

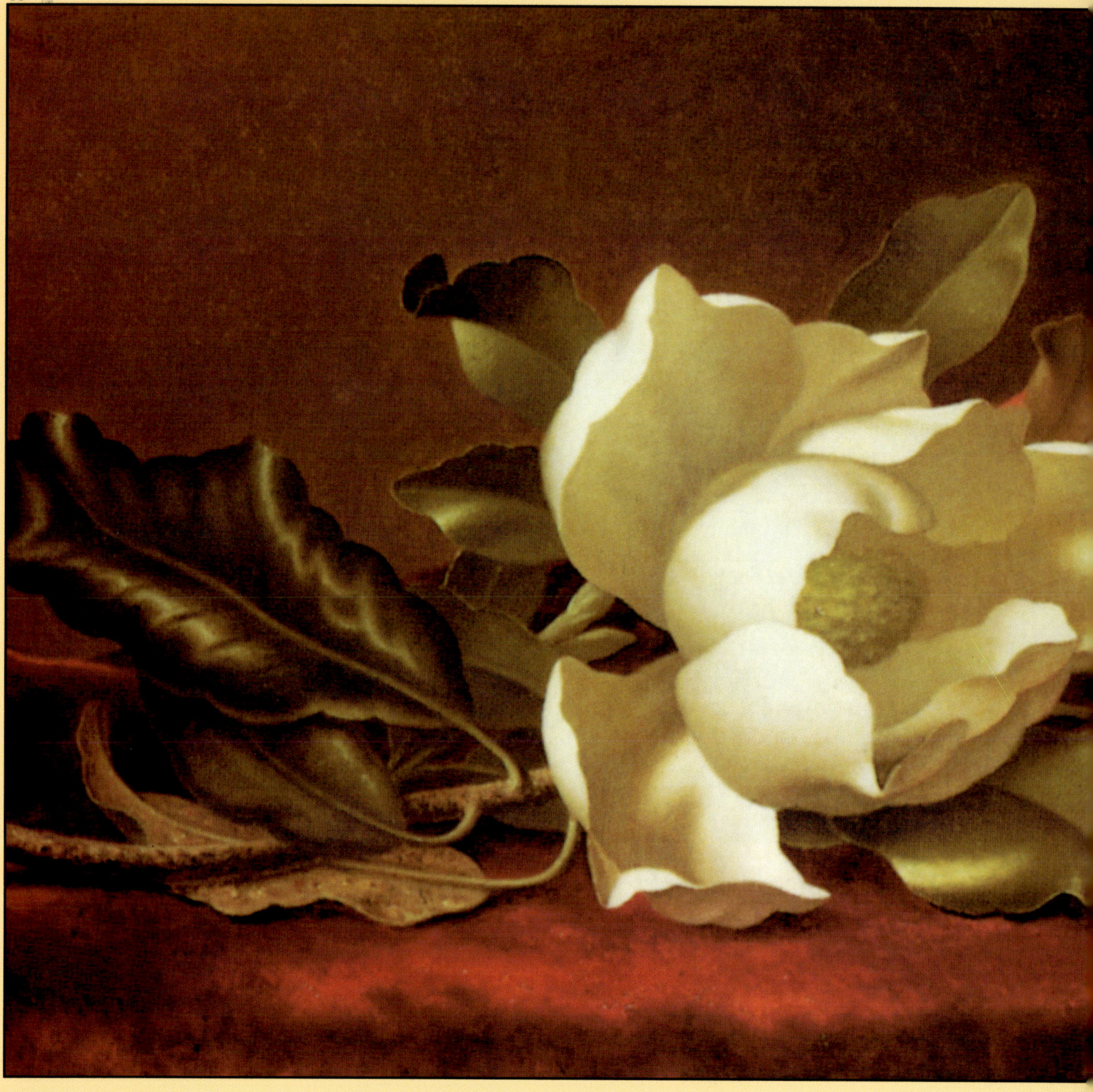

Fig. 38 ***The flower of the magnolia*** **by Martin Johnson Heade (The Putman Foundation of the Timken Museum of Art, San Diego). The enormous amount of detail and chiaroscuro treatment resembles the beautiful floral compositions of the Baroque period.**

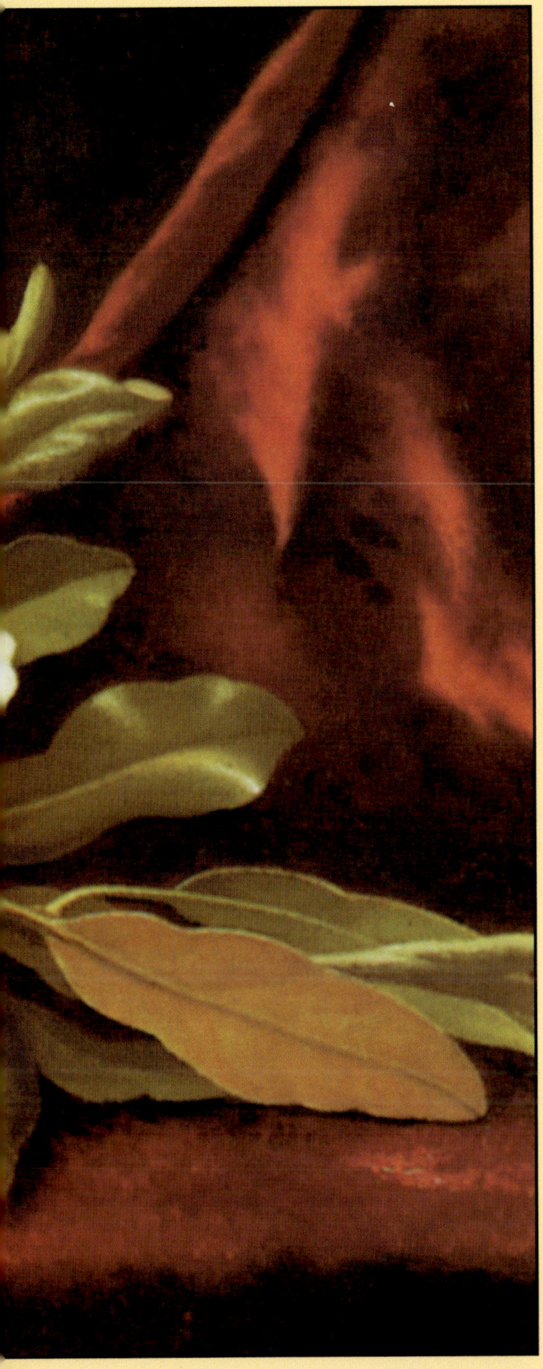

THE SUBJECT: COMPOSITION AND INTERPRETATION

Floral painting has often been wrongfully associated with oil painting, despite the fact that most of the grand masters actually often used watercolors for some of their most important paintings. This is because, although one can produce many more effects and textures with oils, watercolors allow room for more agility and spontaneity that can bring us closer to the actual subject with respect to composition, harmony of color, interpretation and freshness. But, as the following chapters explain, to paint a floral composition correctly, you will need to study several topics first, including the structures both of flowers themselves and the complementary objects that appear with them, the choice of theme and the layout of each element in the picture.

Flowers: Drawing and Structure

To make beautiful floral compositions it is essential that you master the use of the pencil. It is a comfortable utensil and it is crucial for studying the structure and form of a flower, for making sketches and for processing any visual information before considering which colors, tones and textures to use.

All artists are faced with the challenge of representing the third dimension, and flowers can be particularly awkward in this respect, given the fact that they tend to have such complex forms. The best way of avoiding too many headaches is to simplify what you see before your eyes. In other words, flowers, like any other object, can be restructured, or reduced, into far simpler geometric forms (circles, squares, trapeziums, triangles, etc.).

If the flowers are to appear arranged in a vase or as part of a still life, the basic structure or framing of the subject should be obtained by measuring and comparing the dimensions of the flower in relation to the whole picture. This can be done by holding a thin rod or pencil in an outstretched hand. These measurements allow you to find equal or similar dimensions in the subject that will help you to frame it. In other words you create an imaginary frame for the subject and use it to simplify its geometric form without thinking about any details or superfluous forms.

In such cases, the model, made up of a ceramic vase and a bunch of flowers, can be fit into a circle (figs. 40 and 41). The position, dimensions and proportion of flowers and leaves can be drawn from here in relation to the whole picture. The form of the flowerpot or vase is determined, and circles can be drawn for the flowers to be fitted into. As I said before, a few simple lines reduce the elements and forms into simple geometric shapes, and that way they define the best way of positioning the flower in the frame.

Once the structure has been established, there are several ways of dealing with the preparatory sketch, from a detailed study of the subject to a simple drawing that uses only a few lines.

39

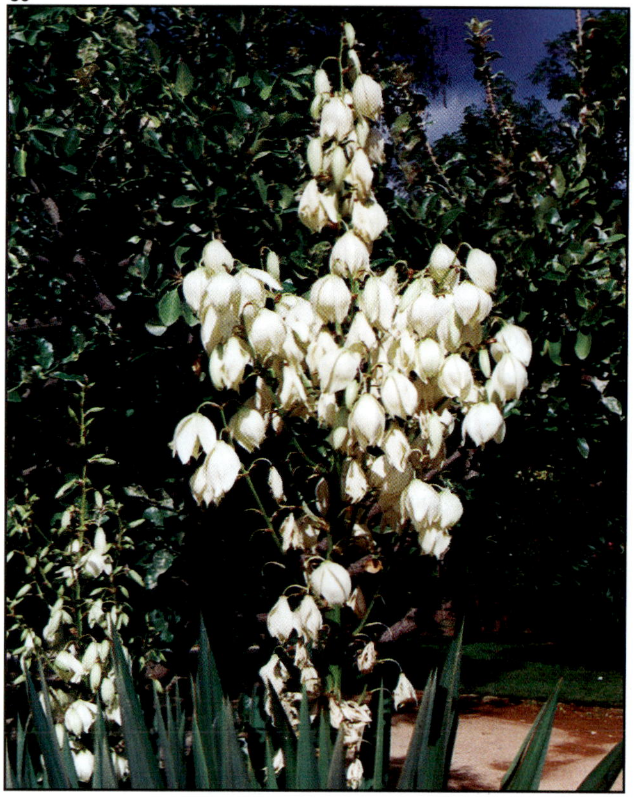

40

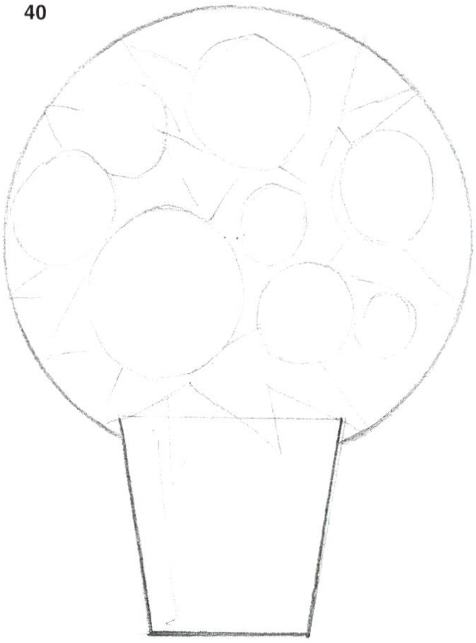

41

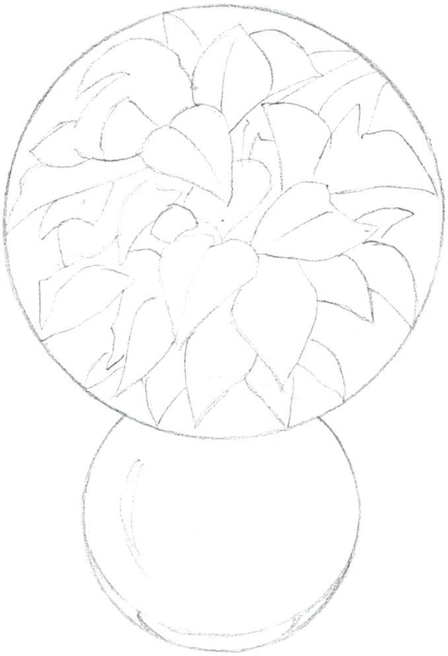

Fig. 39. When painting outdoors, you will often be faced with the problem of drawing the complex structures of flowers like these.

Fig. 40 and 41. When you paint bunches of flowers, the first thing you should do is draw a simple geometric shape around the whole subject, and then indicate the position of each of the flowers and leaves (fig. 40). You should end up with a thin line drawing that describes the outline of each shape (fig. 41).

Bear in mind that floral drawings do not have to be too rigorous. So, concentrate on determining the positions of the flowers on the surface of the paper without worrying too much about modelling, perspective or proportions. Unlike perspective or anatomic drawings, in flower drawings proportion can be falsified without the actual composition being distorted.
With the framing dealt with, you should now redraw and accentuate the outlines of the plant. To do this, I suggest that you use a linear method that will help you determine the real forms of the subject. When you paint with watercolors you should do away with any kind of shadow that highlights volume, because you could dirty the watercolors and spoil the end result.
I strongly advise you to follow this method whenever you draw flowers, because in my opinion it is by far the best for representing the subject properly. If you do this, not only will you be assured of an understandable general subject structure, but you will also achieve a more accurate and realistic drawing, the basis for any decent watercolor.

42

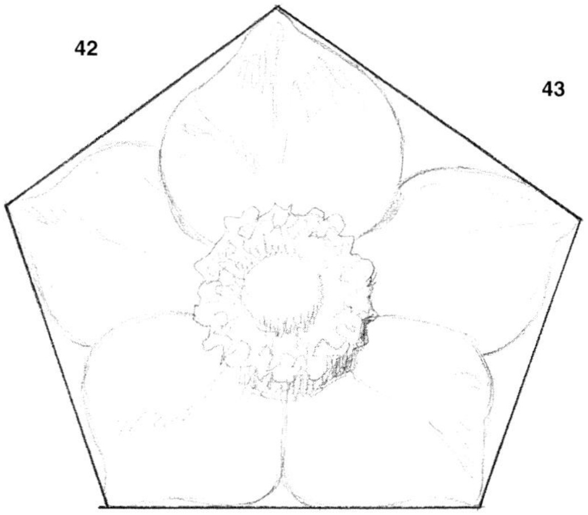

43

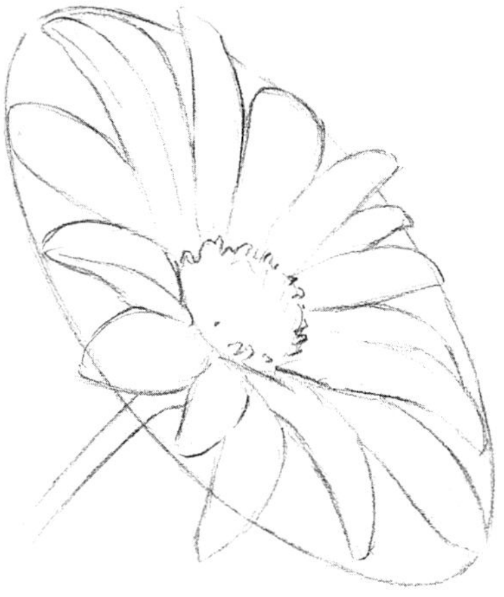

44

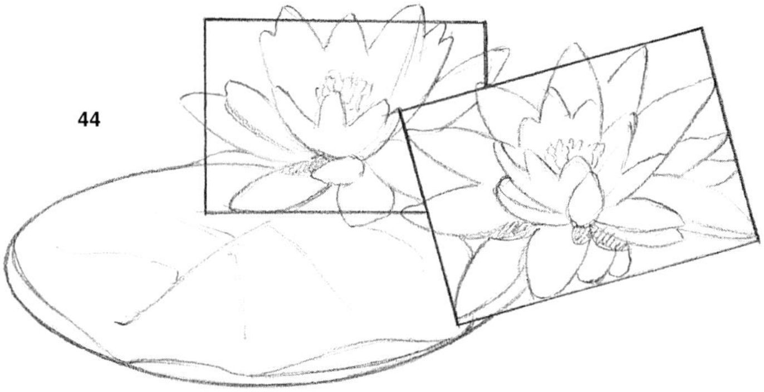

45

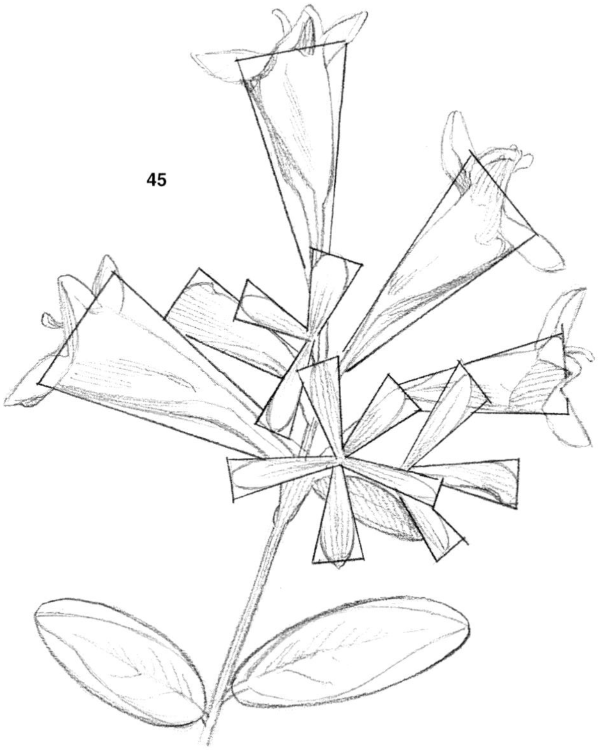

Figs. 42 and 43. The detailed task of drawing flowers also requires a preparatory sketch of the structure that will help you understand their forms better.
Figs. 44 and 45. When you paint outdoors, the process is just the same. Frame the forms of the plant in rhomboids, circles and triangles.

The Importance of the Preparatory Sketch

The different ranges of colors, textures and forms that are found in the world of flowers are an attractive challenge for the artist.

This, like any other theme, requires the artist to have an extensive knowledge of the subject. This means making many sketches from nature to be able to choose the most interesting and characteristic examples. These exercises must allow for the study and memorization of the most appropriate forms, colors, types of lines and brushstrokes for painting the characteristics of the subject.

The aim of a preparatory sketch, which can be made with a pencil or watercolors, is to study the structure of the subject and the repercussion of the colors that appear in it. The sketch should simplify the complex forms of the flower, making it easier to concentrate on its color. Such sketches are usually quite small and are drawn quickly. They should be complete, even if they do not have to look finished. Above all, however, the sketch should give all the basic information about the subject, even if it does not have to be either detailed or exhaustive.

If you are going to paint floral themes, before anything else, I suggest that you spend some time drawing a few simple sketches, which will help you get the right feel of working with flowers. Before ending this chapter, I should like to quote the artist Helmut Ruheman. "Before beginning a painting, make a quick postcard size sketch, and never forget this first, spontaneous idea for anything in the world".

46

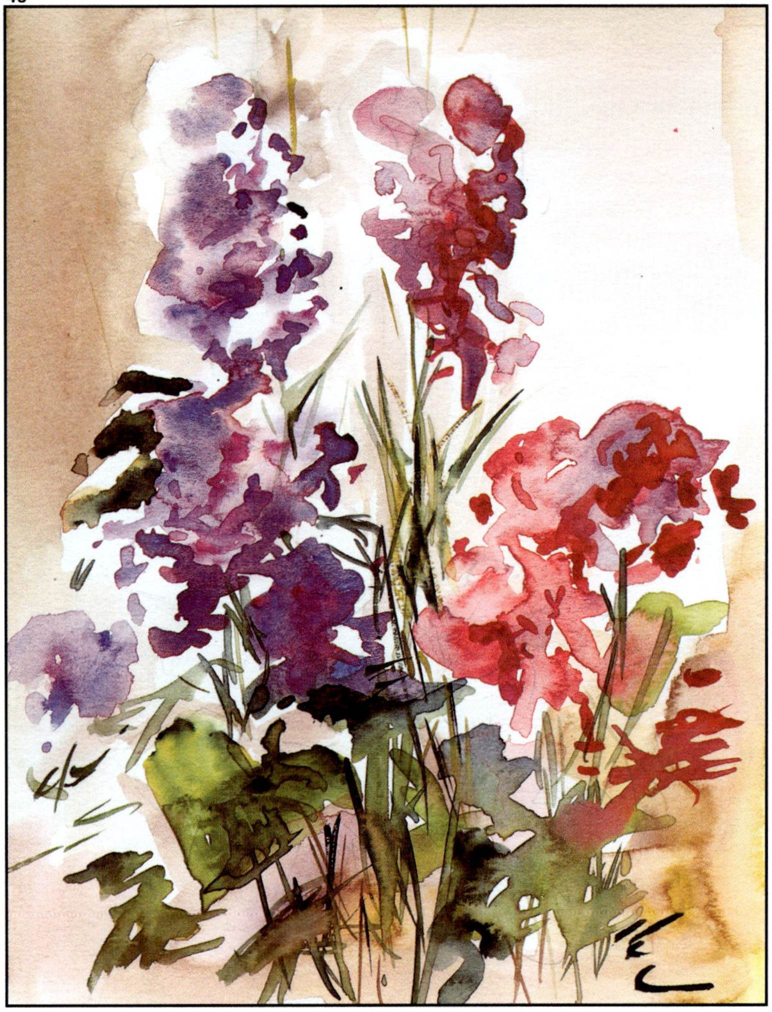

47

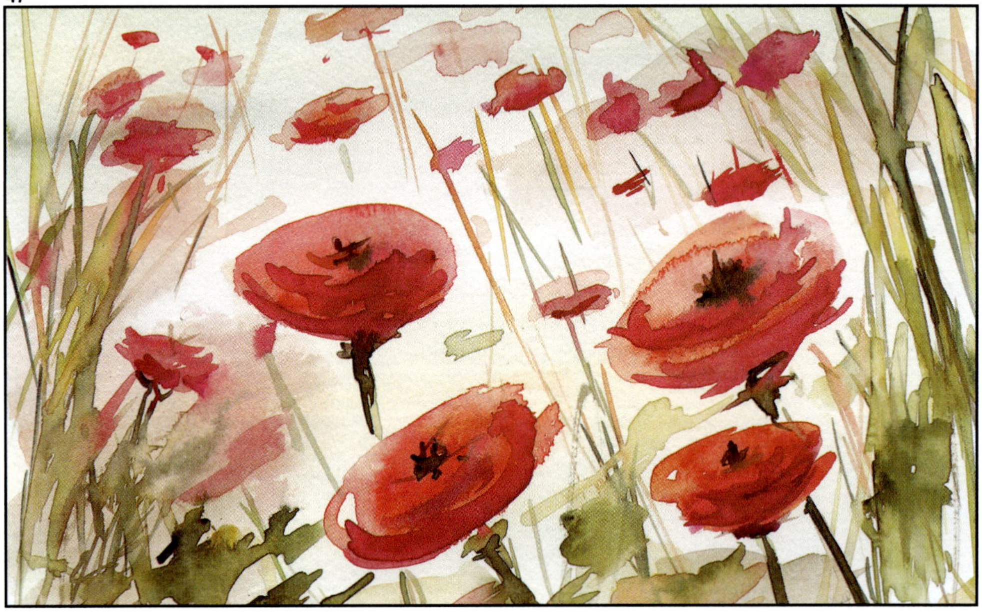

48

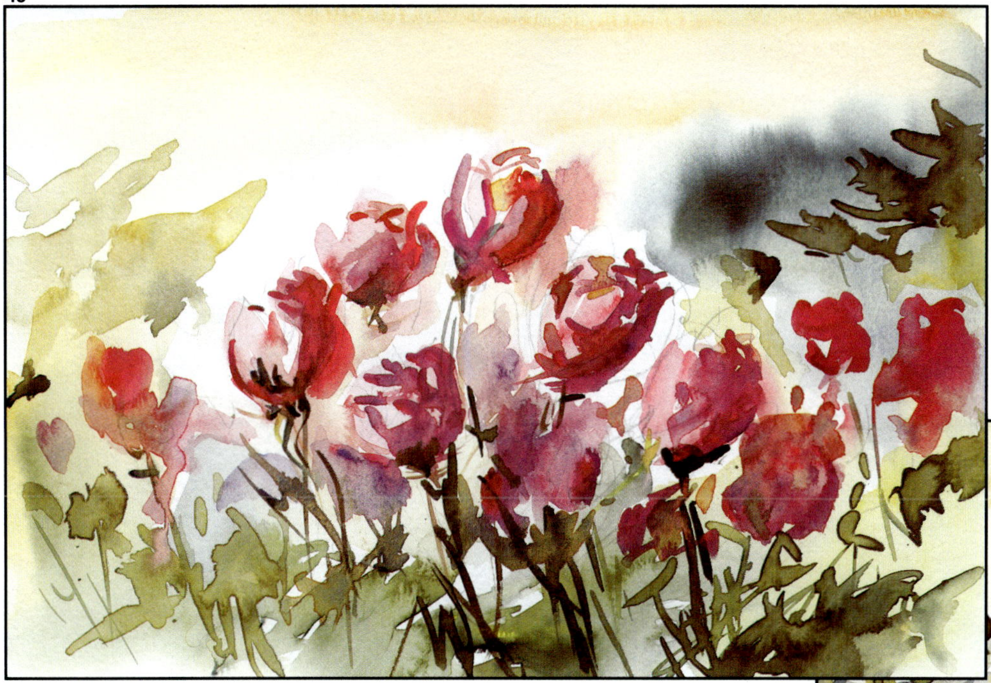

49

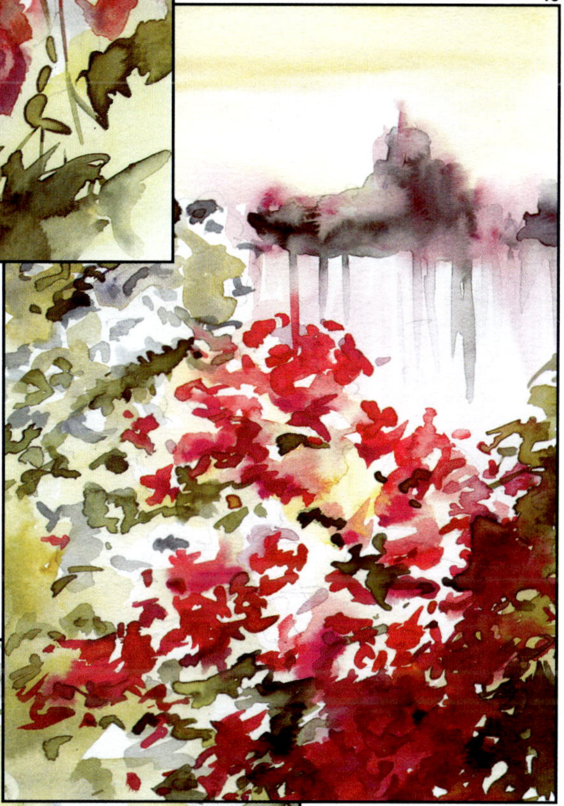

Figs. 46 and 50. Here is a series of five flower sketches by the artist Grau Carod. He has spent no more than five minutes on each one. Notice the simple, restricted colors that he has used in his large brushstrokes, and the total lack of pencil markings. Study how the different forms and directions of his strokes depend on each different subject.

50

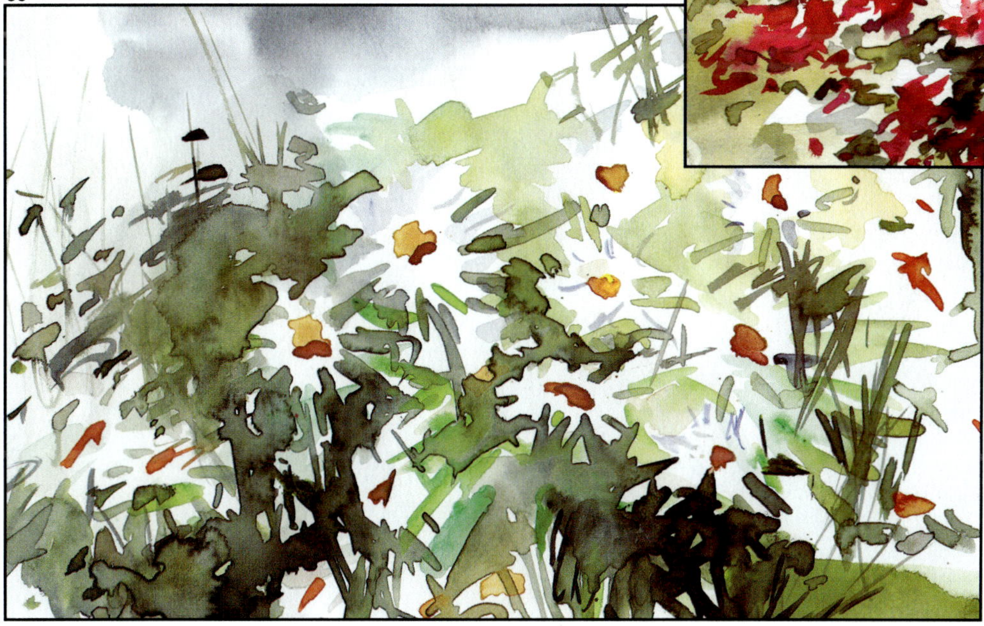

The Art of Composing: Possibilities

The are many ways of distributing objects in space. The layout of the elements, which may often appear spontaneous and random, is frequently the result of several calculations and plenty of earlier attempts. Composing is 'positioning the elements of a picture in a certain way, so as to create the most visually satisfying arrangement'. When you look at a picture, the first thing that you distinguish is how it has been organised and the relationships between each of the different elements and forms. It is composition that makes a picture coherent, and any artist who overlooks it is taking a very dangerous risk.

The artist can manipulate his subject most freely when composing a still life, so it is obviously the best type of theme for the first stages of practice. It is always best if you prepare and arrange your own bunches of flowers. You are more than likely to have a better idea of the composition you are after than the florist's assistant is (fig. 51). You yourself can decide to place the flower that you want to stand out most in the foreground, place differently colored flowers next to each other to force contrast, or prepare flower arrangements with dominant colors.

When you prepare your arrangement, you may find some awkward flowers that refuse to stand up straight or in higher positions than others, and you may need to strengthen the stalk of a damaged flower, so you should have piece of thin wire handy that you can wrap around the stalk (fig. 52). It is common knowledge that flower stalks only stay strong and fresh for a limited amount of time.

In a composition, every one of the elements should be positioned in such a way that it is quite clear what species they are. Look at the example in figure 53, for example. The flowers have been carelessly placed in a way that does not make it immediately clear what species they are. However, after a little rearrangement, the problem is easily solved (fig. 54).

51

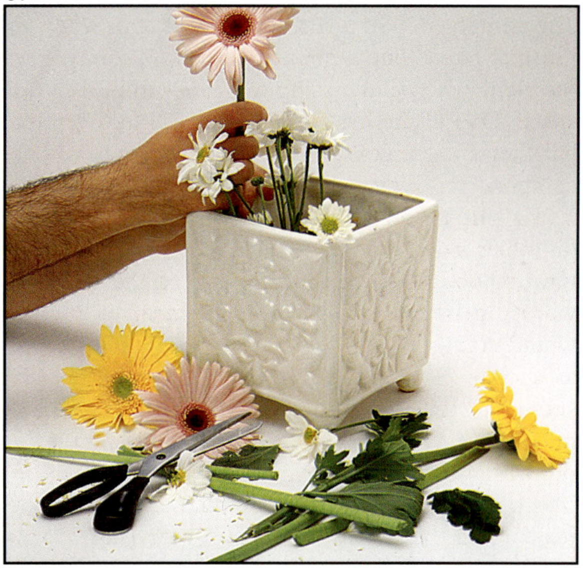

52

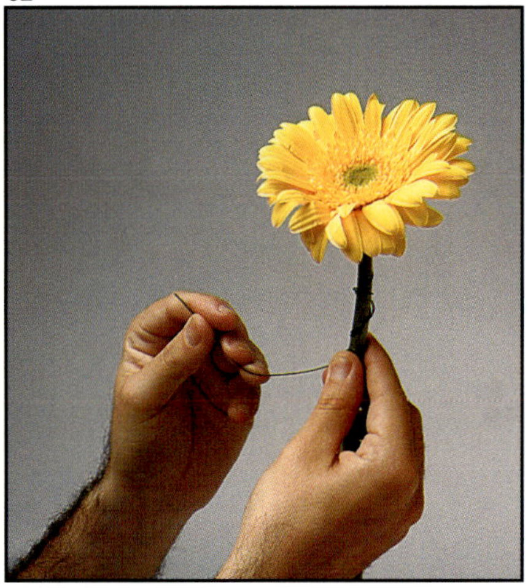

53

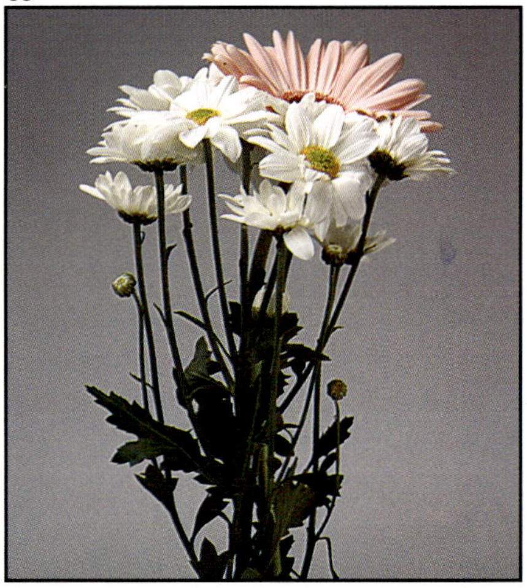

54

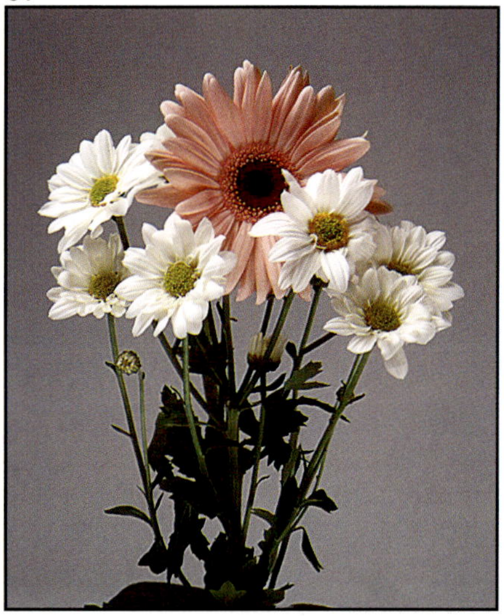

Fig. 51. It is important that you learn to arrange your flowers according to your own needs.
Fig. 52. If your flowers won't stand up straight enough, use a piece of wire as shown in this illustration.
Figs. 53 and 54. It should be quite clear what types of flowers are on show. Look at the difference between this random arrangement (fig. 53) and this much more satisfactory grouping (fig. 54).

The composition of a still life doesn't start when you put brush to paper, but as soon as you start arranging each of the elements you are going to paint within a determined space. One of the first things you will have to decide is whether you are going to use a symmetric or asymmetric composition. Floral paintings are usually symmetrical. You would usually expect to see flowers arranged evenly on either side of a real or imaginary axis, with the features on one side repeated similarly on the other. In other words, perfect symmetry would mean a picture that would coincide perfectly if we were to fold it along that axis. But, don't worry, things shouldn't have to go to such extremes. Although you should keep symmetry in mind, you should add slight variations and additional objects on one or either side of the vase. A vase and bunch of flowers positioned in the centre of the picture, just like in the illustration shown here (fig. 55), corresponds to this kind of symmetry.

On the other hand, asymmetric composition positions objects unevenly in relation to this central axis, creating variety in the composition and a more original frame, without losing that sense of unity. Figure 56 is a good example of this.

55

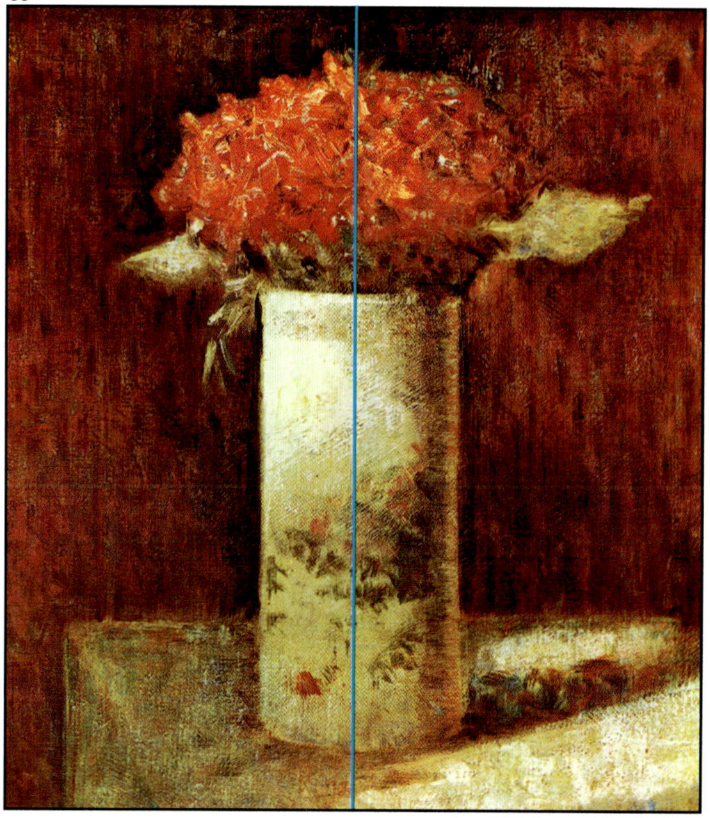

56

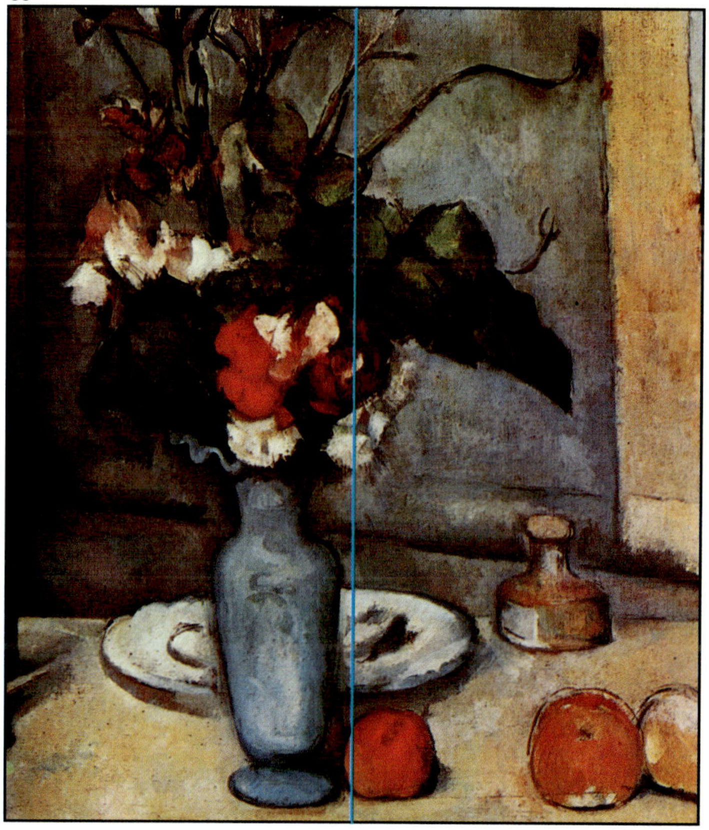

Fig. 55. This painting, **Flowers in a vase** *by Georges Seurat (private collection), is an example of symmetry. If you compare both sides of the central axis, you will see how balanced they are.*

Fig. 56. Paul Cézanne paid very little attention to symmetry in his paintings. See how in this painting, **The blue vase** *(Louvres Museum, Paris).*

Apart from symmetry, there is another more accurate method that can be used for composition. This is what is often called the 'golden rule', a law that positions the set of elements at what could be considered the perfect point, the most aesthetically pleasing position in the picture. According to this theory, to make a proportionately perfect division in the composition, the focal point should logically be moved off centre, either to the left or right of the geometric centre of the frame.

You don't need any special mathematical skills to put the theory into practice; you just need to remember that the golden point is just slightly to the left or right of the centre of the picture. However, if you do so happen to be a firm believer in mathematical precision, you simply have to multiply the height and width of the paper by 0.6. You'll find the golden point just where the two lines you have calculated cross.

This rule, invented by Euclid in the 6th century, bases itself on the need to simultaneously avoid the monotony of symmetric composition and the dispersion of asymmetric composition. Therefore the golden point is moved far enough from the centre so as to attract our attention without making it seem that the picture has been poorly framed.

57a

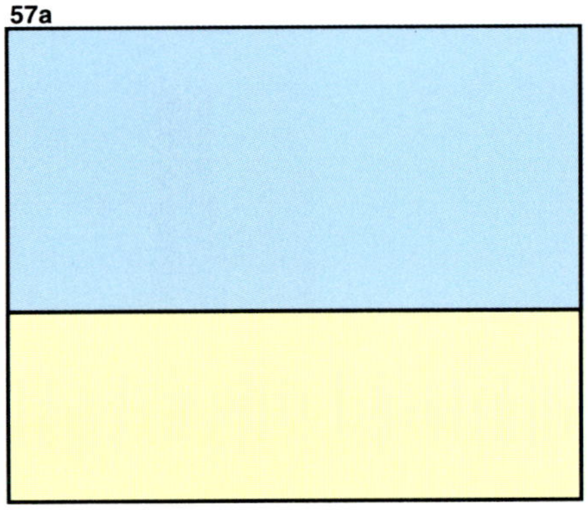

57b

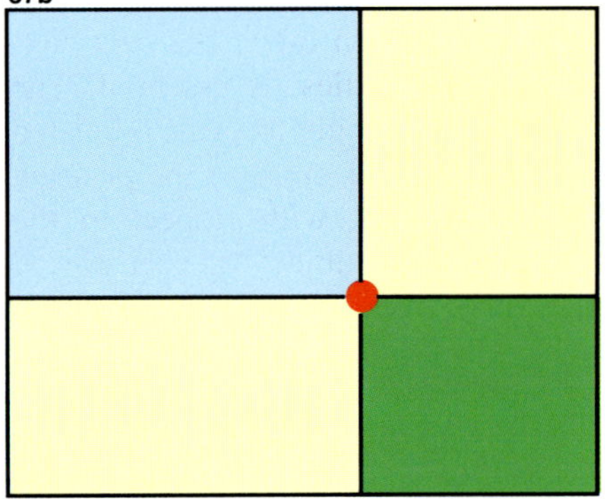

58

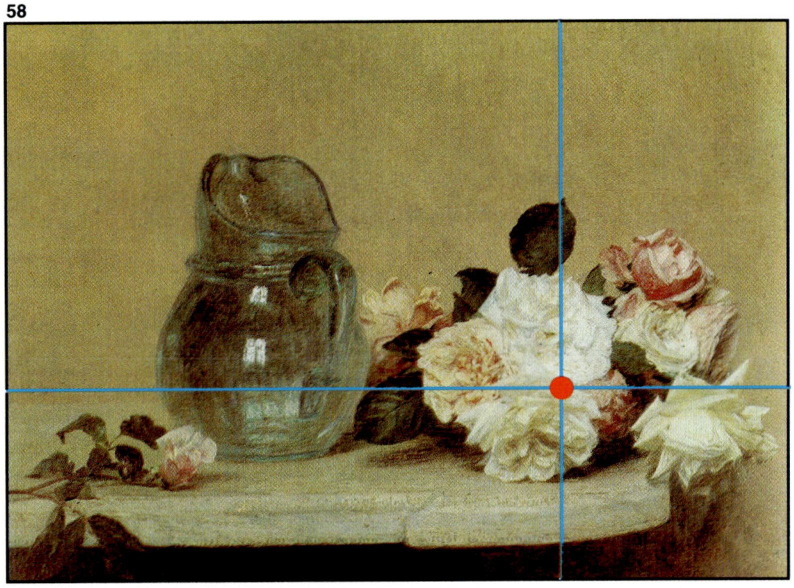

59

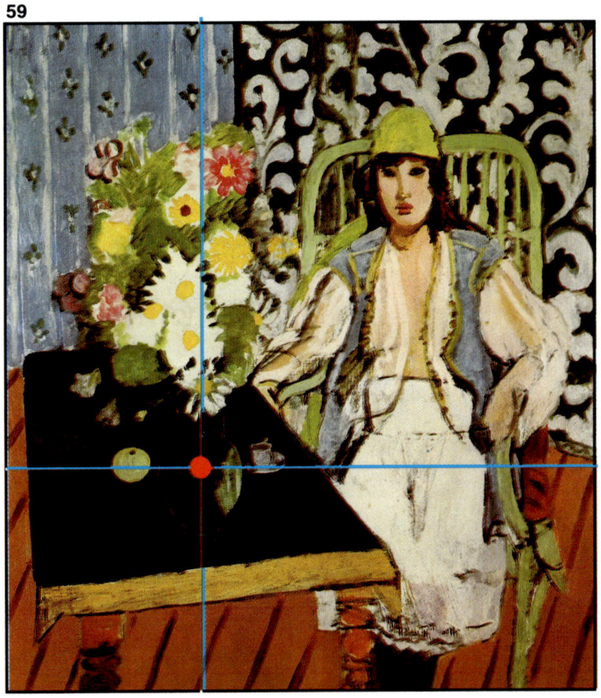

Figs. 57a and 57b. If we divide a horizontal segment of approximately 5 cm into two parts of 2 and 3 cm, we will find that the proportional relation between the smaller and the larger part is the same as the one between the larger part and the total length of the segment: 5/3=3/2. This way we find that, from a practical point of view, if you want to find the exact location of the 'golden point', you should multiply the height and width of the paper by 0.618.

Figs. 58 and 59. Notice how the golden point rule has been applied in these two paintings, **Roses and a glass** *jug (fig. 58) by Henri Fantin-Latour (Museum of Fine Arts, Lyon) and* **Black table** *by Henri Matisse (private collection).*

Choosing the most adequate point of view, that which offers the best pictorial opportunities, is essential. The subject you decide to paint is related in some way or other to the position that you adopt with respect to the horizon. If the subject has been placed on a table, the far end of it will act as the horizon, as is explained in these two illustrations.

– In the first composition, the subject is seen covering the far end of the table (fig. 60), which means that the artist is facing the subject at a similar level. This gives a rather flat, frontal view of the objects, and the shadows are seen as long, thin lines that run parallel to the edge of the table. Most of the elements seem somewhat foreshortened.

– However, if you look at figure 61, you will see that the subject is now below the far end of the table, indicating that the artist is now positioned slightly higher in relation to the subject. This higher position immediately highlights the tablecloth as an element of the composition, and it is now much easier for us to recognise each of the objects in the picture, and we can perceive their volume and form better. Notice how the shape of the shadows has completely changed.

I would advise you to make similar tests before painting any still life. You will soon find how varying your point of view creates completely different images.

60

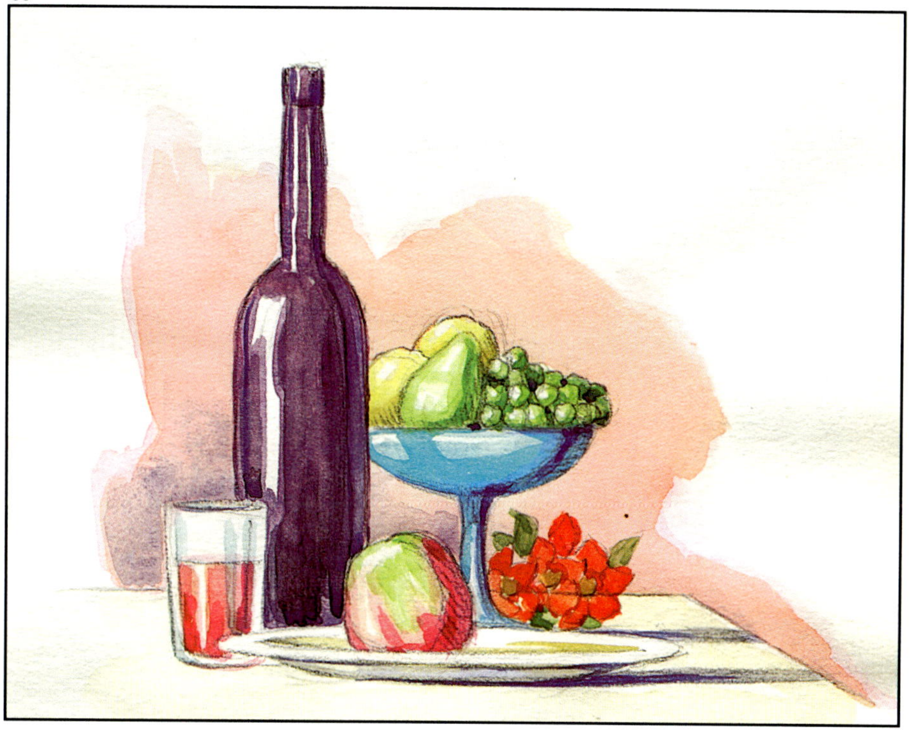

61

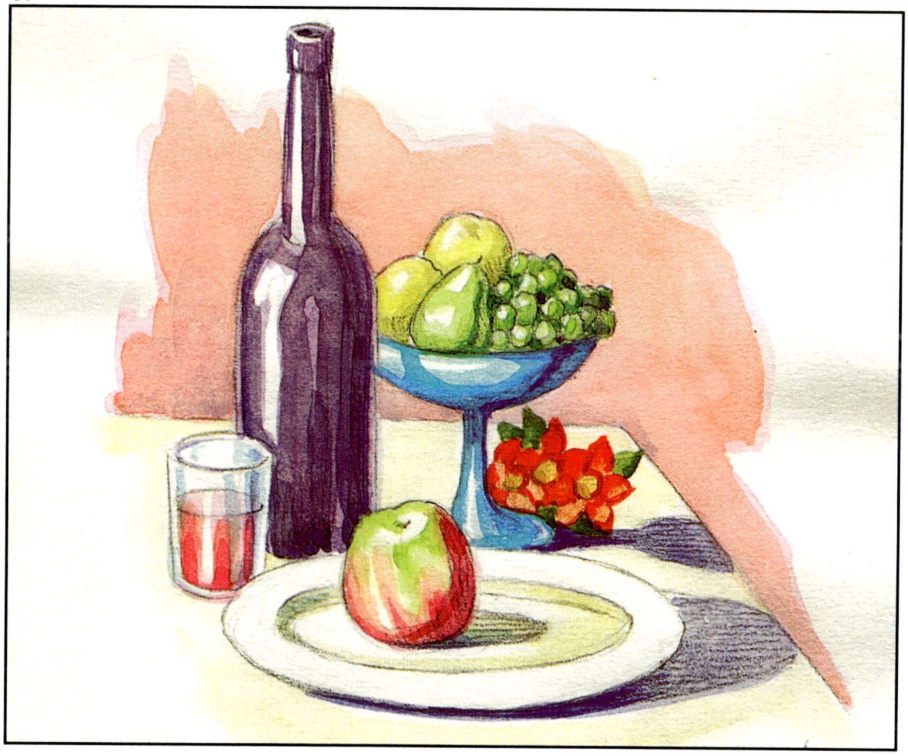

Fig. 60. The image of the subject varies depending on the position of the spectator. In this frontal view, one can hardly make out the surface of the table at all and the shadows seem much longer.

Fig. 61. From a slightly higher position, we get a clearer view of the subject. The surface of the table is much more distinguishable and the shadows appear more rounded.

Composing means organising, and for a clear and organized picture, it is therefore important that the artist has a precise idea of the layout. These exercises in organisation are designed to help you understand how to place and adapt your subject to different types of composition, starting with simple layouts (like rectangles, ovals and squares), which can then gradually be made more complicated. Other classic examples of the composition of still lives are layouts using horizontal, diagonal or pyramid shaped layouts.
If you notice that the still life subject that you are going to paint suggests a certain layout, try to highlight that design, even moving some of the elements if you can.
If we study the floral compositions and their respective layouts on these pages, we will see how this compo

62

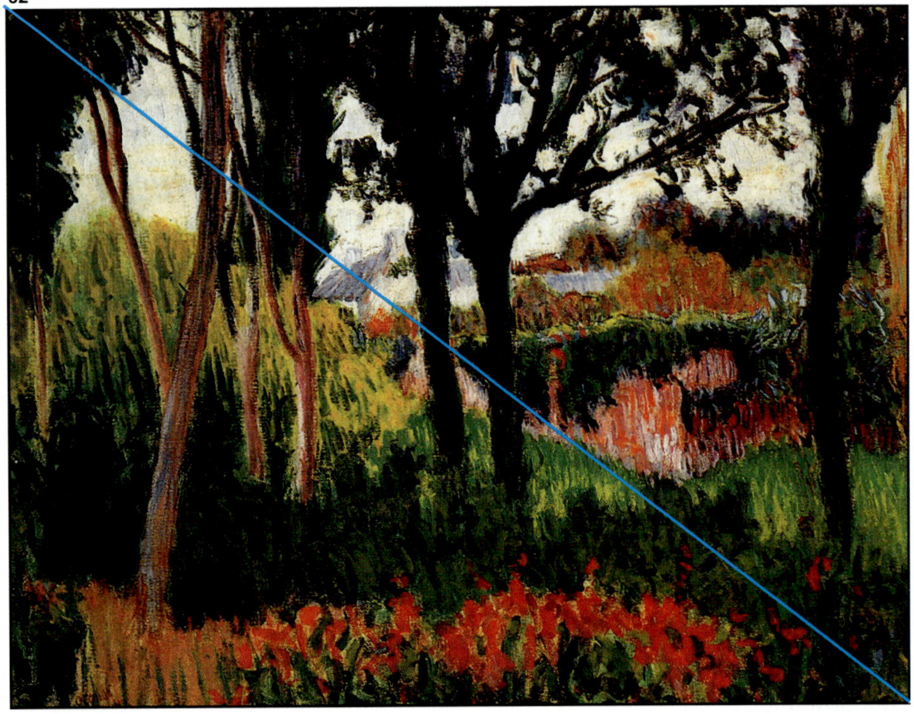

63

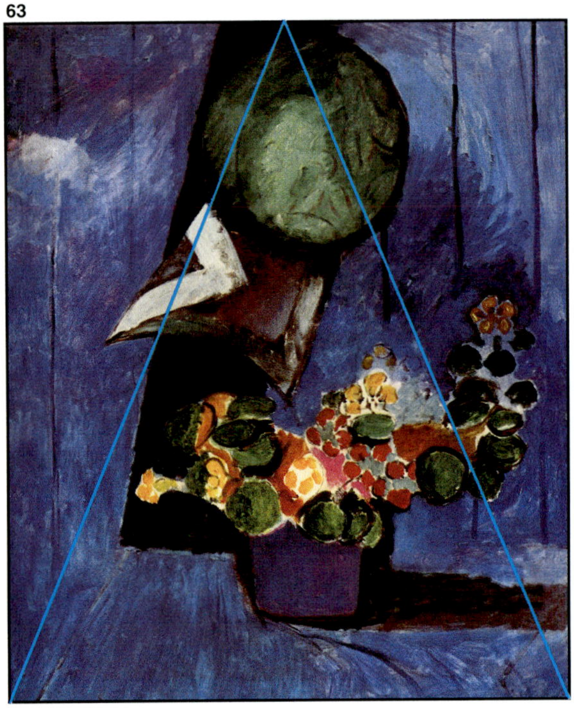

64

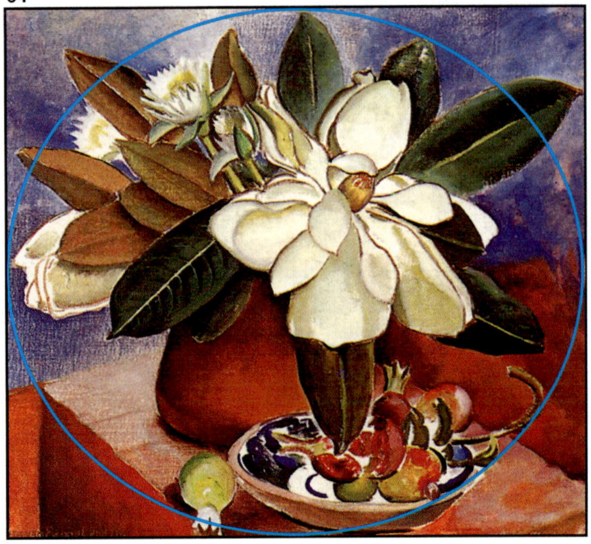

Fig. 64. An example of circular composition, **Magnolia flower** *by Laura van Papplendam (National Museum of Women in the Arts, Abbeville).*

Fig. 62. Notice the diagonal composition of this painting, **The farm in Lezaven, Finisterre** *by Roderic O'Conor (National Gallery of Ireland)*
Fig. 63. Pyramid shaped compositions are particularly popular for floral compositions. **Flowers and ceramics** *by Henri Matisse (Städelsches Kunstinstitut und Städtische Galerie, Frankfurt).*

sitional trick is one of the most important factors when trying to create unity in a picture (I have more to say about that later), which is directly related to artistic composition. The Greek philosopher Plato once said that composition is "variety within unity". He meant that when the distribution of the elements of a picture reveals some kind of basic form of composition, each element can be used to enrich our perception of the image as a whole. For example, objects can be placed outside the geometrical shape, or cloths and materials can divide the picture into attractive diagonal shapes. This is what we call 'variety'. Variety breaks the monotony of the composition and tries to attract the spectator's attention by generating more interest in the theme. The different colors and forms of our choice of flowers help to promote variety. Always try to avoid falling into the trap of monotony. Avoid painting pictures of bunches of identical flowers. A successfully composed picture is only achieved by working out the right relationship between each of the elements of the picture, what I have described as 'unity', and using the right combinations of color and lighting. You should take this well into account when arranging flowers, and you will find that the pre-prepared arrangements that you buy at a typical florist offer far too much unity. You need to think about both factors so that your still life contains "unity within variety and variety within unity".

Fig. 65. Variety can be achieved by introducing lines and forms that break the monotony of the composition. This example is called **Composition with roses** *and is by Juan Gris (private collection).*

65

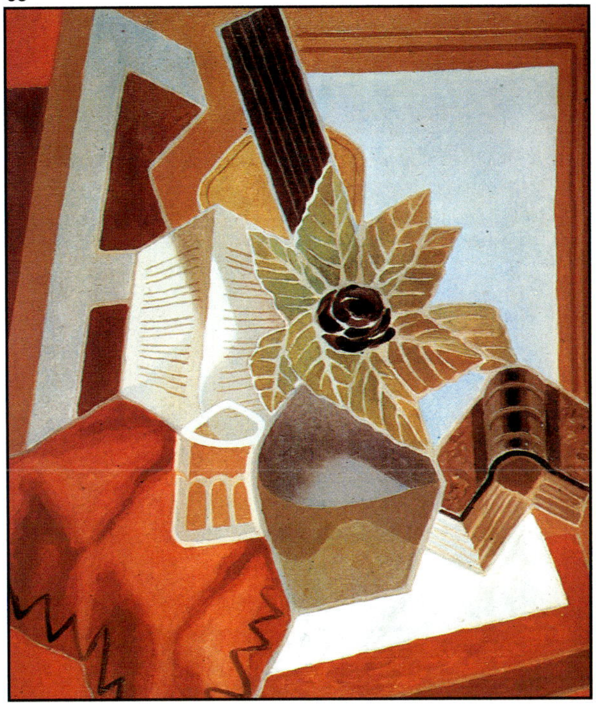

66

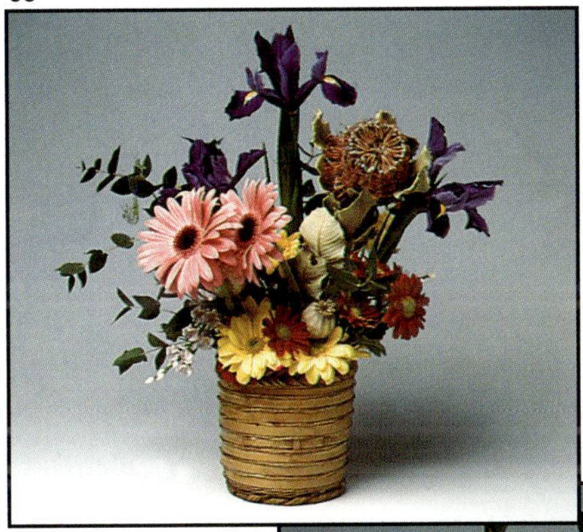

67

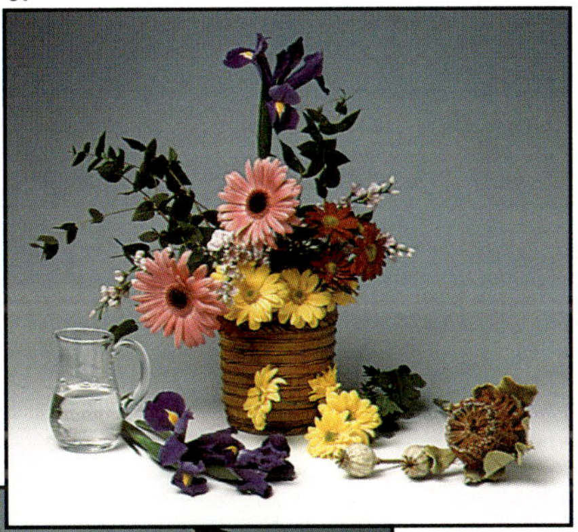

68

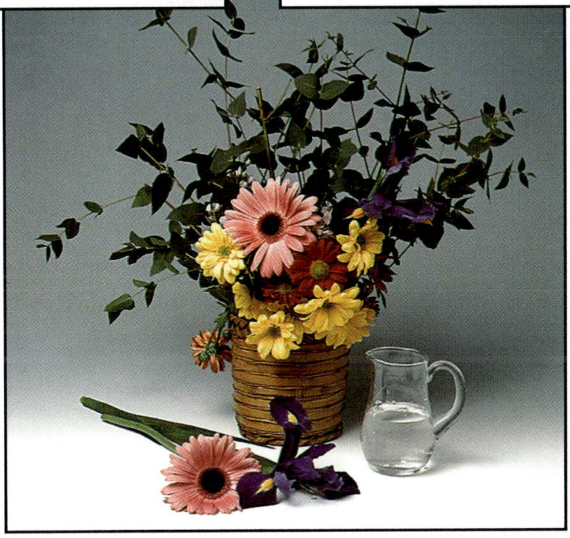

Fig. 66. These flowers, although well arranged, are not complemented by other objects and offer too much unity.
Fig. 67. Sometimes, the artist introduces too many complementary objects, and a composition like this looks far too jumbled.
Fig. 68. As you can see, there is a fine equilibrium in this picture between the flowers and their complementary objects, creating a harmonious balance in the composition

Complements: Plant Pots, Vases and Baskets

There is a wide range of objects that can be used as complements in floral pictures. Each object is given its own value, and plant pots, vases and baskets, whether they be made of glass, china, metal or any other material are painted with great care in keeping with their natural texture. Bringing these additional materials into the painting allows the artist to create more imaginative compositions and to broaden his talents for color and texture.

The secret of correctly reproducing the different textures of these materials basically depends on your ability to express changes in light and color, and reflections on the surfaces of the objects. In short, you need to portray their volumes and give them the right qualities and texture.

These days, there is an enormous range of different plant pots and vases available on the market; this is particularly true of vases. Such supports are used to enhance floral compositions. They offer a wide range of textures: flat, enamel, neutral, rough, glossy, with bas-relief and many more. Earthenware vases have very smooth surfaces that reflect the objects around them. If you use glass vases, remember that they neither hide the stalks of the flowers nor the water inside, which is going to present you with extra problems. I will speak a little more about glass containers in the next chapter.

Wicker baskets, on the other hand, have vegetable rather than mineral origins, and add a natural, countryside feel to the picture. They work particularly well in combination with small arrangements of dried flowers. Baskets come in all kinds of shapes and sizes; you just have to make sure that the one you choose adapts nicely to your composition. Remember that you should paint baskets in colors like ochre and umber, keeping these colors dull, unless the basket has been varnished, which is rather unlikely. The biggest problem with painting baskets is dealing with the wicker patterns. Remember that you don't have to paint an exact replica of every little detail. In some areas you can get away with merely suggesting the line pattern, without aiming for any kind of photographic precision.

69

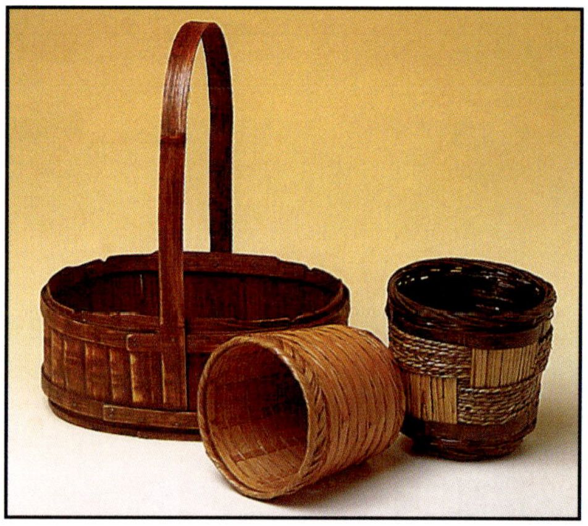

Fig. 69. Baskets, with their rich textures, are the perfect complements for flowers, as well as serving as a stand for them

70

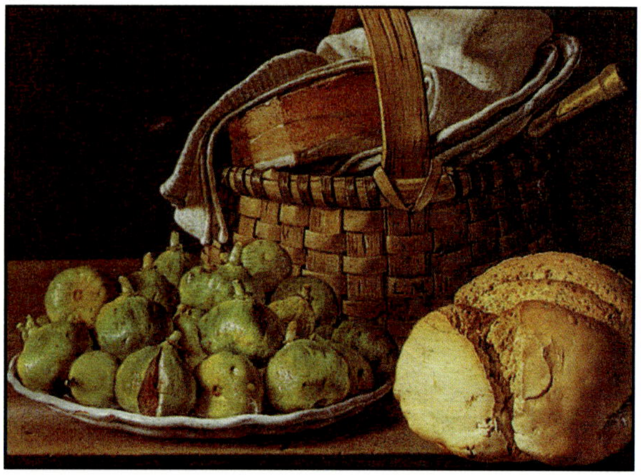

Fig. 70. Here is a very realistic treatment of the surface of a basket. The pattern has been produced by using tiny patches of light that suggest each strip. **Still life of a lunch basket, with bread and a plate of figs** *by Luis Meléndez (Louvre Museum, Paris).*

71

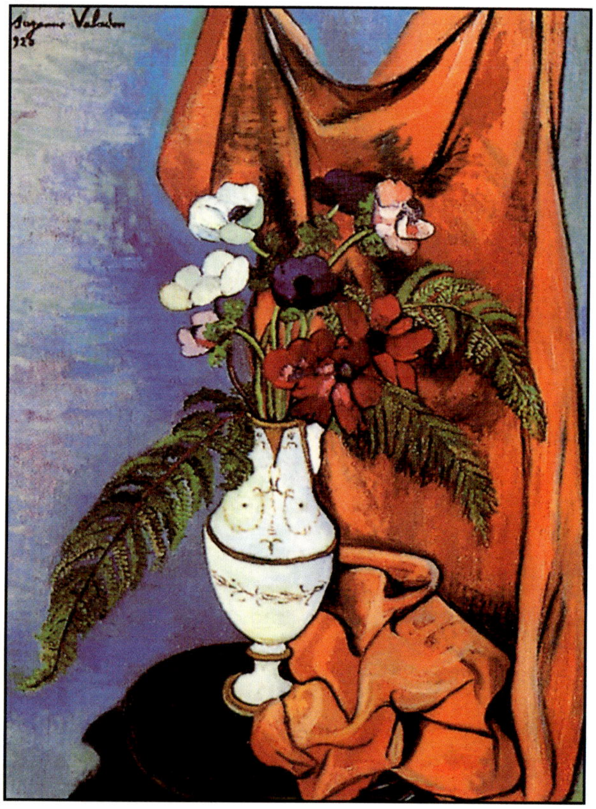

Fig. 71. This vase appears in a colorist painting, where the darker areas appear to have been dyed in a blue wash. **Bunch of flowers in an imperial vase** *by Suzanne Valadon (National Museum of Women in the Arts, Abbeville).*

Textures and Materials of Complements

The tradition of using vases and other glass or metal recipients is still very much alive in floral compositions. The right resolution of the color and form of these materials is vital if we are to surprise the spectator.

To paint glass we need to work from the basic idea that this is a crafted and colorless material (unless, of course, it is a colored glass). Therefore, the volume of the objects inside is seen through a surface that also shines and reflects the lights and colors outside. These shines should be created by using the white of the paper, and should merge into the reflections of other objects, which will modify the tones of certain colors. If there are objects inside or behind the glass container, these items should be seen to be slightly deformed. Their colors, however, should not be altered in the slightest. As Michaelangelo said, "The colors that we see through a glass object or reflected on a surface are as real as those of a table or an apple".

China or clay recipients (unless they are enamelled), need a more rustic treatment, and the reflections and shines are not added until we have already applied the first layer of color. Having painted this first layer, you should make a careful study of the variations of color on the surface of the ceramic object. You should adjust the form, contrasts and textures of the subject with superimposed brushstrokes.

Metal objects are usually represented by successive gradations of color, combining the intense reflections that light creates when it falls upon the object. These colors do not havc any determinate color. Local colors derive from a group of shapes, hues and small gradations that can go from extreme light to extreme dark, passing through carmines, ochres, greens, siennas, sepias, yellows, reds, etc (the latter colors are the most common ones for painting this kind of material). The colors of any nearby objects that are reflected on the surface should also be taken into account.

72

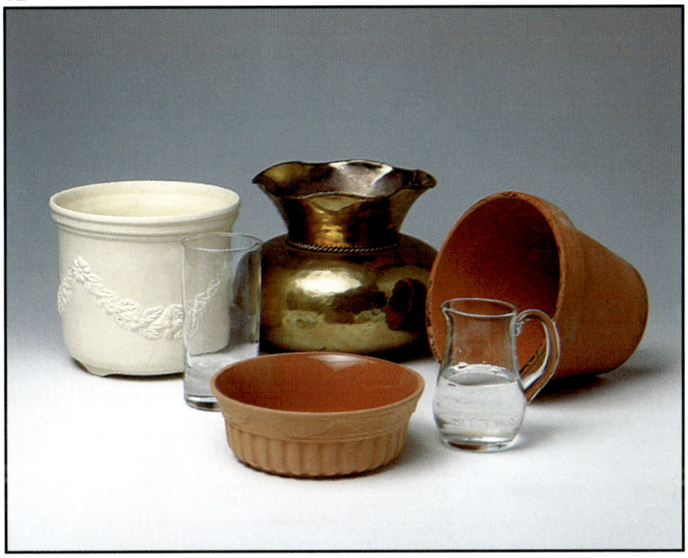

73

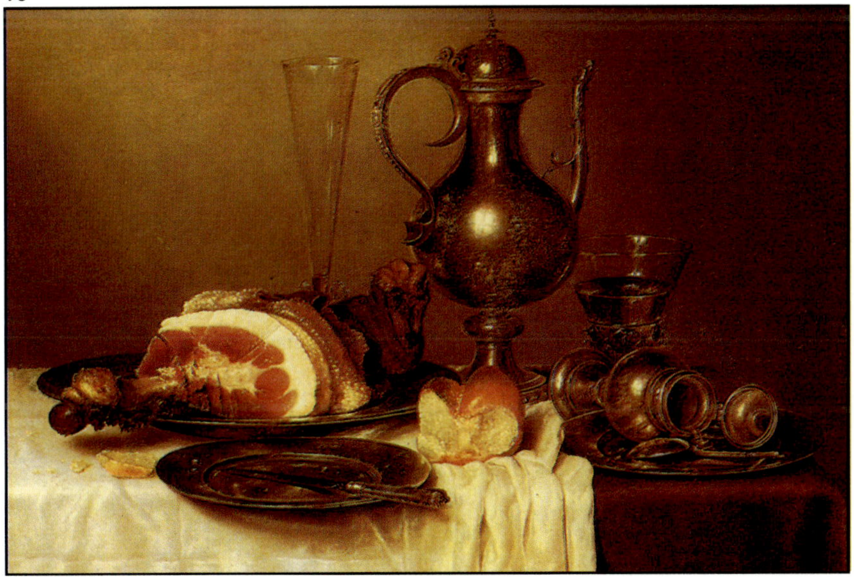

Fig. 72. The biggest difficulty that the artist is faced with when painting vases and plant pots is creating a convincing representation of the texture of the material.

Fig. 73. Study this still life that masterfully recreates the transparency of glass and the characteristic reflections of metal. **Banquet piece** ***by Willem Claesz (National Gallery of Ireland).***

How to Choose a Theme for Painting

The world of flowers is full of surprises; it is a world full of forms and colors that follow on from each other. Wherever you look, you will find objects that you can use in your floral still lives. There are very few places where you won't see flowers. We can find them in our homes, around the patio, in the garden, on balconies, all over the countryside... everywhere.

Painting flowers as you find them is not always a good substitute for a well thought-out composition, but this too can have a certain charm and impact.

If you wander around the countryside in springtime, you will find hoards of flowers all over the place. There is no doubt that this can be a wonderful theme. You will find different ways of dealing with the subject, and each one is made up of several more interesting sub-themes, such as small groups of flowers, hedgerows, wild flowers, cultivated flowers (such as crops of sunflowers) and apple or walnut trees in blossom.

74

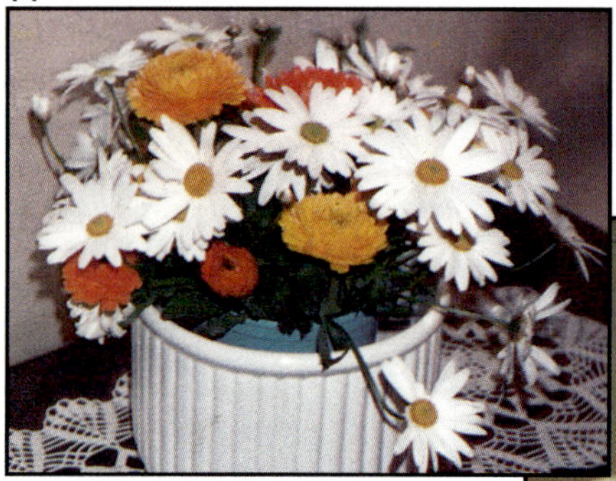

75

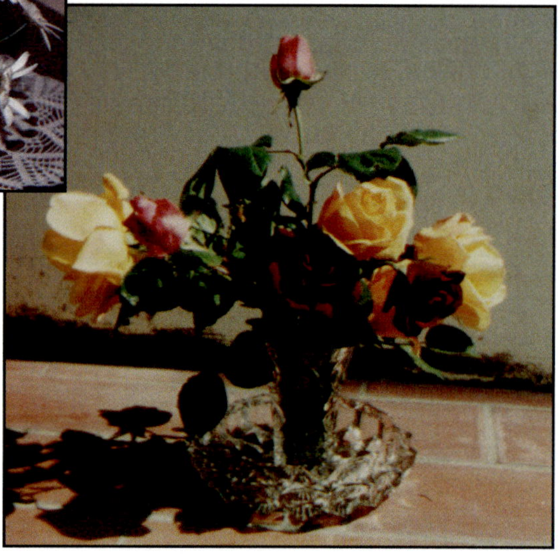

76

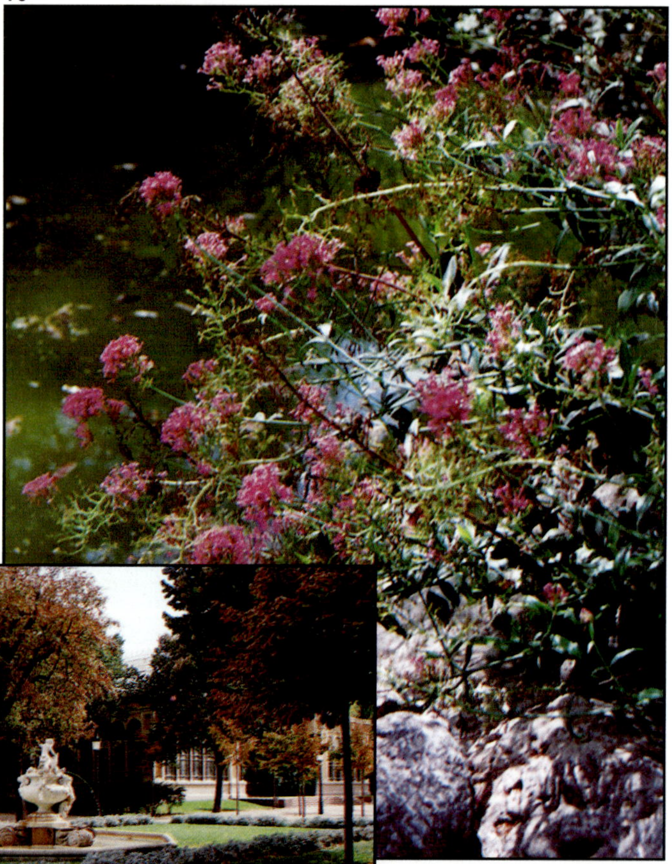

77

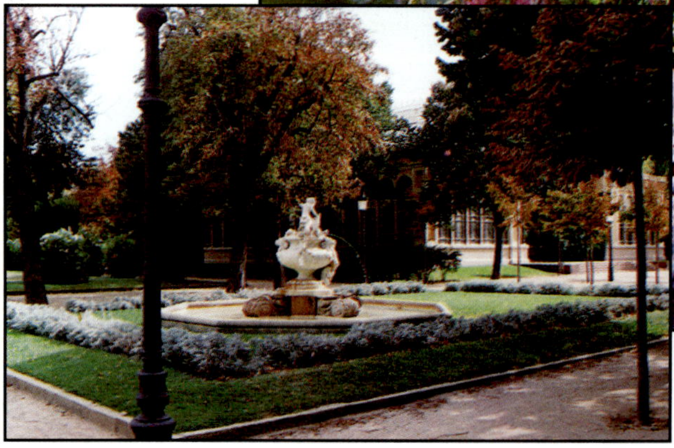

Fig. 74. The bunches of flowers that are so often placed in the centre of tables are an excellent subject for painting.

Fig. 75. If you have flowers at home, take a camera, go outside and take several photos under different lighting conditions and from several angles. You will find that these photographs are an excellent reference when you start painting.

Fig. 76. The countryside is a never-ending source of inspiration. Try walking along riverbanks and streams in springtime.

Fig. 77. If you live in a large city, there is sure to be a park nearby with beautiful flowerbeds and fountains.

Once you have the subject before you, you can start your creative activity. You need to find the right point of view, try out different frames, examine lighting effects and start deciding exactly how you plan to interpret the theme.
If you don't want to go to the country-side, or it simply isn't possible, you can paint flowers in your studio instead. This way, it is easier to get close to the subject and to modify the lighting and its position. You need to remove any elements that do nothing more than crowd the image, and find out exactly what you want to make up your painting. In such a case, you can go to your nearest florist or market and buy natural flowers, dried flowers or pretty sheaves of corn. If you like, you could even buy artificial flowers, as long as they are of good quality and look as realistic and natural as possible.

78

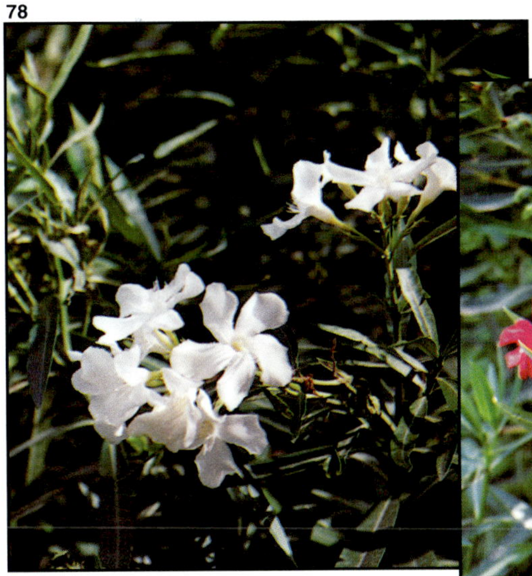

79

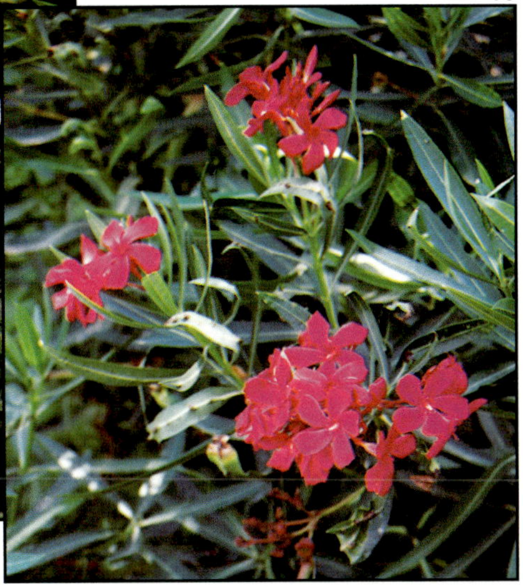

80

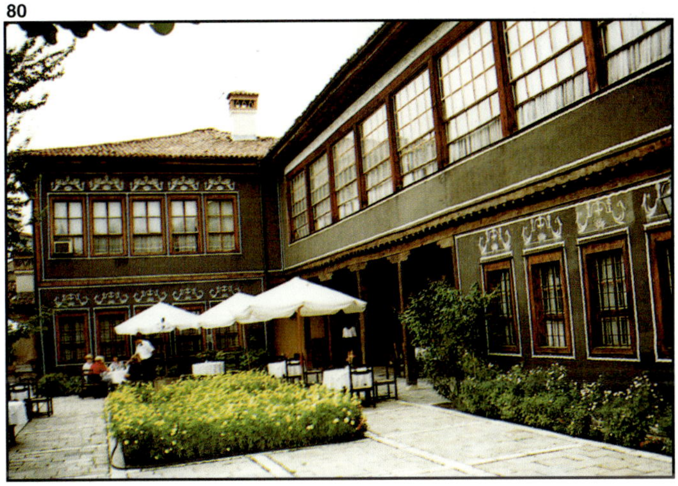

81

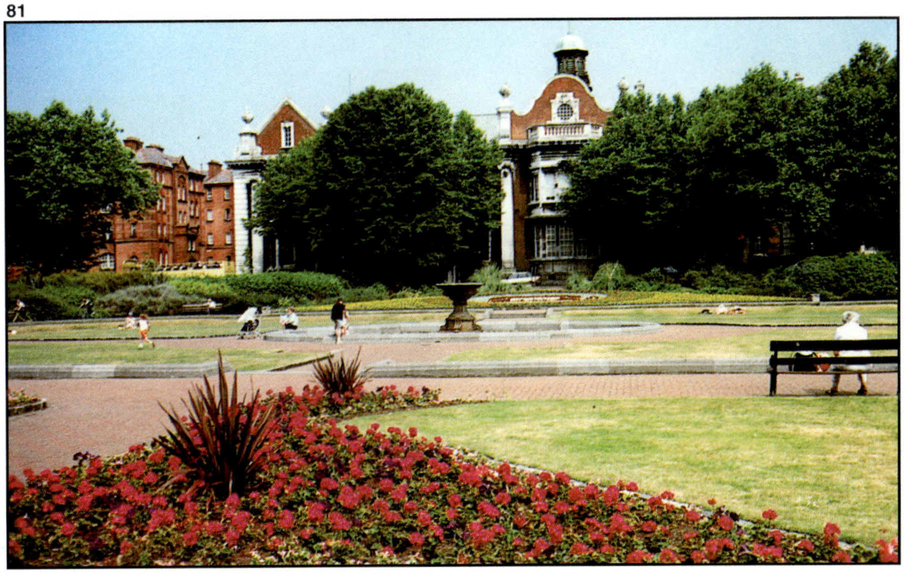

Figs. 78 and 79. Once you have chosen a subject, you should decide upon the right frame by moving about and changing your position to observe the different ways in which light falls upon the petals.
Fig. 80. Large mansions and stately homes usually have gardens packed with themes you could paint. In such cases, you can harmonise the groups of flowers with the beautiful architecture, which would serve as an attractive background.
Fig. 81. City parks also provide attractive subjects, and are ideal places for sketching.

Garden Flowers

If you study garden flowers, you will find that their color, quality and texture greatly depends upon the way in which sunlight falls not only upon their leaves and petals, but also on everything that surrounds them. There is an important difference between the colors of flowers in the garden and those that we paint in the studio. The way in which we perceive garden flowers depends on the intensity of the sun, and also on the way in which they relate to colors in the background. In the studio, flowers are seen in isolation, away from their natural context and subjected to artificially manipulated lighting.

If you have your own garden, you will be able to spend every season of the year painting the flowers and plants that you have grown yourself. This way, you will find out how their colors change as time goes by and how they are affected by changing weather conditions. If you do not have your own garden, there must be some kind of park or public garden within easy reach of your home.

When painting garden flowers you should take the following factors into consideration:

– For painting outdoors, you are going to need smaller instruments that are easier to carry. You should get a small boxed palette (preferably one that you can carry in your hand or fit into a pocket), a small flask of water (in case you don't find any other water source in the vicinity), a piece of cloth for wiping your brushes and, of course, a folio full of paper.

– You will need to work much faster than in the studio because, as you are only too aware, the sun moves quickly, modifying the positions of shadows and brightening or darkening the light in certain areas. The only way you can get around this problem is by indicating areas of shadow with a soft blue wash before moving on to paint the local colors of the plant.

82

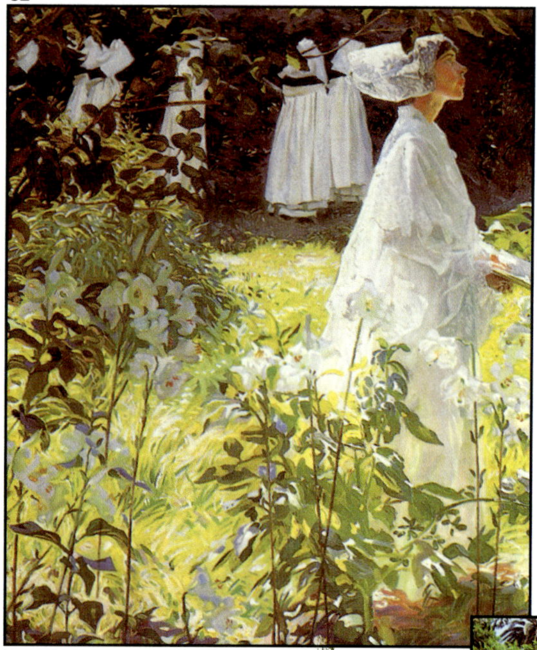

Fig. 82. The neighbouring vegetation should be shown by deliberate shades without trying to go into such details as showing every single leaf. **Convent garden** *by William John Leech (National Gallery of Ireland).*

83

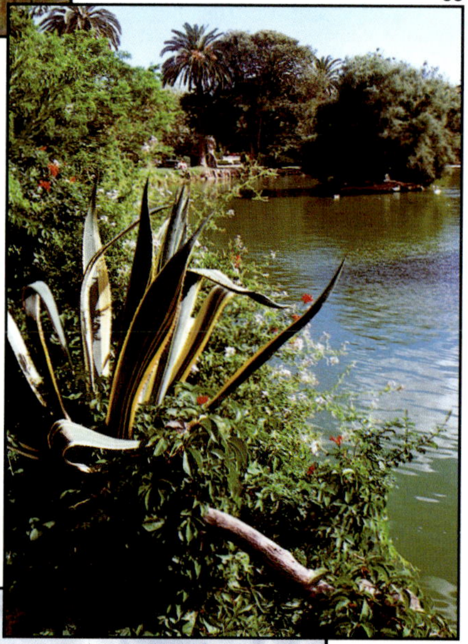

Fig. 83. Flowers rarely appear in isolation in gardens. They form an integral part of an environment full of bushes, plants, ponds and trees.

Fig. 84. When you come across flowers that, because of their structure, never stop moving in the wind, you have two options. Either paint from memory or use a photograph.

84

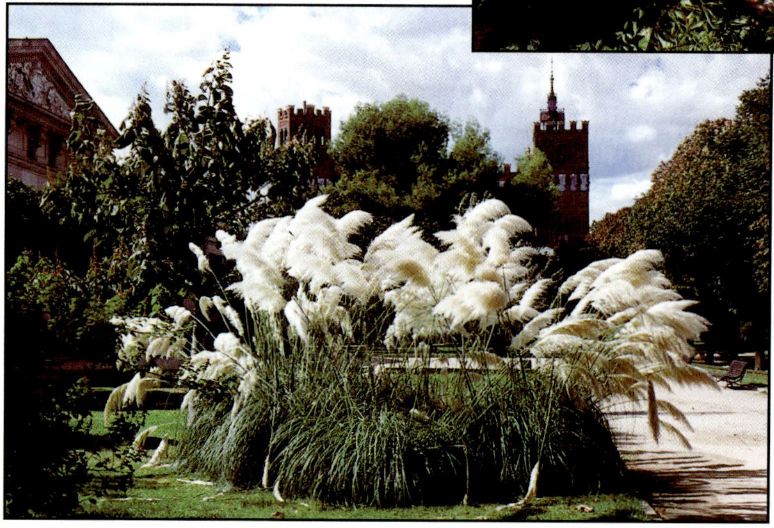

– You will need a lot of patience, because you are going to have to put up with plenty of interruptions. Sometimes, for example, clouds will block the sunlight, or the wind will cause the flowers to move. You will also have people coming up to see what you are painting, sometimes without realising that they are blocking your sunlight.

– If you are planning to spend a long time outdoors, you should take a portable stool and a straw hat to shade your eyes from the sun.

Painting in gardens also involves painting trees, bushes and grass, which tend to become the backgrounds for our floral paintings. These may form irregular shapes, but you needn't worry too much about framing them properly. When painting trees, synthesis is the most important thing to keep in mind, and you can forget about unnecessary details. Don't try to paint a tree by meticulously representing each and every leaf. You don't need such photographic accuracy; just a few simple brush strokes should be enough.

Likewise, you should show bushes and grass with shades of color that synthesise with the whole picture. You can represent them in an almost abstract way, using an explicit synthesis of colors and shapes. They are usually painted in a uniform color, but with a few tonal variations that simulate texture and volume, apparently abstract shades that, when incorporated in the picture, allow the spectator to distinguish a blanket of grass made golden by the sun, the lawn that grows behind a rosary, or a leafy flowering shrub.

85

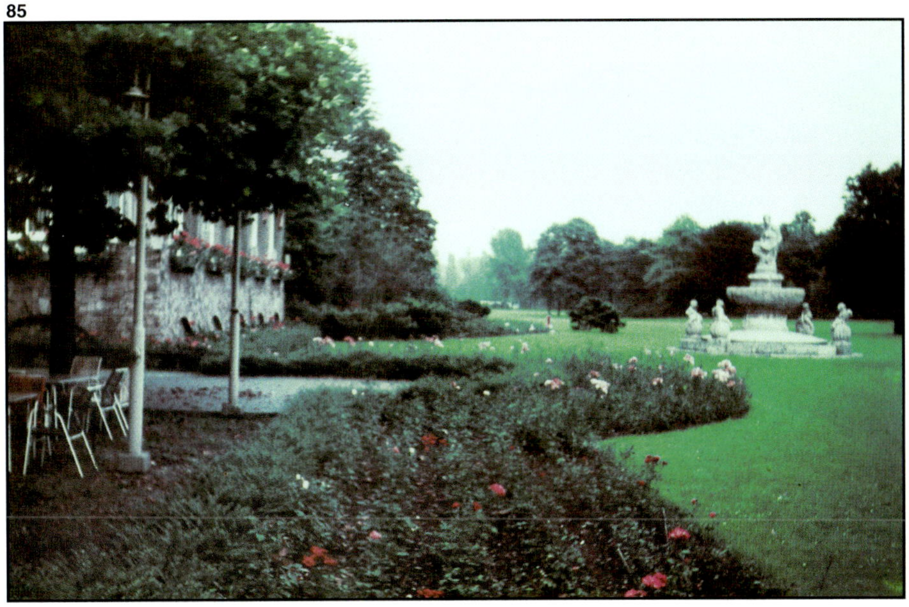

86

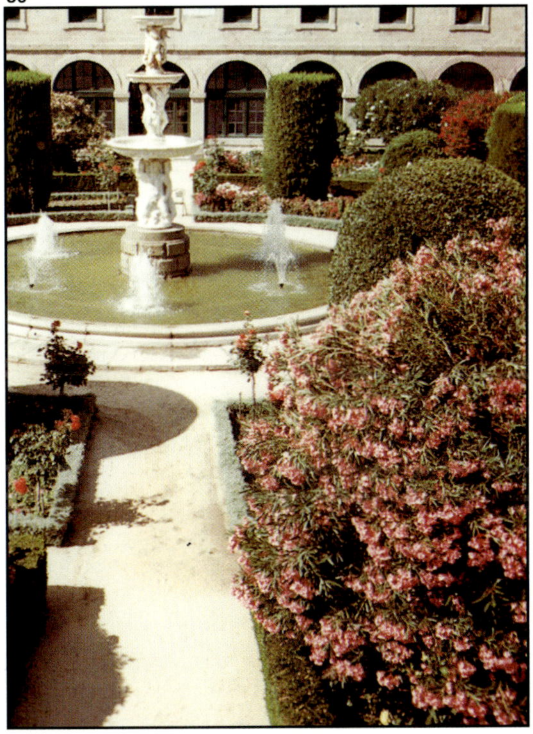

Dig. 85. Just like any work outdoors, the colors of a garden depend heavily on the weather. Notice how the normally bright, vibrant colors of the flowers and grass appear rather dull in this overcast scene.

Fig. 86. On the other hand, sunlight brings the colors of flowers to life and creates much deeper contrasts among the vegetation. This is a much more appropriate scene for a colorful painting.

The Photograph as a Complement to Work

Photographs can be a magnificent aid. The way in which they can so easily reproduce reality helps to reveal several aspects that may pass unseen by direct observation of the subject: images in movement, underwater images, aerial photography or other unusual angles. A photograph can be used as the subject for a painting, or at least as a very useful reference.

Photography is a simple and efficient way of studying the composition and framing of a subject taken from nature, which can later be painted in the studio. You can select the most appropriate frame with your camera, then amplify the image, move nearer or further away, move it higher or lower, to the left or to the right, decide which aspects you will include in the frame and which you will leave out, and ultimately decide upon the most expressive frame.

You don't need any professional gear to make these shots. A reflex camera, manual if possible and with a normal lens, should be fine.

But to what extent can a photograph take the place of a sketch? Remember that a photograph is nothing more than an aid, not the object of the exercise, and it is also important that an amateur artist gets used to sketching from nature. The use of a photograph is most justified in those cases when it is not easy to draw a sketch by hand such as, for example, busy streets, a sunset or sunrise (because they happen in such a short space of time), places that are hard to access or in adverse weather conditions that make outdoor painting difficult (torrential rain or a snowstorm). Although photographs look rather flat and lack depth, you should try to think about interpreting them in the same way that you would interpret real life.

Fig. 87. A photograph is not the object of the exercise, but a useful complement when working outdoors. All you need is an ordinary manual reflex camera and the desire to experiment with nature

87

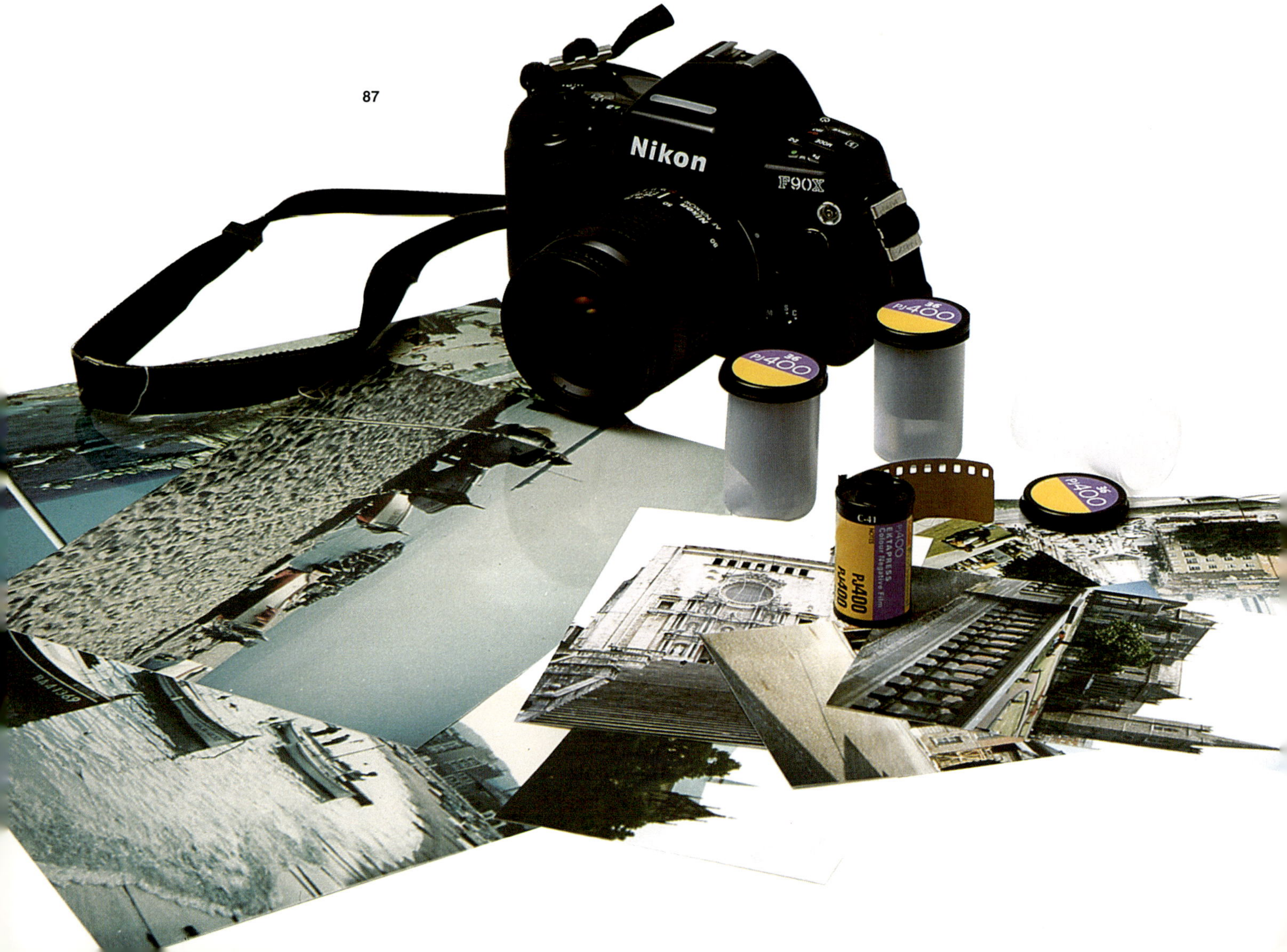

Quality of Light and Contrast

Before you start painting, there are a few basic principles of light and color contrast that you should know about. You can either choose to work with natural or artificial light, it doesn't really matter. Most painters, when they are in their studios, tend to use artificial lighting on their subjects. This can make the subject look slightly redder than normal, an effect caused by incandescent bulbs, while natural lighting tends to have a more bluish appearance. Whatever you do, don't try to mix both types of light together, or you will create conflicting effects and color ranges. Neither should you attempt to paint flowers under fluorescent light, which falsifies colors, and makes them look artificial and takes the naturalness out of the color.

The quality of illumination greatly influences the value and contrast of light and shadow. The possible forms of lighting can be summarised by two qualities and four directions of light:

– Quality of direct light: this is what creates heavy shadows and accentuates color contrast. Direct sunlight and artificial spotlights come under this category.

– Quality of diffused light: as suggested by its name, this is the kind of light that softens the contrast between lit and shadowed areas. Good examples are overcast daylight or the light that comes from a window high above the position of the actual subject.

88

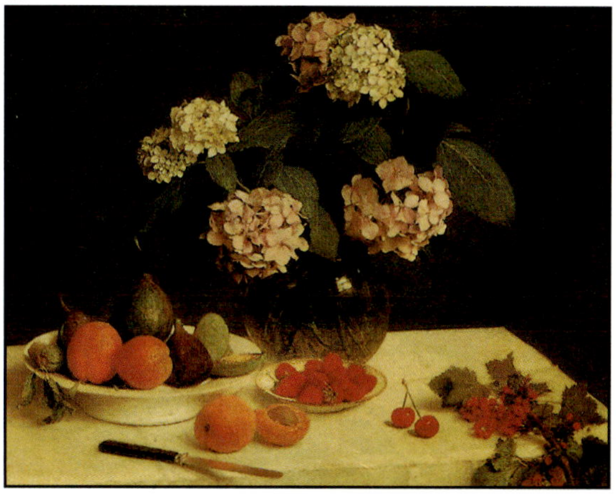

Fig. 88. Even if you are working in your studio, I would suggest that you try to use natural lighting as often as possible, just as the grand masters did. **Still life** ***by Henri Fantin-Latour (Museo Gulbenkian, Lisbon).***

89

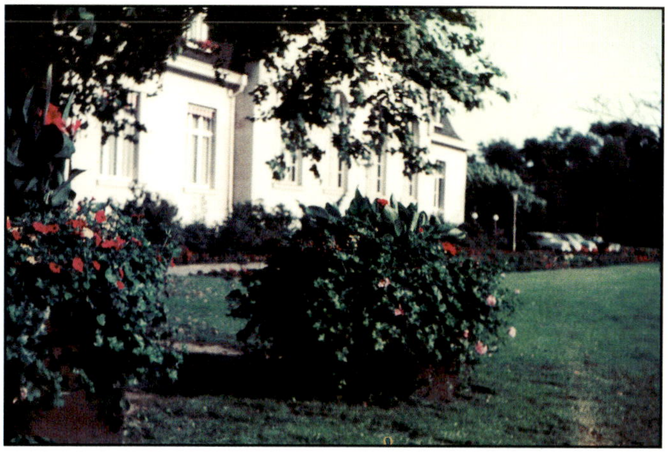

Fig. 89. Diffused light tends to blot our perception of colors and forms, softening silhouettes and possible color contrasts. See this effect at work in this pretty German garden.

90

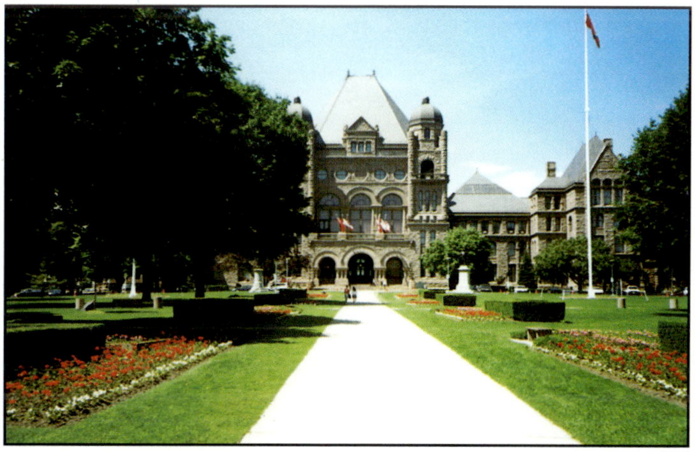

Fig. 90. Direct light brightens colors and creates more contrast between light and shadows.

– Frontal lighting: when light hits the subject from the front. It hardly produces any shadows and is perfect for painting colorist style flowers (fig. 91).
– Frontal side lighting and side lighting: light strikes the subject on one of its sides and projects a shadow on the opposite side. This is the most normal type of lighting, and the best one for explaining the form of the flowers thanks to the volume that the contrast between light and shadow infuses (fig. 92).
– Zenith lighting: the source of light is placed high above the subject. This is ideal for drawing or painting, although the presence of shadows is less evident (fig. 94).
– View against the lighting: light strikes the subject from behind, creating a shadow in the foreground and a halo of light around the outside of the floral shapes (fig. 94).

As you have seen, up until now we have been exploring illumination from basic lighting, using just one light source. However, a complementary screen can also be used on the opposite side of the light to soften the shadowed areas. Be careful not to put the screen too near the subject, or it will reflect too much light onto it. If the subject receives light from both sides, volume is lost and the effect will not look very realistic.

Before you start painting your picture of flowers, you should study every lighting option and decide which is most appropriate, taking color and form into account with respect to the background.

91

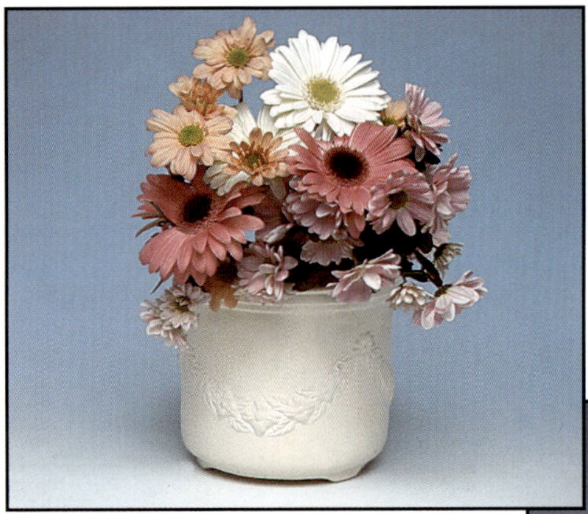

92

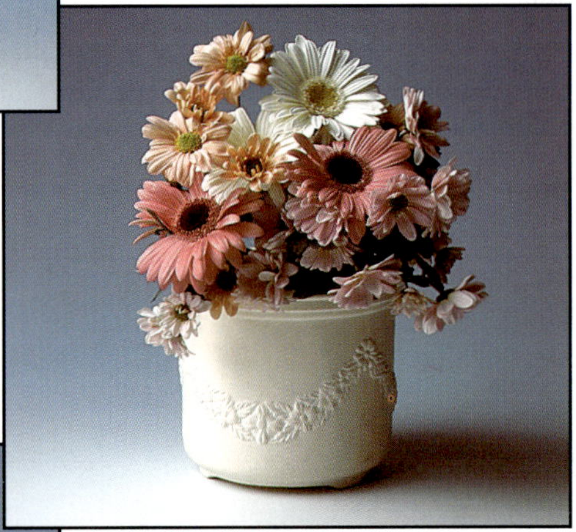

93

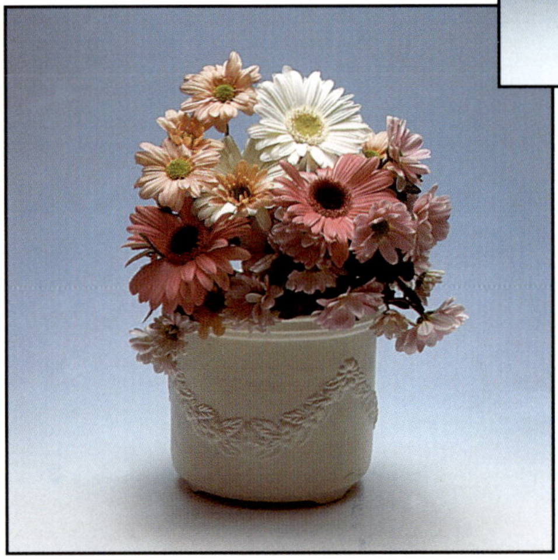

94

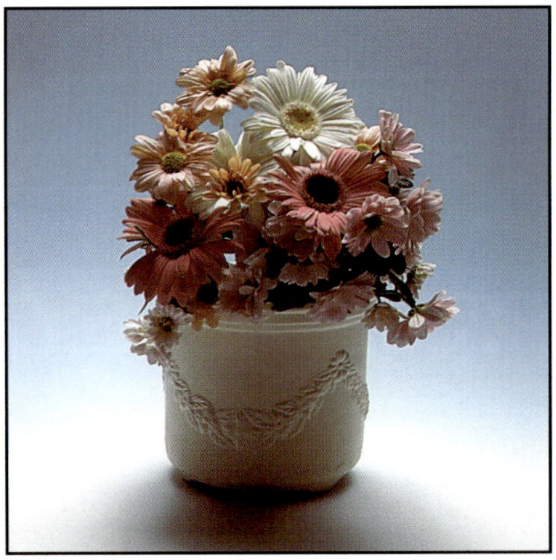

Fig. 91. Frontal lighting hardly produces any shadows, and is therefore the best option for colorist painting.
Fig. 92. Frontal side lighting and side lighting create more contrast between shadow and light, giving greater value to the subject.
Fig. 93. Zenith lighting is the most common option for floral painting. Baroque still lives used it frequently, with a tenuous light coming from a skylight at the top of the room.
Fig. 94. Views against the lighting give the flowers an unrealistic phantasmagoria effect.

By 'contrast' we are referring to the juxtaposition or clear difference between colors. Two clearly different colors are placed next to each other, which intensifies their dissimilar characteristics. There are basically three factors that vary color contrast:

– Tonal contrast: this when contrast is obtained by placing two different tones of the same color next to each other. The most obvious example of this is the use of different tones to color petals. Although the petals are all the same color, different tones make it easier to distinguish each different one.

– Simultaneous contrast: this works on the theory that a color appears lighter or darker depending on the color it has surrounding it. The colors of a flower can be modified by adjacent areas, in this case the background. Look at figure 96 to see how the flower on the right stands out more clearly because it has a lighter color behind it, making it easier to make out its shape and outline.

– Complementary contrast: the carmine or vermilion color of a flower surrounded by a green background creates an extraordinary contrast, because the discord between the two colors is sharper when made by complementary colors (fig. 97). The same happens when yellow and violet, red and green, or orange and blue are juxtaposed.

95

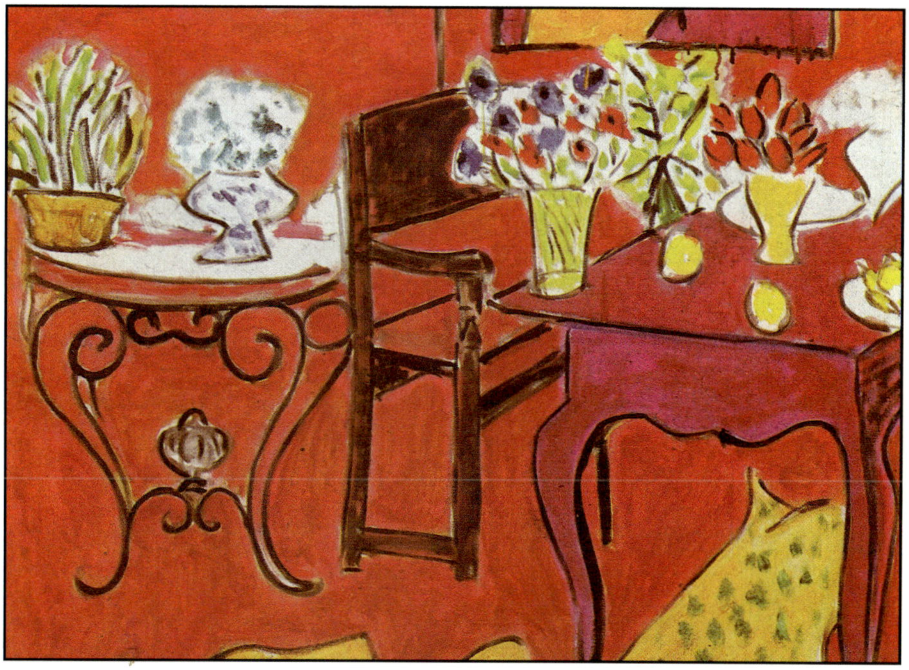

Fig. 95. Fauvists like Henri Matisse quickly understood the relationship between colors by provoking sharp contrasts in their floral paintings, as we can see in this fragment of **Large red interior** *(National Museum of Modern Art, Paris).*

96

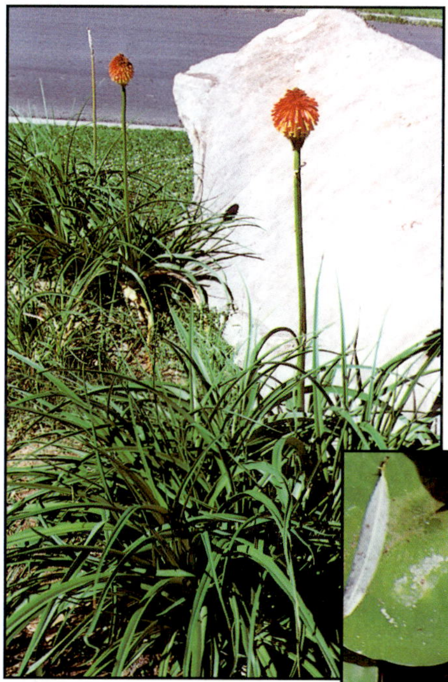

97

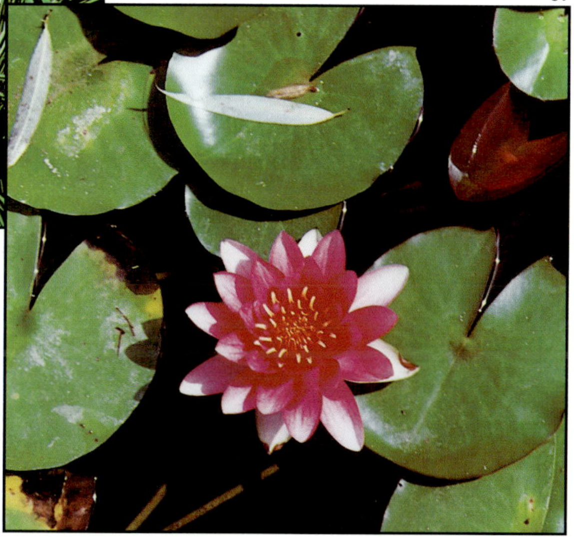

Fig. 96. The color of a flower depends largely on the color that surrounds it. Look at how the shape and outline of the flower on the right seems much sharper when it is surrounded by a lighter color than the flower on the left.

Fig. 97. The maximum contrast between colors is produced when both are complementary, as is the case in this photograph. The pink appearance of the flower contrasts with its complement, the green of the leaves in the background.

Harmonic Relationships

If, as we have seen up until now, the relationship of contrast is made by colors of a different range, harmonic relationships are established between colors that belong to the same family or that have similar values, integrating nicely into the picture as a whole. This is because a color means very little on its own, its meaning comes from how it relates to other colors, and there is a certain level of mutual dependency.

These chromatic tendencies come from nature itself. If you paint the flowers in a public garden early in the morning on a clear, sunny day, the light will appear slightly orange. After five o'clock in the afternoon, when the sun starts going down, this orange will return. On a cloudy day, colors will take on a more greyish appearance.

Harmonic relationships can generally be divided into three types: the ranges of warm colors, of cold colors and of burnt colors.

– Warm color range: made up red and its derivatives, with red being considered the color that generates the greatest feeling of heat. Although red is most dominant, we should also classify colors like green, yellow, orange, carmine, purple and violet as part of the range. We should also consider transitory colors that could be classed as either warm or cold such as violet and yellowish-green. The flowers that most represent this range include yellow and red roses, hyacinths, anemones, tulips, auroras, mimosas, yellow chrysanthemums and geraniums. Brightly colored gardens that are dominated by warm colored flowers are very eye-catching.

– Cold color range: identified visually as the opposite sensation to that offered by the warm color range. It is based on blue and its derivatives, and therefore includes cyan, ultramarine blue, dark blue, permanent green, emerald green and the aforementioned transitory colors. The flowers that best represent this range include red roses, hydrangeas, hyacinths, forget-me-nots and veronicas.

98

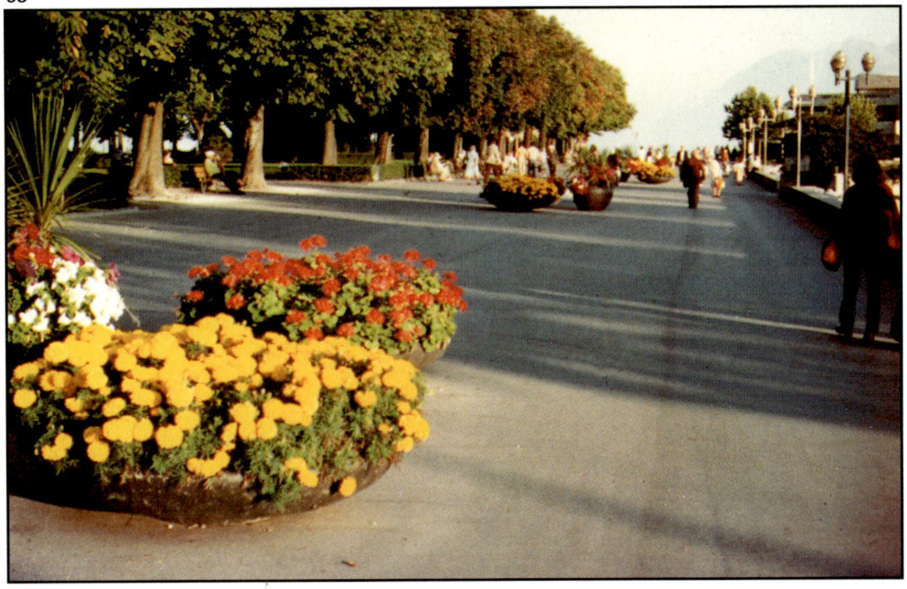

Fig. 98. When the sun is either rising or setting, the atmosphere tends to look rather orange, and this affects the colors of the flowers.

99

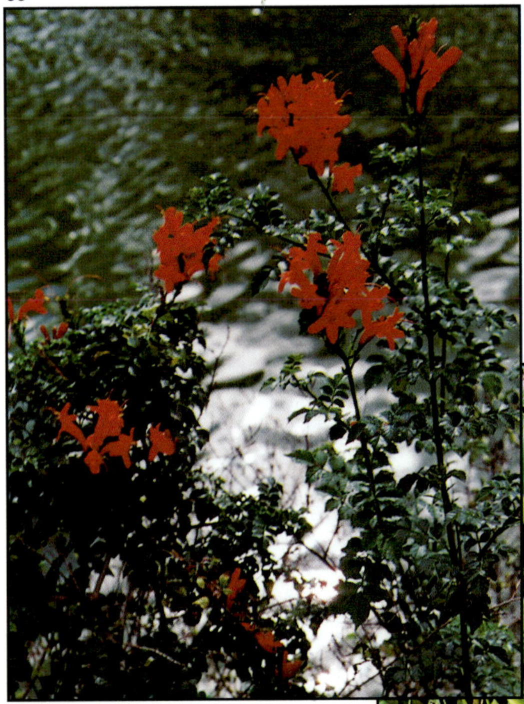

100

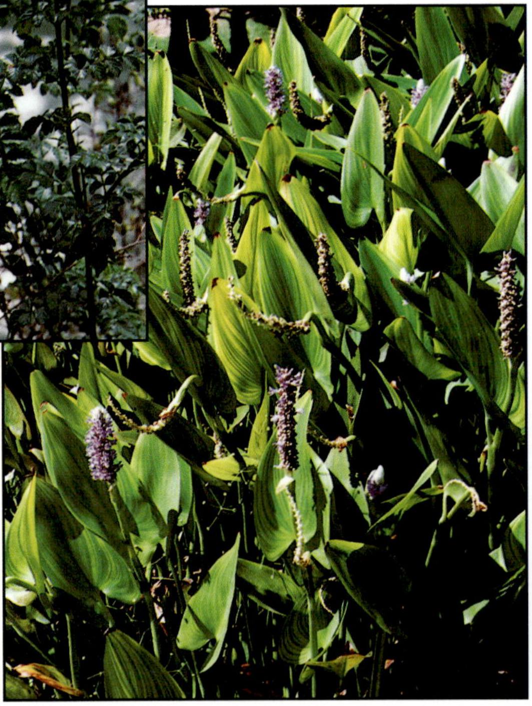

Fig. 99. Warm colored flowers stand out from the background, making them much more eye-catching.

Fig. 100. Cold colored flowers, such as these violets, do not stand out from the background so much, and make the picture look more integrated.

Cold colored flowers harmonise better with green backgrounds of vegetation. Because they contrast less they are more balanced and the colors less striking.

– Burnt color range: is preferred by many artists because of the quality of its colors, a product of the mix of complementary colors in unequal proportions with the intervention of white (in the case of watercolor painting, the white of the paper is already active). It results in a greyish tendency, which can be either warm, cold or neutral. Dried flowers lose a lot of their color during the drying process, and they generally have burnt colors. Flowers that belong to this category tend to have a rather monochromatic appearance, and hardly contrast with surrounding vegetation at all.

101

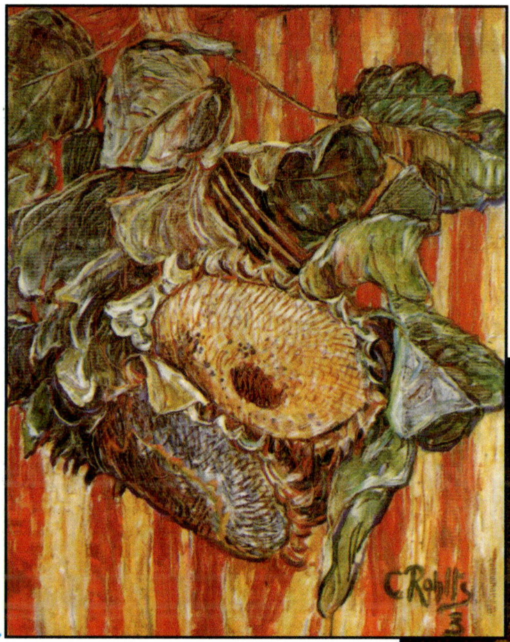

Fig. 101. **Sunflowers** *by Cristian Rohlfs (Ostwall Museum, Dortmund). This is a clear example of the use of warm colors.*

102

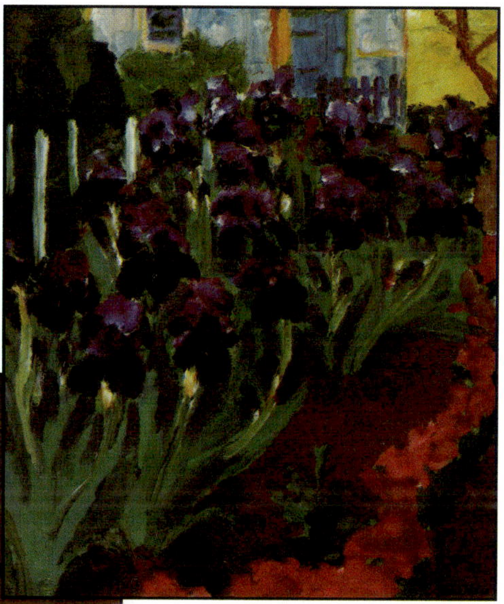

Fig. 102. **Blue irises** *by Emil Nolde (Kunstmuseum, Basle) shows the corner of a pretty garden painted with predominantly cold colors.*

103

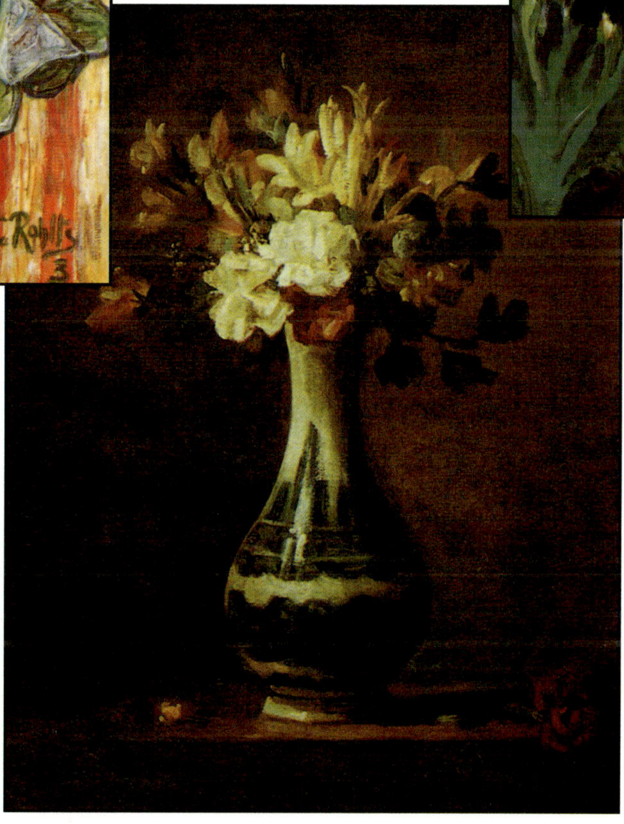

Fig. 103. This outstanding painting by Chardín, **Vase with flowers** *(National Gallery of Scotland) has been painted using burnt colors.*

Styles and Coloring Techniques

As you know, floral paintings are one of the most popular themes for still life painters. This can easily be explained by the colorful nature of flowers and the never-ending quantity of chromatic possibilities that they offer. Nowadays there are two main styles of painting: valuist and colorist. Valuist painting takes careful care over volume, lighting and shadow effects, modelling and, in short, attempts to represent the third dimension. Volume of flowers is shown by chiaroscuro in the strictest sense of the word, meaning the successive gradation of the colors from light to darker tones. Light is shown by brightening colors, and shadows by darkening them. The different values are distributed on the surface of the painting just as much to suggest the volume of the flowers as a sense of depth.

Colorist painting involves the idea that colors can be used to express everything, without needing to worry about volume and modelling. It is colors that lend value to the painting, with shadow and light being represented by saturated colors. Colorists show form with flat colors, without shadows, justifying this with the fact that "color diversifies, separates and explains the volume of objects by its own devices". This type of artist generally opts for frontal or diffused lighting, which involves less shadow, and objects are modelled with large areas of color.

104

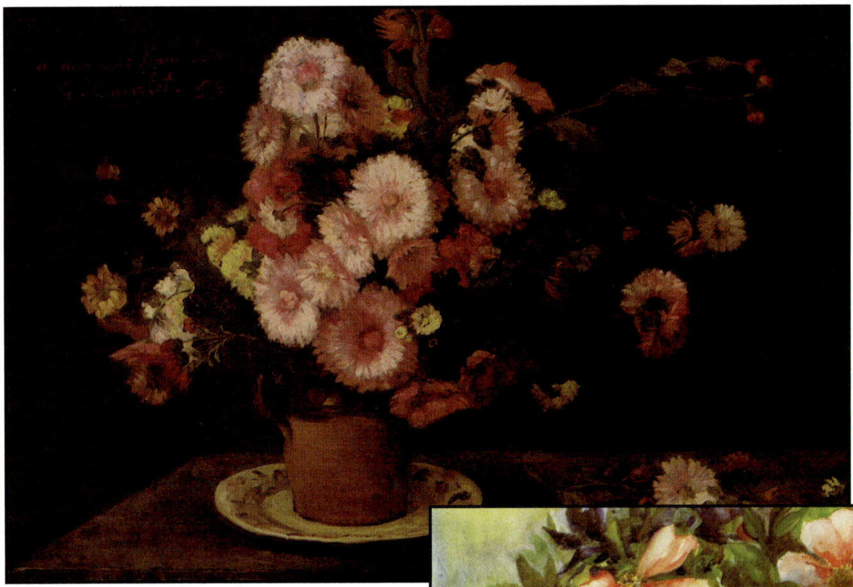

105

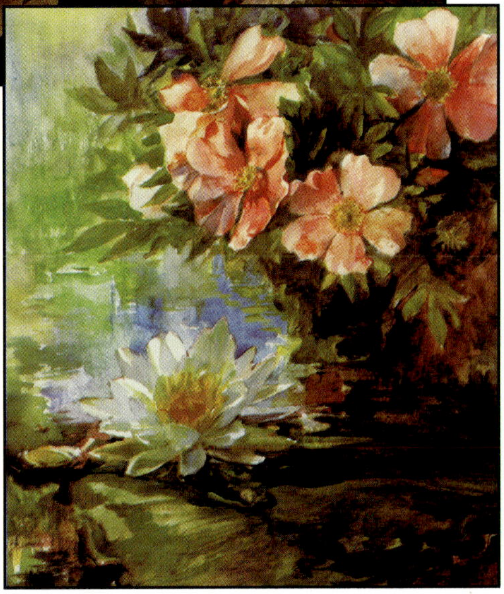

Fig. 104. The valuist technique is associated to modelling, in other words, the detailed description of light and shadow.* Bunch of flowers *by Gustave Courbet (Kunstmuseum, Basle).

Fig. 105.* Wild roses and water lily *by John La Fargue (private collection). If you look closely at the tones of the petals, you will see how they show the volume of the flower, suggesting the valuist nature of the picture.

106

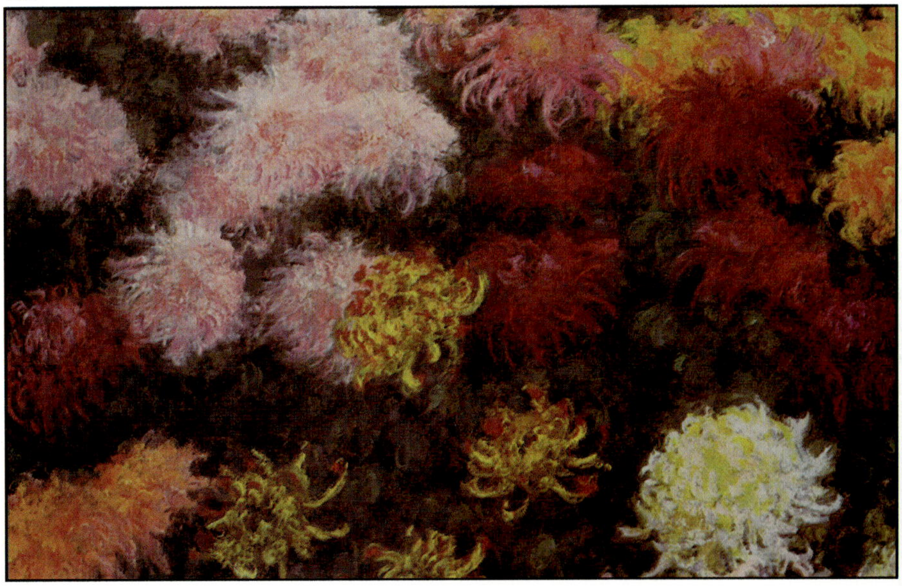

Fig. 106.* Chrysanthemums *by Claude Monet (Kunstmuseum, Basle). This painting lies somewhere between valuism and colorism. However, it seems clear that the artist has taken a great deal of interest in tonal values.

It would be wrong to suggest that a colorist style is more appropriate for painting flowers because there are so many possibilities for working with color, so rich in tensions and emotions. If you look around any museum or gallery, you will see that there are still many artists working masterfully in the valuist style, with some delightfully realistic floral paintings. It would also be wrong to define valuism as a classical or academic style that belongs more to centuries gone by than the present day. In 20th century art there have been several wonderful valuist painters who are still admired and imitated by young art students today.

107

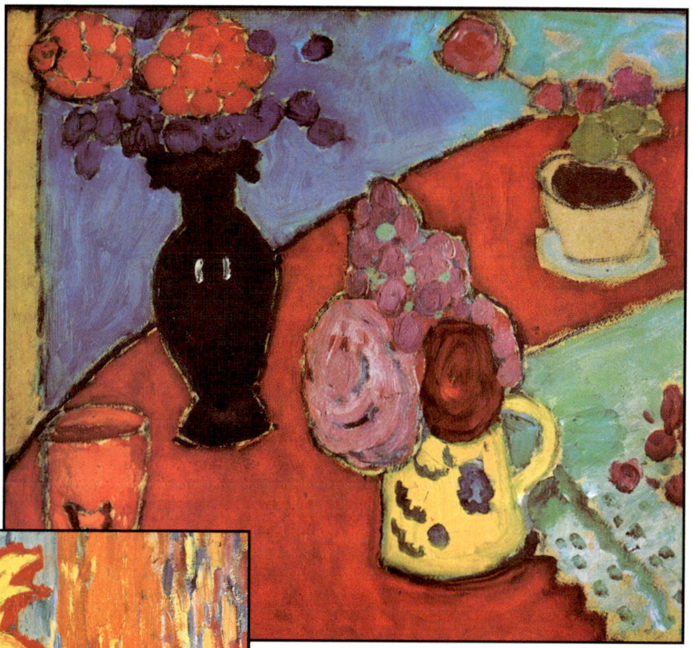

108

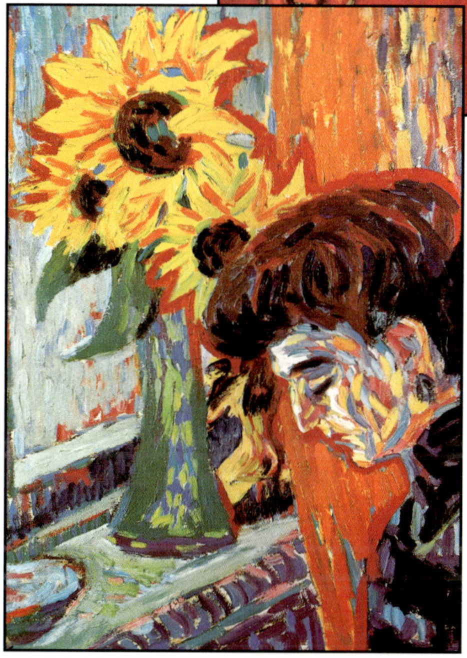

109

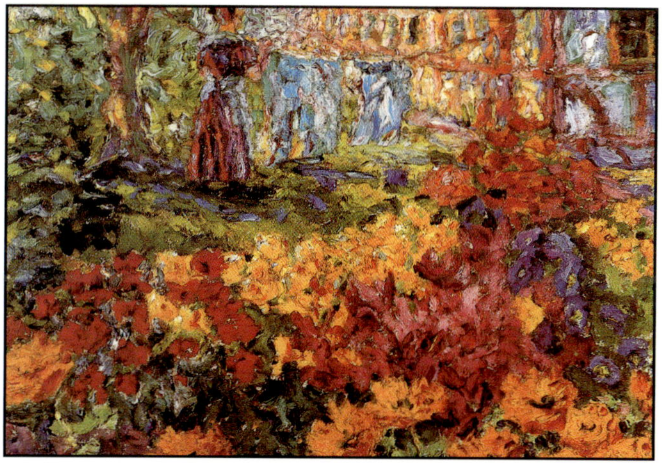

Fig. 107. **Still life with vase and jug** *by Alexej von Jawlensky (Ludwig Museum, Cologne). In colorist compositions, elements are distinguished by sharply contrasting colors.*
Fig. 108. **Woman's head in front of sunflowers** *by Ernst Ludwig Kirchner (Burda collection, Offenburg). If colorism is combined with divisionist techniques, the results offer a vibrant image.*
Fig. 109. **Garden of flowers** *by Emil Nolde (Kunstmuseum, Düsseldorf). This type of colorist treatment favours thick shades and the use of matt colors.*

The Interpretation

Painting is not simply a question of applying the suggestions and rules that I have been giving up until now. Painting means modifying reality in accordance to our own inner feelings. To help you do this, you should look carefully at the example paintings in this book, and learn from the work of the grand masters, studying new and interesting points of view, changes in illumination, composition and so on. I suggest that when you are studying your subject, you should decide what it is that you want your painting to convey, and working from there, find the corresponding interpretation. This is done by enlarging, highlighting, decreasing or exaggerating contrasts, and taking out or introducing new forms and details to the picture. You have to let your imagination and creativity run freely.

On these two pages, you are going to be shown a few of the more concrete options that you might be interested in trying out when you are thinking about how to interpret a theme.

Look at these paintings. The first (fig. 110) shows a bunch of iriscs superimposed onto a grey background. They seem sculpted, and their volume is clearly expressed. The forms are accurate and the colors are dull. The artist has represented this composition by aiming to symbolise human vulnerability and fragility. There is no doubt that the lack of bright colors and evident brushstrokes conveys an idea of solitude and sadness.

110

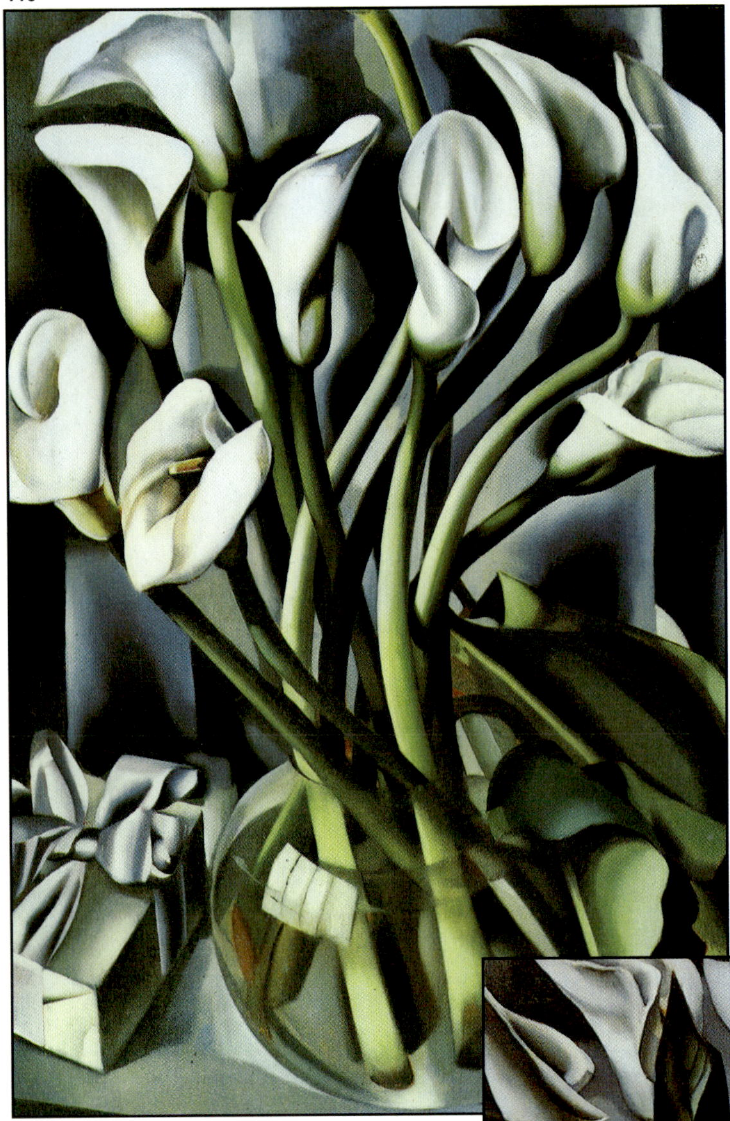

111

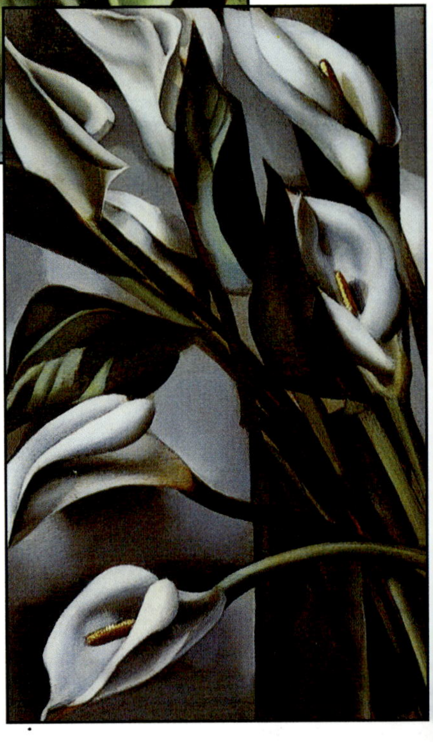

Figs. 110 and 111. These two paintings by Tamara de Lempicka, **Cala lilies** *(Cresswell Mathysen-Gerst, New York, fig. 110) and* **Cala lilies** *(private collection, fig. 111), reflect sadness and melancholy. Despite the linear sculpted appearance, the colors do not allow the forms to contrast with the background, meaning the picture has a monochromatic feel to it.*

Study another way of expressing volume and color. This time I want to show you the effect of a watercolor that has been worked onto a washed background in a gestural way (fig. 112). The contours of the objects are diluted, and merge into the colors of the background. If you look closely at the flowers, you will see how each transparent brushstroke that has been applied on wet can be distinguished. Also, look at how the artist has left spaces for the white of the paper to show through. The colors and the visible brushstrokes are therefore perceived as much warmer.

On the other hand, in figure 113, the artist is able to recreate flowers in a most peculiar way. He seems to have managed to convey the emotion of a whoop of joy by using colors and a pictorial treatment on the surface of the painting.

Through these examples I have tried to show you how the interpretation of a theme is highly related to the level of enthusiasm and mood that the artist is capable of portraying.

112

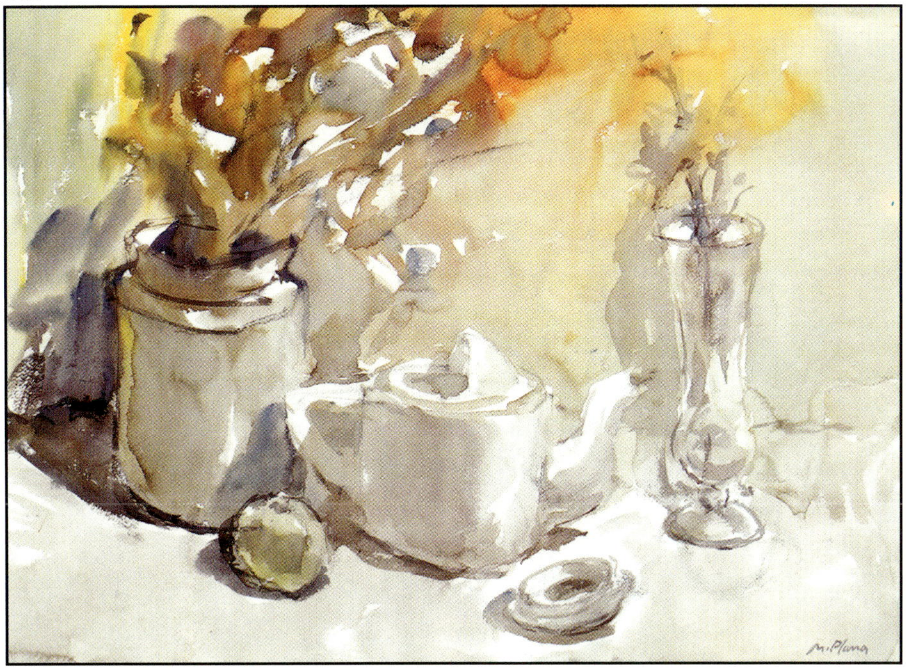

113

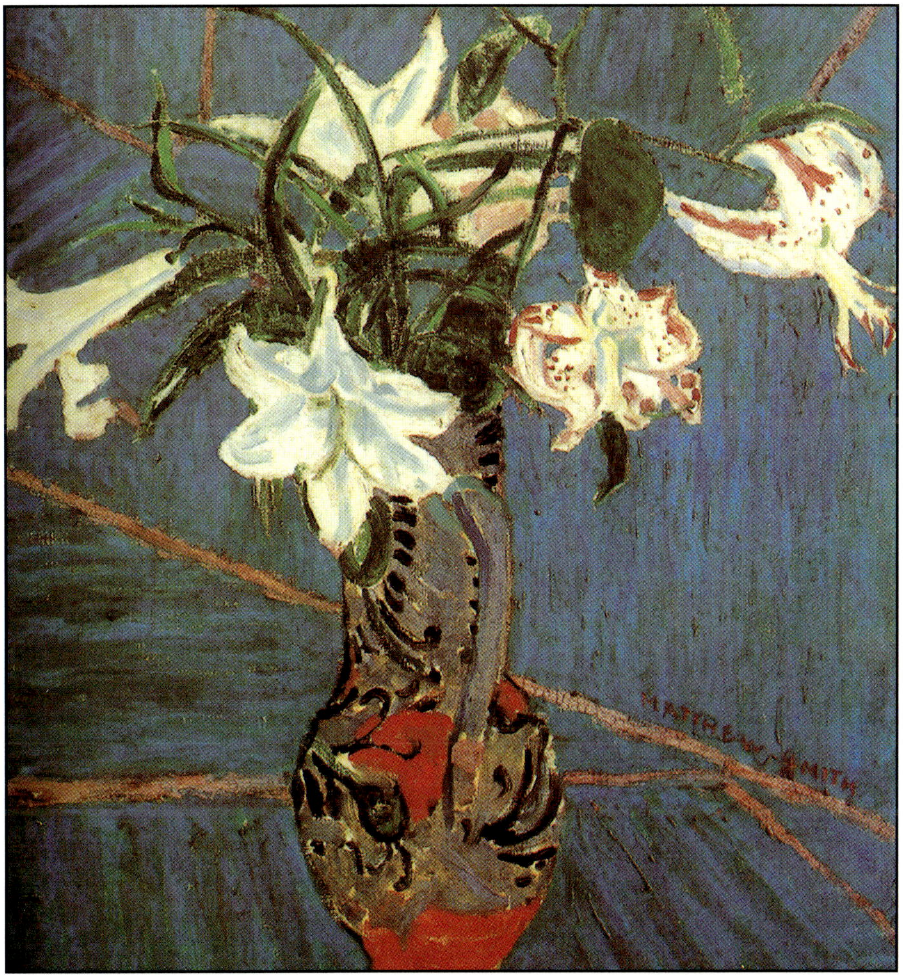

Fig. 112. This painting, **Still life with teapot** *by Manel Plana, has a much more spontaneous treatment; it is much more fluid. Light floods the composition and creates gestural washes.*

Fig. 113. **Irises in a vase** *by Matthew Smith (City Art Gallery, Leeds). This painting has much more vitality owing to a more colorist, less detailed treatment. See how important the visible brushstrokes are in the interpretation of the theme.*

PRACTICAL EXERCISES

In the following chapter a series of practice exercises begins with the step by step development of the study of flowers as carried out by professional artists. We are now talking about you learning by practicing. These pages should be a reference point for you to be able to study in a practical way the techniques and skills for floral painting, the peculiarities and tricks. As such it is recommended that you copy each of the following exercises without deviation. As you will see some of these exercises are accompanied by pages with outline-guide drawings which will help the work. You will also find an easy to understand teaching text accompanying each of these exercises so that you can faithfully follow the development step by step. And given that this is not only a book to be read, but also basically one to be practiced with, I invite you to go back to each page and begin working and dedicating the necessary time to each exercise.

Painting a Basket of Flowers

In this first exercise the artist Carlant will paint a flower basket in a simple and clear manner, allowing you to understand the way in which the flowers are structured and how the effects of light can be represented. This is a good exercise to begin this section, working with a very limited range of colors and without superimposing too many of them. I invite you to also practice doing it by taking the outline-guide drawing no. 1 which can be found at the end of this book.

Notice that the basket is in a well lit position, against a flat or gradated background just as shown in the model (fig. 114).

First of all, make a sketch by skimming over the surface of the paper with the point of a graphite stick without applying any pressure (fig. 115). Draw the outline in a way that frames all the basic shapes and gives the idea of a whole. If you prefer you can use outline-guide no.1 as your sketch.

As you are making the strokes, constantly establish a connection between one area and another, constantly measuring and joining them with lines, or identifying the places where the flowers and leaves will be positioned by using circles or rough marks. Go over the outline putting more pressure on the graphite point. When the motifs are more complicated it becomes more comfortable to show the position of the elements with geometric shapes instead of directly tackling the subject. In this way you will always

114

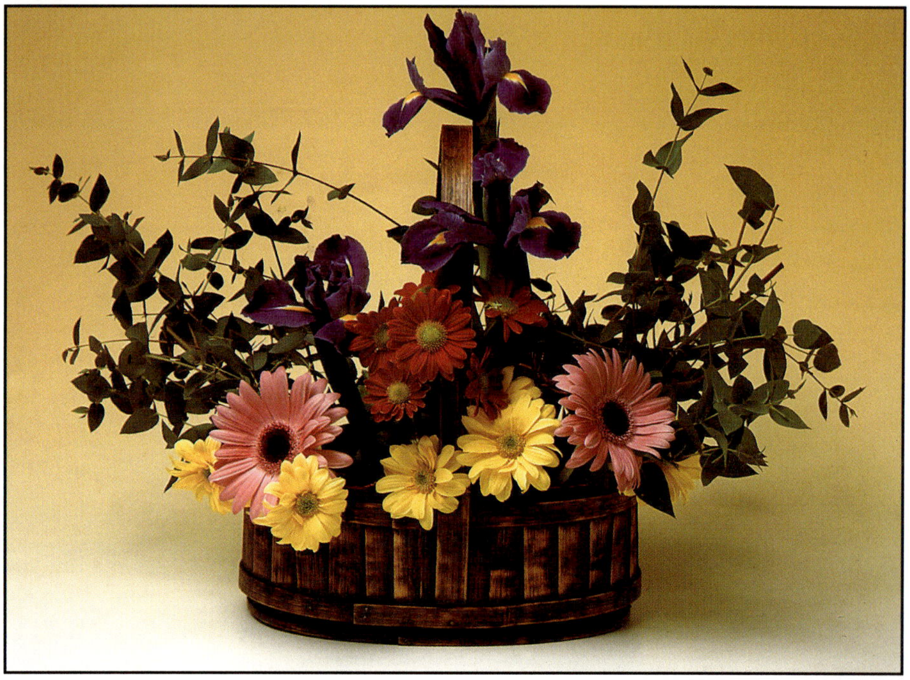

Fig. 114. This is the flower arran gement, still life, which you are going to paint. It has been decided to maintain the light directly above the subject to make the contrast between the dark and light aspects much clearer.

Fig. 115. The sketch is made by using a pencil. Your main concern has to be how to compose and distribute each one of the elements making up the subject.

115

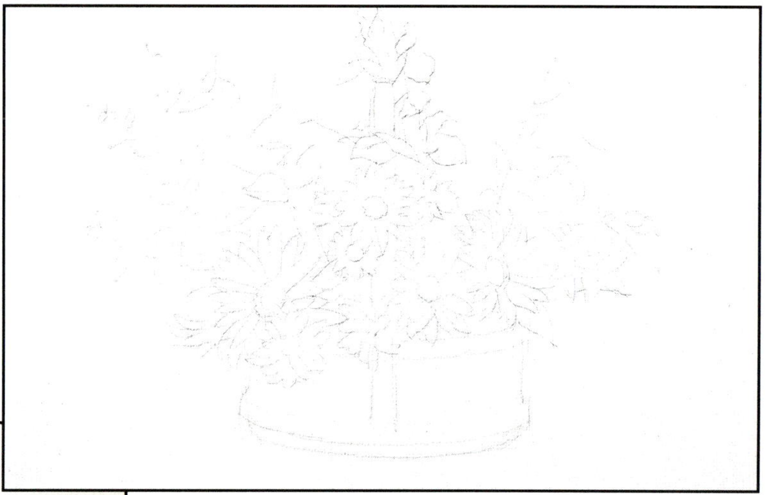

116

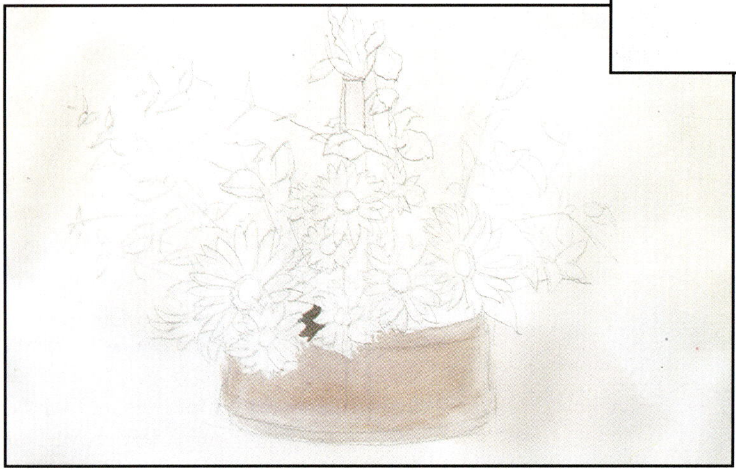

Fig. 116. When the outline is finished begin extending the first washes in the background and in the basket.

117

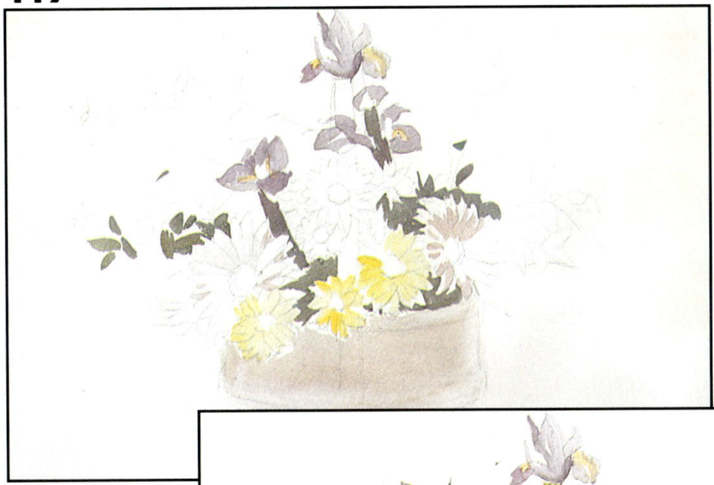

118

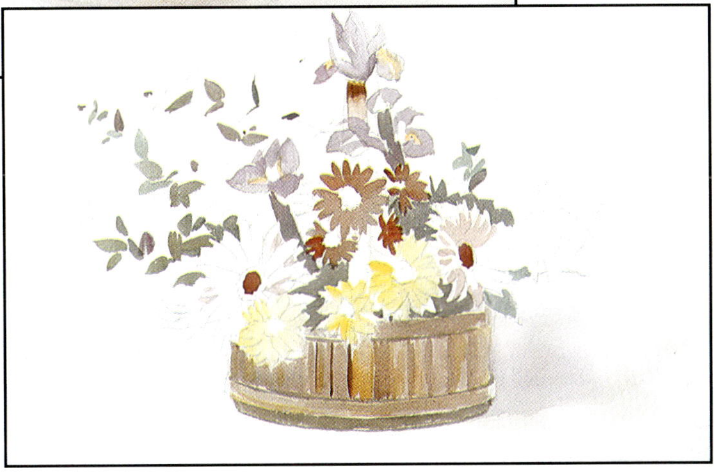

Fig.117. Draw the flowers on the upper part with uniform washes which appear cut back. The harmonious range of grays bring these colors together with the rest of the subject.
Fig. 118. Continue working on the flower petals with uniform washes, without paying attention to the volume or the contrasts in shade.
Fig 119. Gradually the composition is beginning to fill up with small details. Notice the chromatic variety presented by the group of leaves to the left.

119

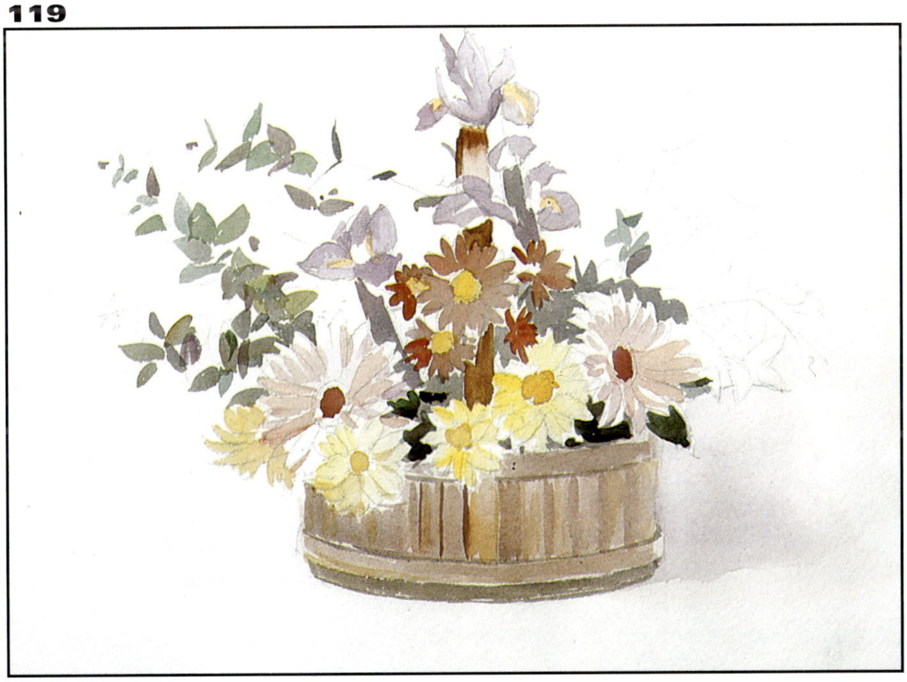

preserve the original outline as well as the relationship and proportions established between the different parts of the model.
Once the drawing's structural lines have been determined begin to apply the paint: take a thick paintbrush and add the first wash with a diluted burnt umber earth color for the basket. With the same, but very diluted color tinge the background (fig. 116, previous page). Begin with the group of violet flowers, which should be done with uniform washes applied by a medium-sized round paintbrush. With Payne gray paint the small dark spaces between the flowers. With cadmium yellow paint the petals of the group of flowers in the center of the bunch, and with a little diluted carmine begin to fill in the flower in the right (fig. 117). Continue adding colors and painting more flowers. With a little vermillion and umber earth paint the petal corolla of the three central flowers, those with a brownish-gray color. With Payne gray mixed with emerald green, violet and cadmium green begin to paint the series of leaves. Now begin to work on the basket details, doing so by washing it over with a darker mixture than the earlier one. The aim being to reproduce its texture. As you can see, the washes applied by the artist are uniform and clean, having been treated delicately and with subtlety (fig. 118).
Painting follows its course: paint the basket handle and the center of the flowers, patiently continuing the job of painting the leaves. With emerald green and a drop of brown complete the group of leaves which have the most intense color, in the lower part of the bunch (fig. 119). Once finished painting the leaves the work has to be complemented with a small paint-brush. Draw lines for the stems in a broken and subtle way, with a little Sienna color. Mix in large washes with smaller paintbrushes, this giving the work a greater and richer textural quality. With the model now somewhat advanced see how the central part shows the "empty horror" of the flowers which completely cover the white background spaces (fig. 120).

Despite having represented every one of the elements making up the bunch, the work is still a collection of areas with differently washed surfaces and few details. Continue then to decide on the main areas and then highlight them with respect to the tone of the painting, profiling the small shapes with more detail and superimposing washes with more intense colors on those done earlier. Give the basket the same treatment as the rest of the painting: add new washes of natural umber and burnt umber colors, although doing so in a simplified way (fig. 121). Last, adjust the shades to achieve a natural contrast . Use different types of paintbrushes and intensify the tone to establish the relationships between the different parts of the plant. As you can see, the circular centers of the flowers have also been retouched and profiled more realistically.

The finished painting is an example of how a motif can be dealt with by using a limited palette and by superimposing a small quantity of materials. The method used involves the gradation of different areas through contrasting tones (fig. 123). The main difficulty of this work lies in the synthesis that you have to develop, meaning that you have to be capable

TIPS

-Remember to periodically move away from the painting to look at how the combination is going together. In this way it will be easier to balance the information carried by the different parts of the painting.

-To give a faint shadow in an even smoother and more delicate tone, and to also give a less broken look to the brushstrokes shade off the watercolor with the finger.

-Change the water in the bottle often, with the aim of not dirtying the colors and always maintaining a palette with clean colors.

120

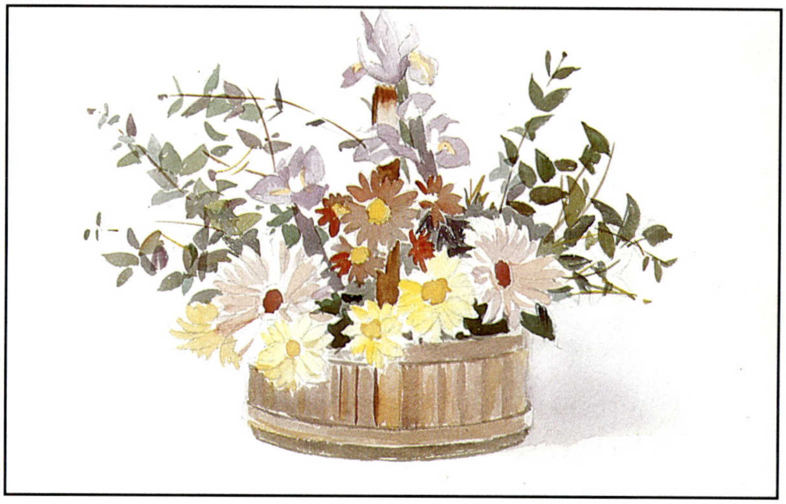

121

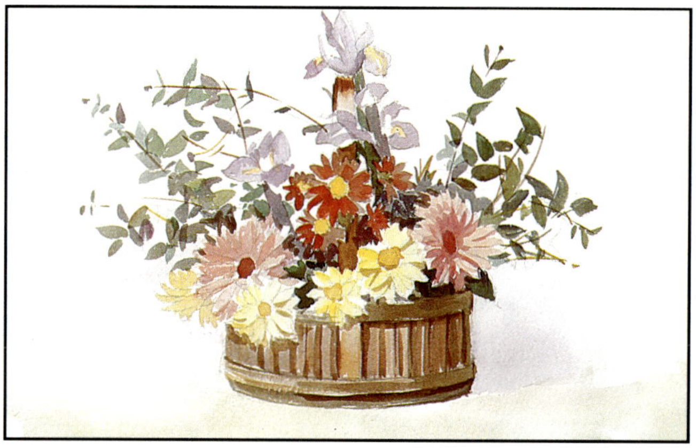

122

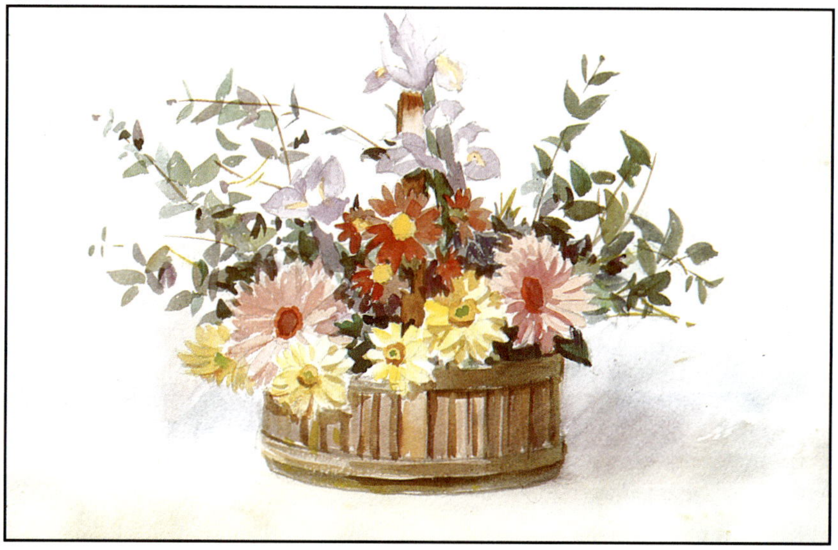

Fig. 120. The painting should continue being developed until it reaches this state. At this point each one of the elements in the painting are represented. However, the subject now appears to have little volume and also little contrast amongst the features.

Fig. 121. Take the localiced colors into consideration, defining each element in characteristic tones, giving them shape, drawing with accuracy, forming them by superimposing more intense color washes.

Fig. 122. Now the work appears to have more contrast and is more defined. The background has been darkened and the shadow of the subject has been projected by extending a diluted wash to the right.

123

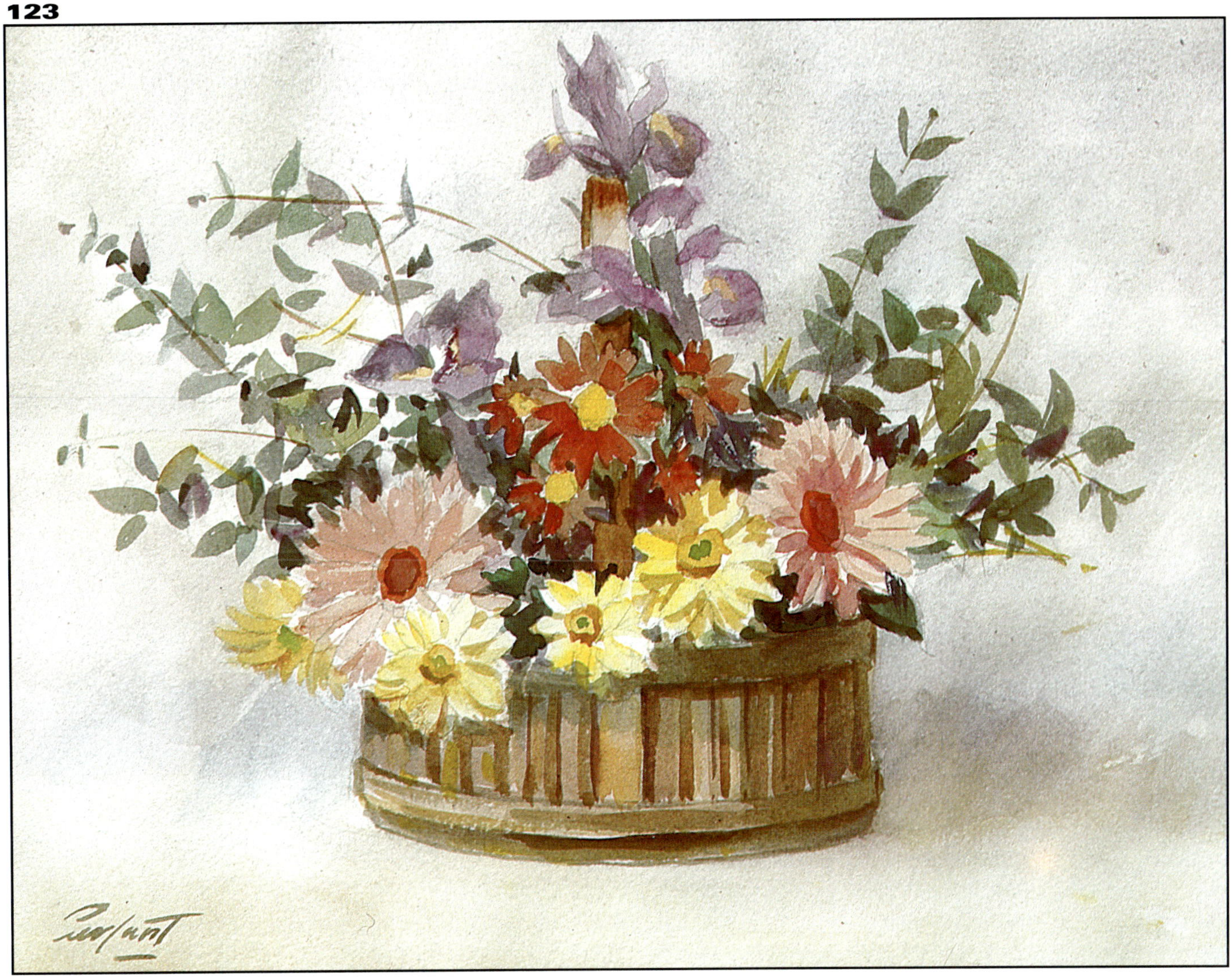

of reducing the motif from the use of a few basic brushstrokes. It will be easier to simplify the object if you look at it through halfclosed eyes. When working on the motif you will be tempted to superimpose excessive details, lines, branches, stems, but getting closer to the model the composition appears very defined, in fact I would say too defined. However, moving further away you will discover that the shapes and the tones merge, and in some cases even blend together. Maintaining this spirit means that instead of treating it as a photograph, you are simplifying the subject so that the essential features of the composition stand out. Try to keep the paint clear, with clean and well-defined colors and don't mix colors unnecessarily to try and make the work more realistic; lighten the tones only when it is really necessary to do so. Some uneven paintbrushes can strengthen the appearance of the leaves on both sides of the composition. However, see how the violet leaves on the upper part are still simple sketched shapes. Leave them like this indefinitely (fig. 122). Finishing off, intensify the background colors and slightly project the shadow of the bouquet.

Fig. 123. The finished work gives a result offering volume, light and shapes which are much more defining. The work, despite not giving detailed or photographic precision comes across with many artistic qualities including subtle changes in tone and an appearance which is visually satisfactory.

Painting a Park in an Impressionist Style

The artist Oscar Sanchís is going to paint the beautiful view of a park using the wet watercolor technique. As you can check from other exercises in this book, this is a technique which is normally used for painting floral compositions. It basically consists of first dampening the area with water, doing so lightly, and as such controlling the limits of the area or shape that we are going to paint. The model is a view of a sunny urban park, with flower beds, in the historic center of Dublin.

Take a pencil and make a preparatory sketch with a careful estimate of the dimensions and proportions. It may seem difficult with the level of complexity of elements, including trees, buildings, benches, vegetation..., but it is exactly this number of elements, as well as their ordered distribution, which will help us to come up with a composition with a satisfactory result.

First of all, you should begin drawing, with a pencil, the line of buildings located in the background, given that in this case the architectural features are the ones which will present the greatest difficulties (fig. 124).

Begin the watercolor by painting the sky with a mixture of cobalt blue and yellow, applied from the upper edge of the paper until the row of trees and houses, in a way which gives a gradated tone (fig. 125). Note that in this first phase you must not only paint the sky, but the tops of the trees. With this last part the limits should be well controlled so that the green of the trees does not mix with the wash used for the sky. This type of control means that, on occasions, it is necessary to dry the wash with absorbent paper, this applying to cases where unwanted drops of paint drip or the color over-runs the predetermined space. The green used is a mixture of Payne gray, permanent green and burnt umber colors (fig. 126).

Take into consideration the fact that because the colors have been mixed on wet areas you will have to work quickly (fig. 127, on the next page).

124

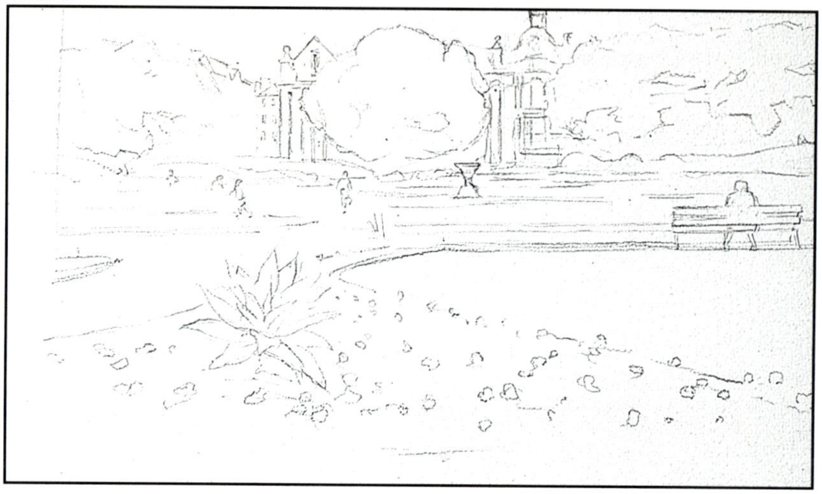

125

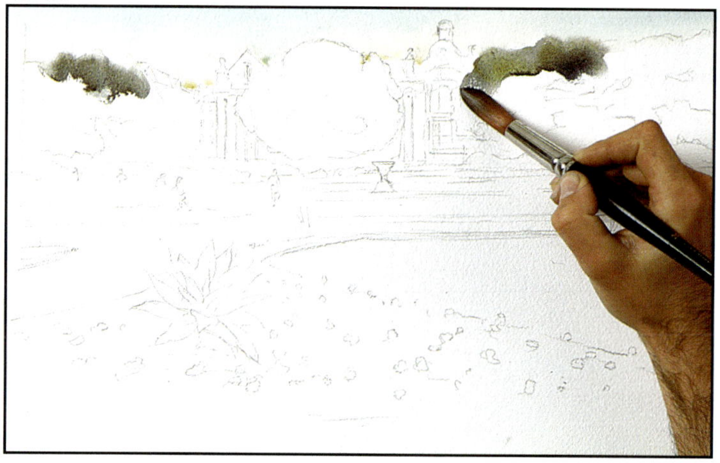

126

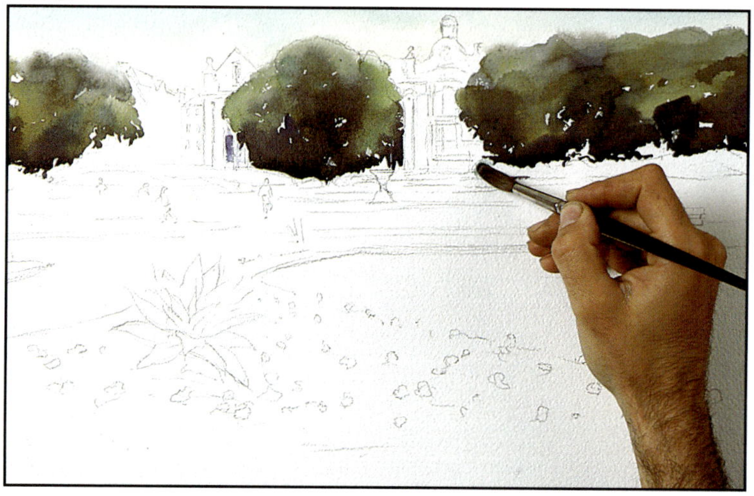

Fig. 124. The spatial extent of this scene obliges us to make a planning sketch in pencil, drawing the series of profiles corresponding to trees, buildings, the edges of the lawns and flower beds.

Fig. 125. First of all, paint from the top down, gradating the sky and distant boundaries.

Fig. 126. The process continues with the sky wash drying out and the painting of those areas which correspond to the group of trees.

Next, paint in the colors of the lawn with a first wash; in the first attempt, cover the white of the paper to avoid false contrasts. Note what the condition of the painting is like, in figure 128, when this phase is finished.

Now comes the first of the elements. This concerns the flower beds, something which is simple enough. First of all, take a small paintbrush and using a pink color paint the flowers in the appropriate positions, but without any great detail, instead doing so in a semi-abstract way with strokes of color. After leaving the pink colored layer (corresponding to the flowers) to dry slightly, use the same brush to paint the surrounding vegetation with an olive green. Do this with a lot of care, without superimposing colors, endeavouring to go around the color of the flowers. It is advisable to leave small spaces so that the background paper shows through, the aim being to achieve a surface with a richer texture and more spontaneous result (fig. 129). In a few seconds you will have the flower bed painted in. As you can see the plant which takes up the main position has been kept in white. Now paint this *alla prima* using the wet into wet technique (fig. 130). Paint the effects of light and shade on the plant. For this, work with three basic tones: a semi-transparent wash of green bluish-yellowish for the back leaves; a green-purplish one for the central part and blue with a little burnt umber color to highlight those parts where the contrast between light and shade is most obvious (fig. 131). Next, with the same greenish wash used for painting the

127

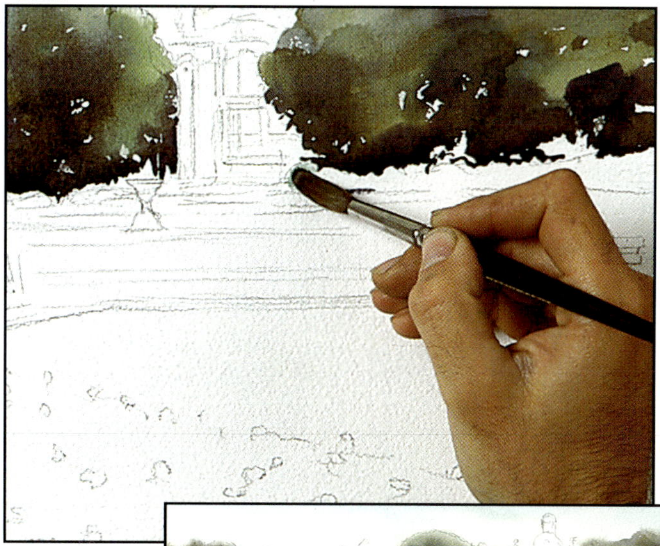

128

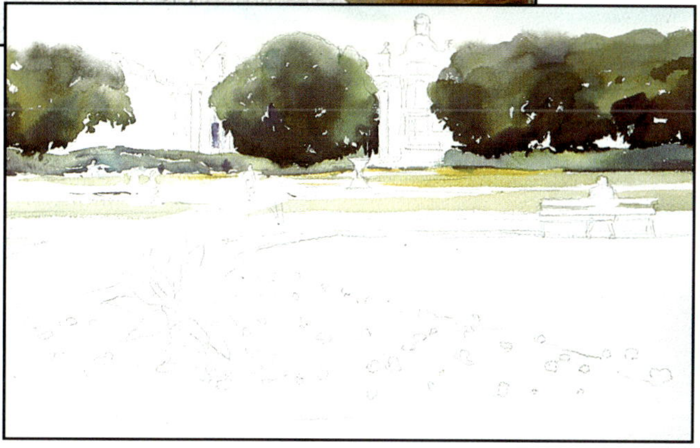

129

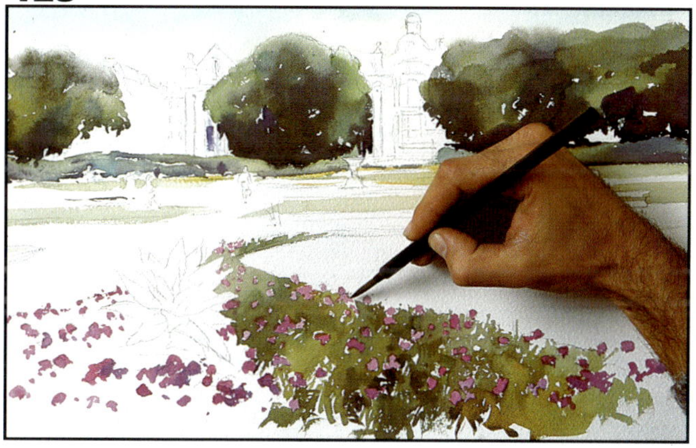

130

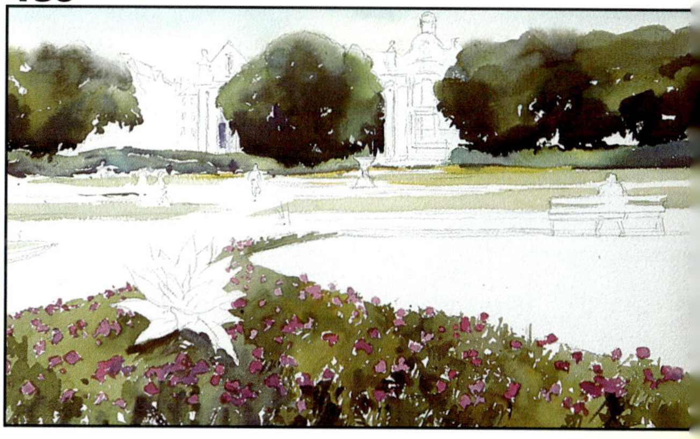

Fig. 127. In this detail we can see the spontaneity and swiftness of work necessary, with colors being mixed on wet.
Fig. 128. Paint the lawn in this last part and its light effects with a paintbrush dipped in cadmium yellow.
Fig, 129. In this image observe how the artist has painted the flowers. First of all their position has been marked, this then followed by the extension of the green color, endeavouring to silhouette each one of the flowers.
Fig. 130. In a few seconds the first of the flower beds has been painted. If you look at it the green color is not uniform, but instead presents its own qualities and effects which are related to the technique of painting on wet.

lawn below the line of distant trees, paint the grass covering the ground in the front and middle views of the painting. Do this with a uniform wash. Begin the last phase of the painting by painting in the shape of the buildings positioned in the background and the people passing through the park. This is a laborious process which requires a lot of attention on your part because of the necessity to paint many small features on the building facades. This means that these areas must be worked on with a small paintbrush (fig. 132). Go back to the foreground to continue painting flowers. The artist has decided to add more groups of flowers to both sides of the composition. Before painting, open up white areas on the earlier wash by rubbing the surface with a paintbrush soaked in water. Next mark the rose positions with bright and intense colors (to the right) and a group of anemones (to the left)- see fig. 133. Finally, with a small paintbrush give a second appraisal to the nearest group of flowers with the aim of showing the contrasts, to describe the definition and shape of the flowers better and also to add new groups of flowers, such as the collection of purplish flowers emerging from the plant in the center (fig. 134, next page). Also work on the middle section of the painting adding new flower beds which, given the distance, have to be dealt with from the viewpoint of using small strokes, coming together as a group of superimposed points.

131

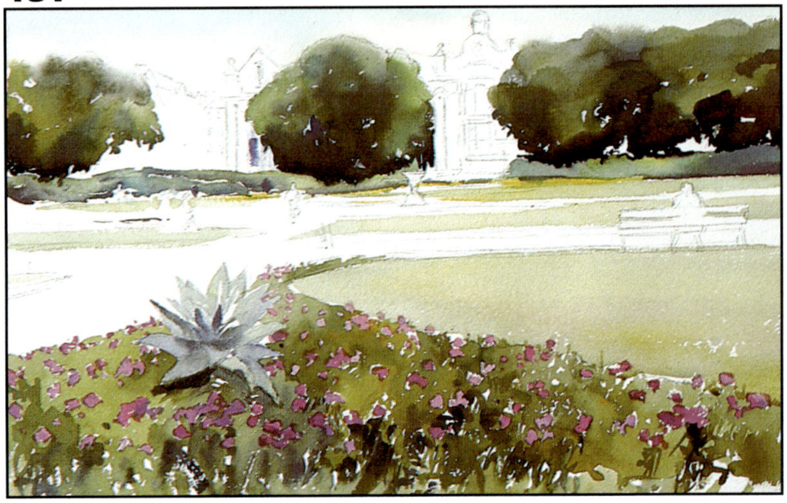

132

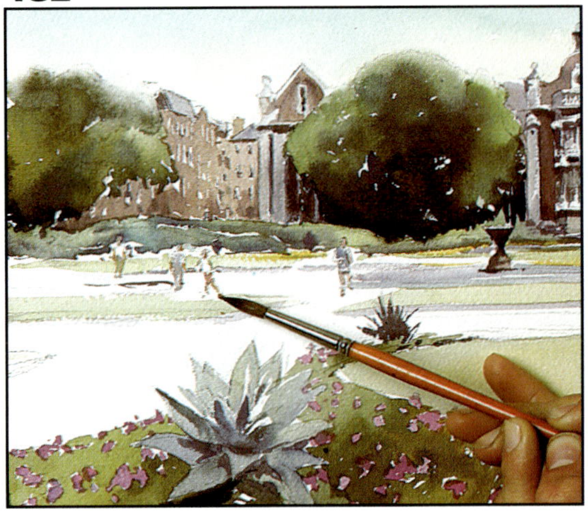

***Fig. 131.** With a wide brush paint the middle section by extending a uniform wash over the area.*
***Fig. 132.** The street furniture and people passing through the park should be painted with a small brush and the shapes worked on as much as possible.*

***Fig. 133.** Go back to the foreground and form new flower groups by adding new color. Before applying these colors it is necessary to remove some of the earlier paint.*

133

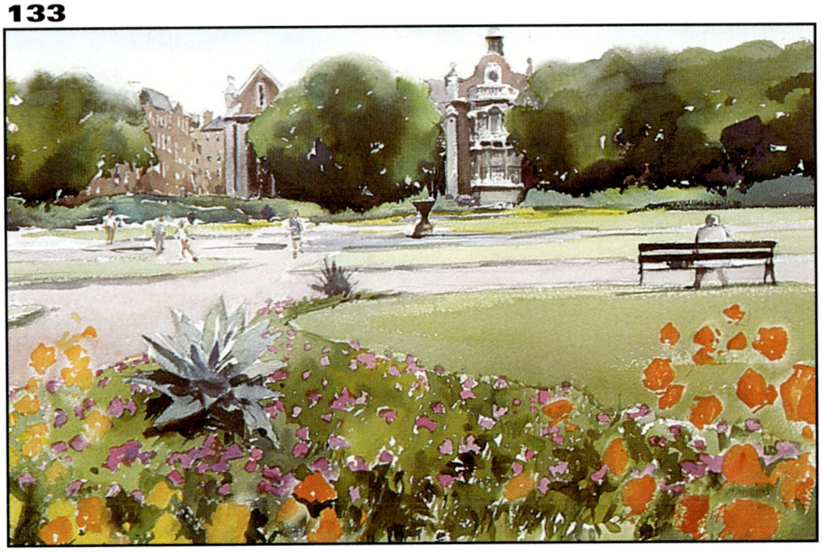

TIPS

-When painting the sky do it with the paper reversed, in other words, upside down, so that the wash will run down with the sky left darker in the upper part.
-The professional watercolor artist will also turn to opening up white parts of the painting by using his nail or the end of the paintbrush, doing so on a surface which is still wet to produce a texture effect or the impression of growth (to represent the vegetation).

134

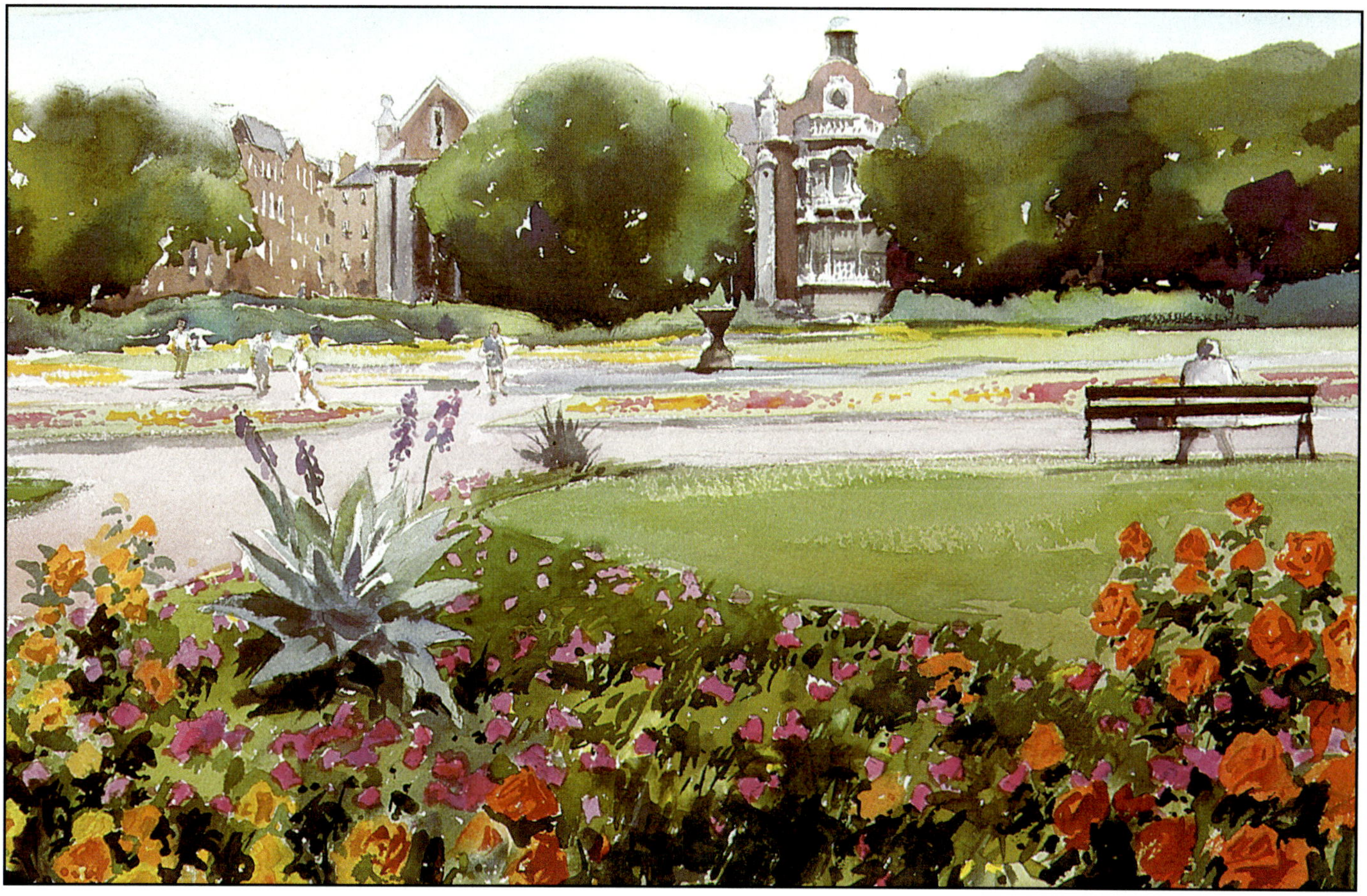

Almost certainly you have tried to give great detail to the figures which appear in the park. Do not overly complicate this because it is not necessary. Notice that in the work painted by Oscar Sanchís there are no facial features to identify any of the characters, because it is not necessary in a painting like this. Possibly, when you are working naturally you will have problems painting groups of figures incorporated in urban scenes, but this is generally the case. As such when doing an outdoor painting like this, which requires a certain amount of speed, deal with it by avoiding the details and paying attention to the interpretation of the model: paint in synthesis.

Apply this same principle to the vegetation. As you can see it is also not necessary to express the flowers and the foliage of the trees in a realistic manner when these are to be found in such a distant view. Manage to bring them across in an impressionist style, this meaning that they should be painted with only a few strokes, doing just what is necessary. At the same time look at the model through halfclosed eyes. In contrast, it is appropriate to take some care over the flowers in the foreground; first painting them in synthesis filling out the painting in a style which borders on the abstract, in a way which manages to reproduce the texture of the elements being represented. This then gives content which is more intense, working with volumes and contrasts. All in all, this makes the shape more recognizable, in ways which can allow the type of flowers being dealt with to be identified.

Fig. 134. And this is the final result. Apart from those watercolor effects coming from the application on wet note the variety of brush strokes and textures offered by this work from the first details in the foreground to those further away in the background.

Painting a Still Life with Flowers in the Old Style

The artist Ester Llauder is going to paint a still life which offers particularly strong similarities to those which used to be painted in the baroque style. As you can see, the bouquet of flowers provides a profusion of earth colors, pinks and yellows which stand out even more when superimposed with the dark background, this completely lacking spatial references with regards to depth. Furthermore, it is lit by front-side lighting, the cause of the intense contrasts between light and shadow (fig. 135). In this way the strong lighting and marked contrasts create the sense of volume in the subject.
In this exercise, the content of the flower bouquet will be managed through chiaroscuro in the classic sense of the word. This means that the modelling of the subject will be expressed through a successive gradation of color towards black or white. You can also practise this exercise, beginning it with outline-guide no. 2.
Using a model with these characteristics, the best way to proceed is by producing a solid and accurate drawing. It must be linear and will have to indicate the position and specific shape of each of the flowers represented, in a way that will allow us to color each one of the elements more comfortably. The lines should be intense and visible so that they can serve as a guide during the course of the exercise (fig. 136). Also remember that the outline-guide no.2 can be used as the drawing base.
Sketch the leaves sticking out from the flowers. Begin with these, using an earth color. The group of leaves shown with more of a tendency towards a reddish color is done with a little ochre, sienna and vermilion. Those in the center have Payne gray in the mixture and in the upper part a large amount of burnt umber is used. As you get on with painting the leaves, add shadow and some details (such as folds and veins). The darkest parts of the shaded areas are generally achieved by mixing the local leaf color with a little burnt umber and Payne gray (fig. 137).
Now paint the falling greenish colored leaves, hanging or angled over the edge of the vase with washes of emerald green in the clearest places and the same green deepened by Payne gray to highlight the darkest areas. When you

135

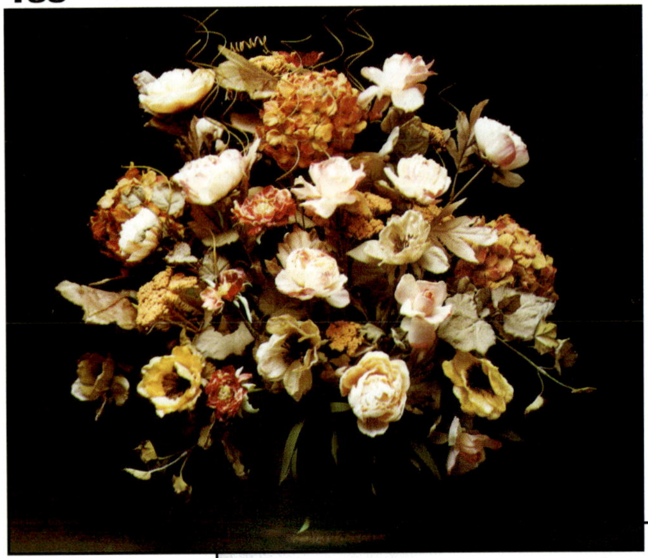

136

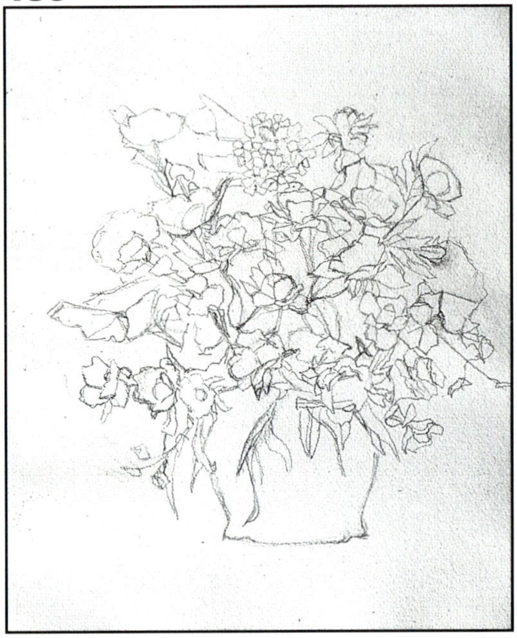

137

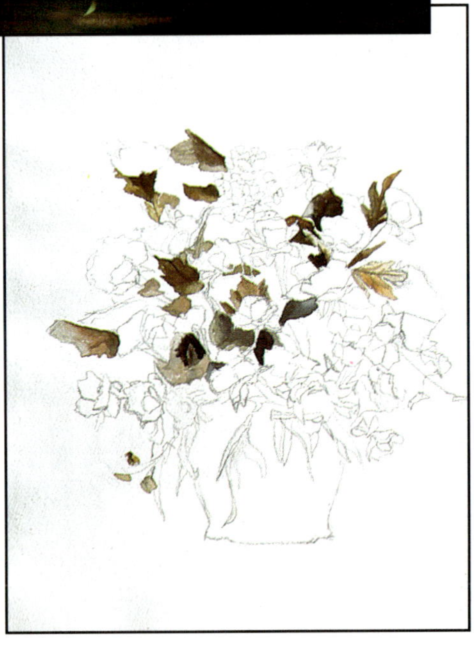

Fig. 135. As you can see, the subject is reminiscent of a baroque composition with earth and pink colors, all in all, an elaborate work which accentuates the chiaroscuro effects.
Fig. 136. The drawing must be precise given that it will be greatly used to correctly paint each one of the elements represented. Mark the lines heavily with a pencil because they must remain visible until the work is finished.
Fig. 137. Begin painting those leaves which share the same chromatic and textural qualities.

have finished this operation it is the appropriate moment to begin working on the vase. This is made of ceramic, although the dark patina is bronze colored. For the moment apply a uniform wash with burnt umber earth mixed with a little Payne gray to identify both its volume and profile, on what is still a white background (fig.138).

The characteristic features of the flowers are painted with a small brush using the dry paint technique and which is managed with various mixtures of yellow ochre, natural umber, a purplish color, cadmium yellow and crimson. This is done in such a way that the different shapes are distinct from each other and not confused. The washes are left to stand for a moment and when they seem to be virtually dry add new features and paint to bring the work closer in accuracy to the subject, making it much more realistic and detailed (fig. 139). Observe how the artist has first painted those flowers which have a less striking chromatic tendency, and in fact are more similar to the colors of the leaves. He adds other flowers, this time more colorful, those which with their colors add a lot more life to the bouquet. As you can see working with the paintbrush is not as free and uninhibited as was the case in the previous exercise. Instead it is much more controlled, precise and methodical. Pay attention to the small details, such as the orange flower in the upper part which show a variety of petals going from a vermilion red color to the most intense of oranges and then to cadmium yellow (fig. 140). As you will see for yourself painting flowers is a laborious process which requires a lot of ability with regards to skills of observation and patience.

138

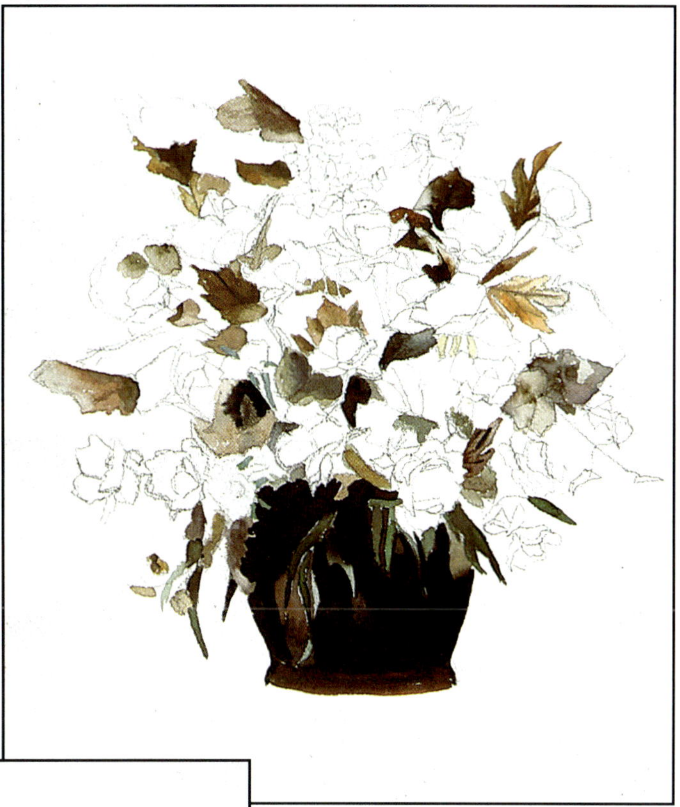

139

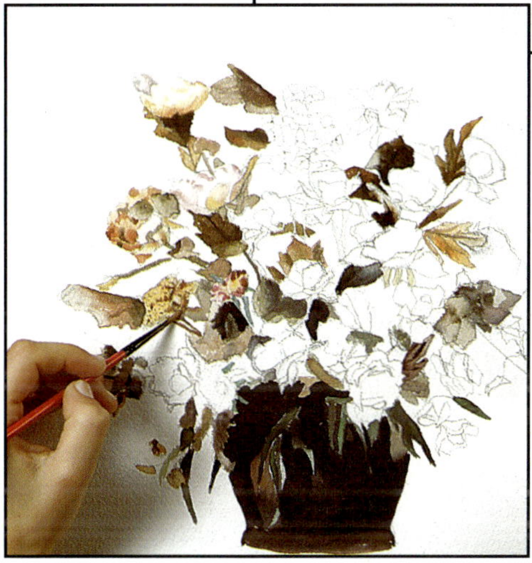

Fig. 138. In contrast to what has been explained up to now, painting this work involves working with fragments instead of a collection of parts, and as such means that an elaborate drawing is of great importance.

Fig. 139. With patience and a small paintbrush work with the flowers individually, endeavouring to maintain the chromatic harmony of the whole.

140

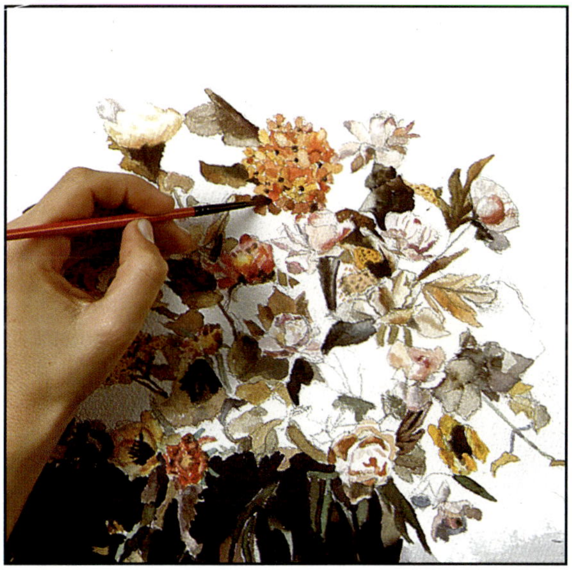

Fig. 140. You will have moments in which flowers similar to these will require good powers of observation from you, and ability, allowing you to translate the visual image onto paper.

Leave the work on the flowers for a moment to paint the background. In this way you will avoid making mistakes brought on by contrasting the colors of the flowers with the white of the background. Take a wide brush and start to cover the background from the bottom up. The painting of the background is done with various mixtures of ultramarine blue, Payne Gray and a little burnt umber, these giving this so characteristic blackish color. Leave some flowers white, these to be painted later on (fig. 141).
Continue covering the background until you reach the upper part. Now leave the brush to the side and take a small one. With this now paint the spaces between the flowers the same color, in such a way that the white background is completely covered. After this operation you will, perhaps surprisingly, discover that the brightness of the flowers has been intensified. This is based on the fact that the color displayed by a body depends in great measure on the color surrounding it (fig. 142).
From this point finishing off the work is simple. When the background color has dried only the white spaces left on the inside of the bouquet need to be painted

141

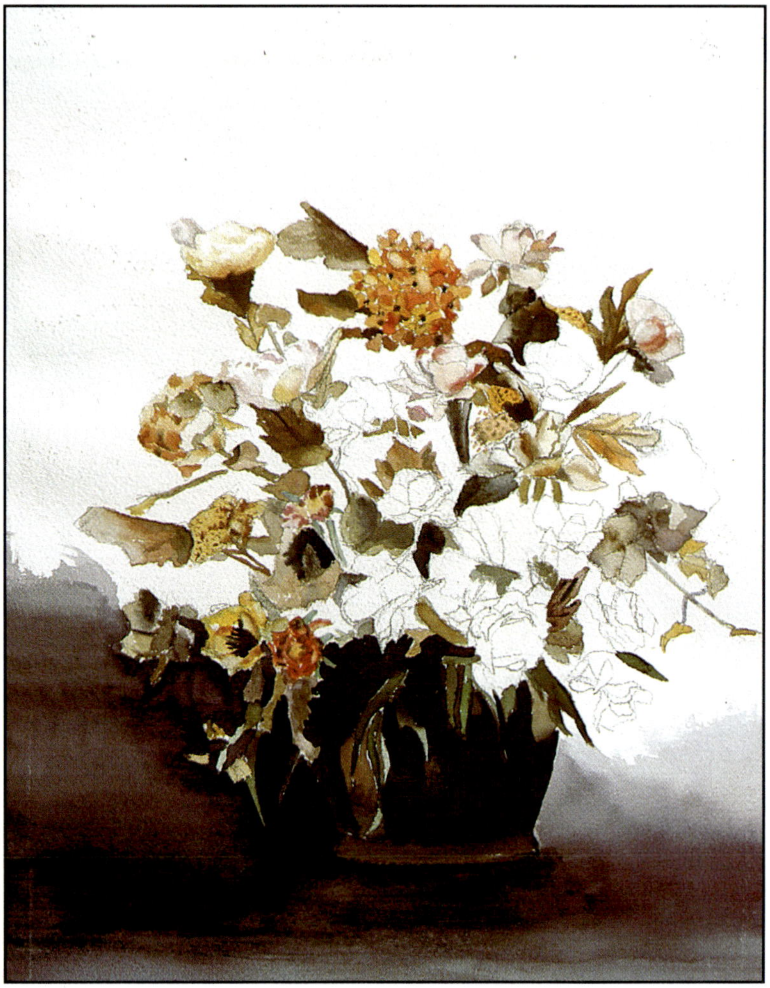

142

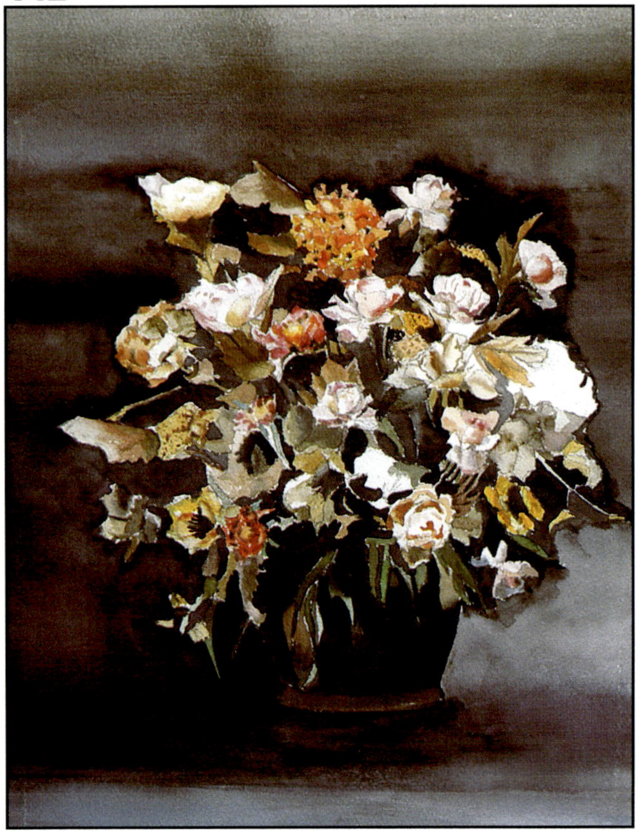

Fig. 141. Work on the background by applying washes with the blackish color. This avoids having the contrast of the flower colors against the white of the paper.
Fig. 142. Painting the background dark makes the colors of the bouquet brighter and the form of the flowers more precise and profiled.

TIPS

- If you are working on the painting and see that it is not doing so well try not to loose your motivation. Keep on painting and you will see that there are solutions for many of the problems. It was Renoir who said that "For a painting to be good it has to go through bad moments".
- Do not paint this work in only one day because it is a complicated subject which requires precision and patience. This way you will not allow your rush to overcome patience and therefore lead to making mistakes.

143

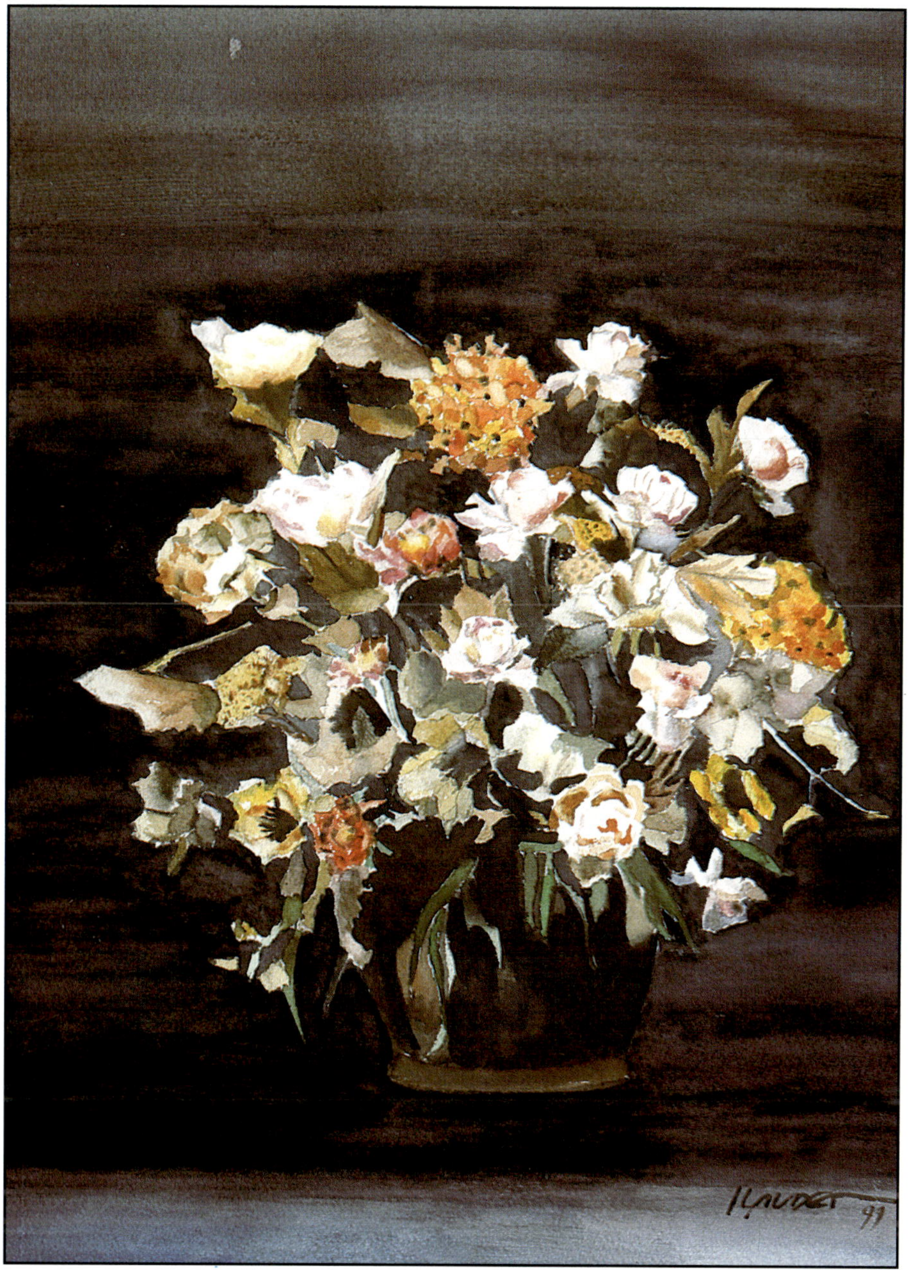

and finished. In other words, only those flowers which still remain.

This exercise is a very positive one, given that it is something of a challenge for you, with the need to work with fragments and deal with real details. It is the complete opposite of the majority of pictorial methods which first advise that the main features of the composition should be set out and the details worked on later. Despite the fact that the second method is the most advisable and usual, I recommend that you forget about this for the moment because once in a while giving up this kind of method for exercises such as this one are very useful. These types of exercises offer new challenges and new ways of working and I am sure that you will learn much from them (fig. 143).

When you work on these flowers avoid drowning the painting with gray colors, taking into consideration that painting shadows does not mean adding gray to every single flower. Deal with the colors in a more creative way: darken the flowers with ochre, with carmine, with umber earth or, if you like, also use some blue (according to some impressionists shadows were blue colored). In addition, be patient and do not start painting when the earlier wash is still wet because this work requires a great deal of accuracy and painting on wet surfaces can lead to the color expanding and therefore leaving the edges without any profile. I do not advise this. I have often recommended in other books that you should not be excessively careful about painting the delicate and lovely forms of flowers. However, we have to make an exception in this exercise because here it is better to get lost in the details and their delicate shapes and changing tones.

Fig. 143. The final result is this excellent watercolor painted by Ester Llaudet, presenting a subject painted in meticulous detail, with patience and showing the marked effects of chiaroscuro.

Painting Flowerpots with Different Colors

After painting a bouquet of flowers inside a house, why don't you try to paint the flowers in a more natural setting, such as this terrace. The artist Oscar Sanchís is going to do exactly this, painting a terrace full of flowerpots with flowers of different shapes and colors. What this means is that it is important to be conscious of the composition, to take good note of the shapes and the textures of the plants and to work with intense contrasts between light and shade. To do this exercise take the outline-guide no. 3.
The exercise begins with a simple enough sketch of the interior, in this case showing those architectural elements which limit the terrace, these being the walls, the door, the windows and the bench (the last of which can be found in the center of the composition- see fig. 144). Instead of making the sketch you can, if you prefer, use the outline-guide no. 3.
The window, which acts as a backdrop, is the first to be painted after the initial sketch is completed. First give the shutters a wash of medium intensity burnt umber and then work on the vegetation with cadmium green, painting on wet and *alla prima*. You will paint the glass later on, so for the moment leave it white.
With a medium-sized round paintbrush continue working on the vegetation. Paint the green mass below the window with permanent green and a little yellow. Try to leave a white space in the area between the stems and flowers of the plant at the front, the aim being to silhouette them better. With the same permanent green and Payne gray paint the shaded area of the right shutter. With Prussian blue and emerald green paint the elongated leaves of the exuberant plant in the center. Look at how working on wet means that the colors mix on the paper and therefore make it unnecessary to be done on a palette (fig. 145).
Now take a small paintbrush and continue the task of painting the vegetation. Continue going down the paper painting the flowerpots to the left with only two colors, enough to give the desired sensation of volume. Now paint the group of red flowers: treat them as undefined monochrome

144

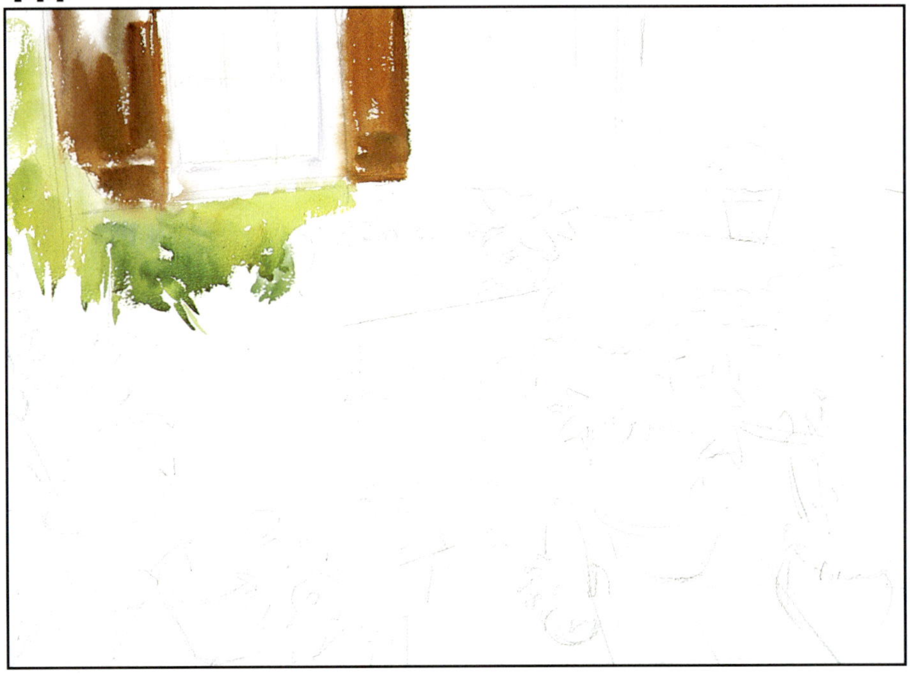

145

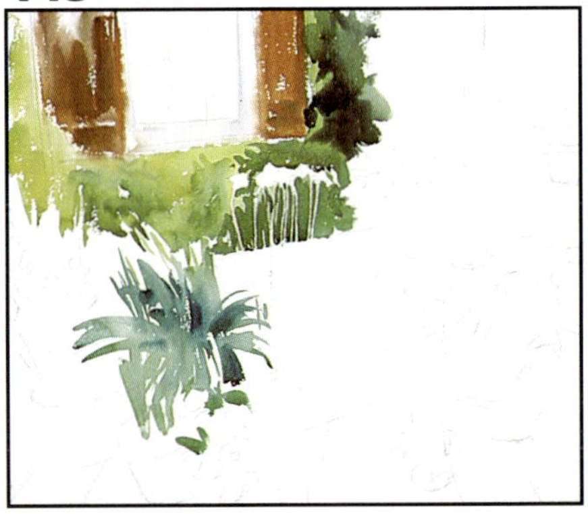

Fig. 144. Just like any step by step exercise this should be started with a sketch of the model, or alternatively, using the outline-guide no. 3.
Fig. 145. When beginning a watercolor it is preferable to start from those perspectives furthest away and to then move down the painting from the upper to the lower part.
Fig. 146. Paint the plants and flowerpots with some washes applied on wet and alla prima, this meaning without superimposing other layers.

146

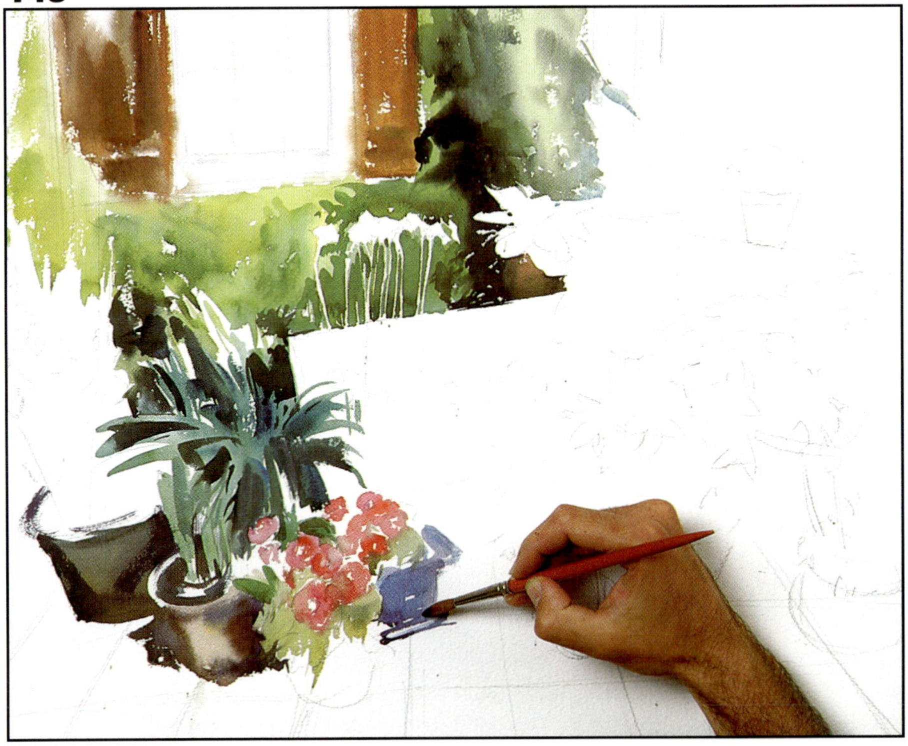

colors keeping the center circle of the flower white, which will be painted with a yellow wash. Finish this phase by painting the flowerpot to the right with an ultramarine blue. It is important to always work with clean colors, because in this way the paint will come across in shining terms and with a chromatic energy which really stands out (fig. 146, earlier page).

Take the medium paintbrush and prepare a wash with Payne gray and medium intensity natural umber. With this paint the background, this being the floor and walls of the house wherever the vegetation allows this to be visible. The wash should be spread in a gradated way, from top to bottom, such that the closer it gets to the windows the darker it gets. Alternatively, the closer it gets to the lower part of the paper, the lighter it gets. When this wash has dried, draw lines on the floor with a small paintbrush to show the tiles coming together (fig. 147).

Now begin to paint the gaps. First, paint the window frame to the right with a purplish wash. With the wash still wet superimpose a little gray and natural umber, this allowing the mixture of the three colors to diffuse in the way you can see in figure 148.

Once you have finished the background continue with the perspectives closest to the viewer. See how the plants to the right should be painted, these being dealt with by using more grayish shades (emerald green and Payne gray). As with the earlier cases keep the white spaces occupied by the flowers for later when you will add pale pink washes (fig. 149). With ultra-marine blue apply an uneven wash to the bench in the center of the scene.

147

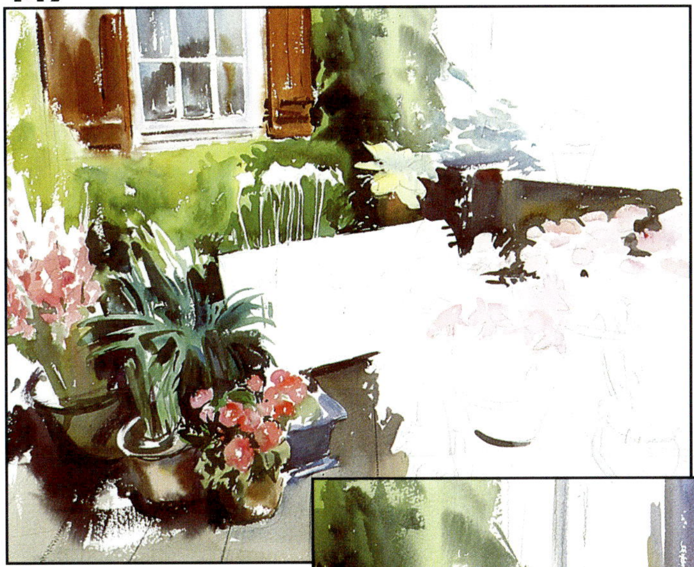

148

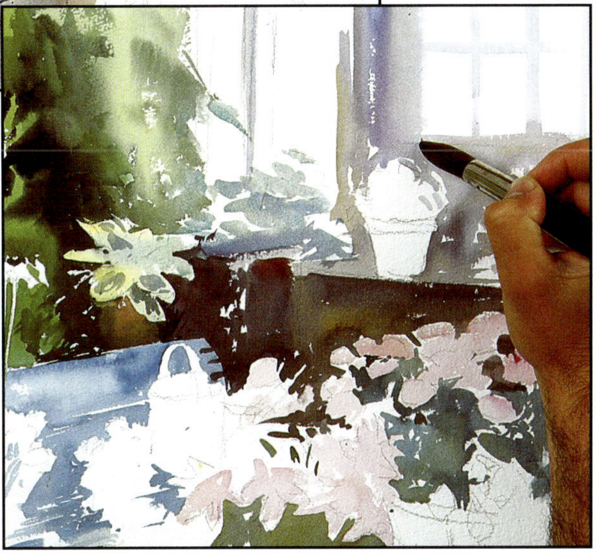

Fig. 147. Work on the details of the window glass and contrasts the shapes by adding more substance.

Fig. 148. Paint the window frame to the right **alla prima** ***and work with three colors: violet, natural earth umber and Payne gray, allowing the washes to shade off and settle on the surface of the paper.***

149

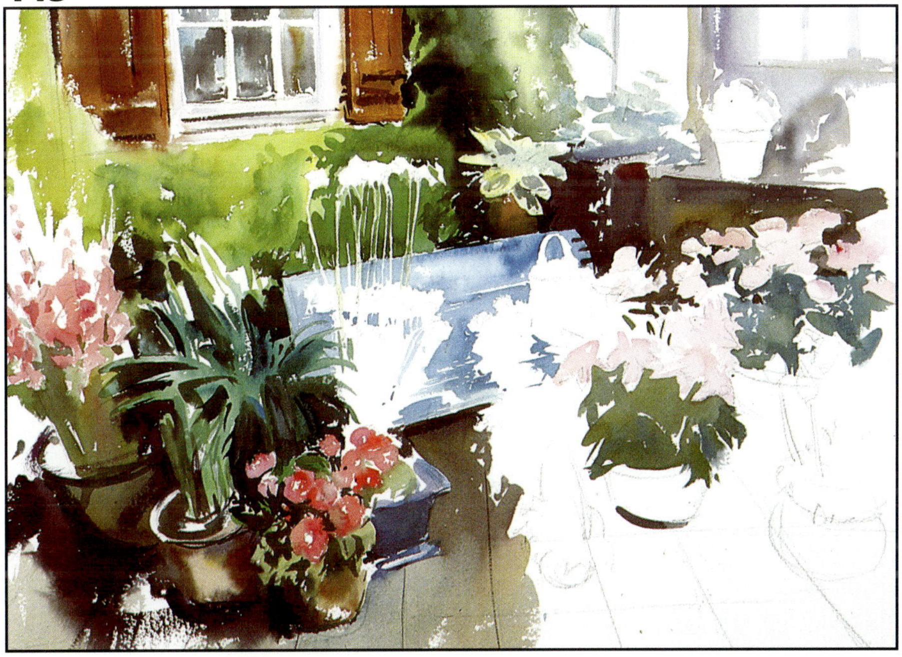

Fig. 149. Begin highlighting the flowers with washes of carmine diluted with water. Similarly, do the bench in the center with an ultra-marine blue wash and the walls with gradations in color.

As you can see the main plants and flowerpots have been painted. Now it is time to paint the flowers (fig. 150). The watering can sitting on the bench is painted a blister green color, but do it carefully to portray its volume. To do this a purplish wash is applied to the left side of the can to give it more of a cylindrical appearance. The flowers recently painted are made up of pink, ochre, and carmine colors in the clear parts of the painting, whereas the colors of the darker parts are obtained with emerald green and Payne gray. It is important to take into consideration the morphology of each of the plants so that once painted they are easily identifiable (fig. 151).
This is now the best moment to paint the bench. Take a small paintbrush and with an intense ultra-marine blue paint parallel lines to represent the horizontal strips running up and down the length of the bench. With the mixture of ultra-marine blue and burnt umber earth paint the shaded spaces between the stems, leaves and flowers with a more intense color. After doing this the watercolor will have taken on a much greater contrast (fig. 152).

150

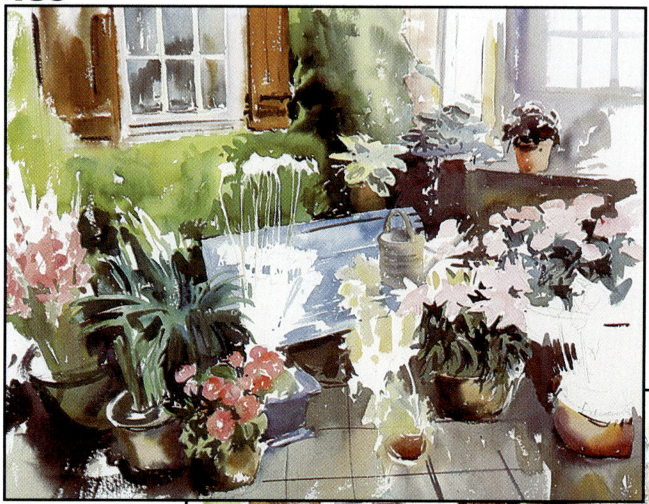

151

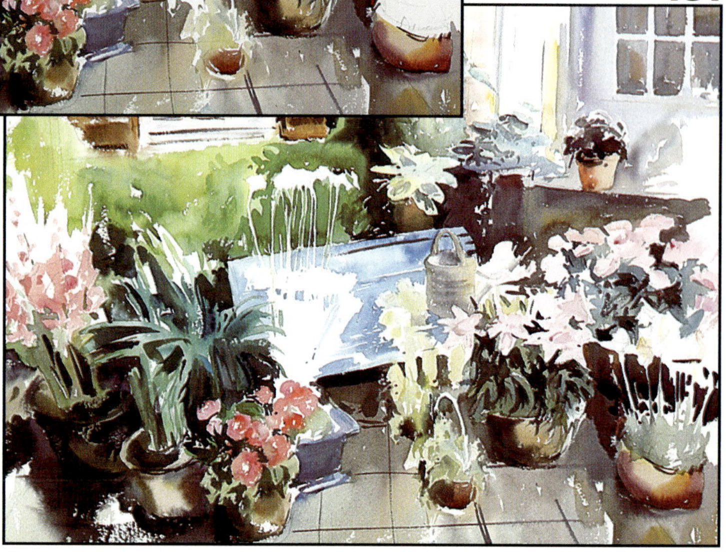

Fig. 150. After leaving the earlier washes to dry, and given that this operation should be carried out on a dry surface, detail the contrasts of light and shadow in the group of plants to the right.

Fig. 151. Continue detailing this first part, but paying attention to each of the plants' shapes and textures.

Fig. 152. With a small paintbrush add the details of the texture to the bench and darken the spaces between the leaves and the flowers to allow them to stand out from the darker background.

152

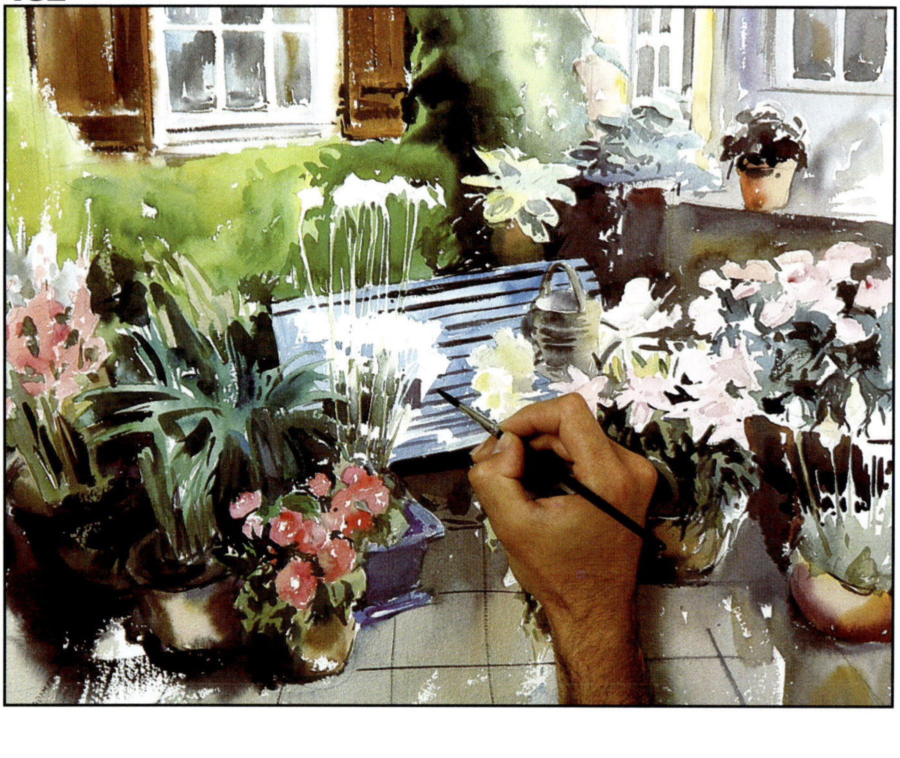

TIPS

- Something which should always be taken into consideration by any beginner is the need to try and enrich the tonality, this meaning the enrichment of areas which are not made up of different colors.
- The small white spaces, the small holes, which are usually left by many professional artists when painting watercolors, give a kind of vibrancy to the color and form which accentuates the vitality and realism of the subject. They also give the work a spontaneous and fresh finishing touch.

153

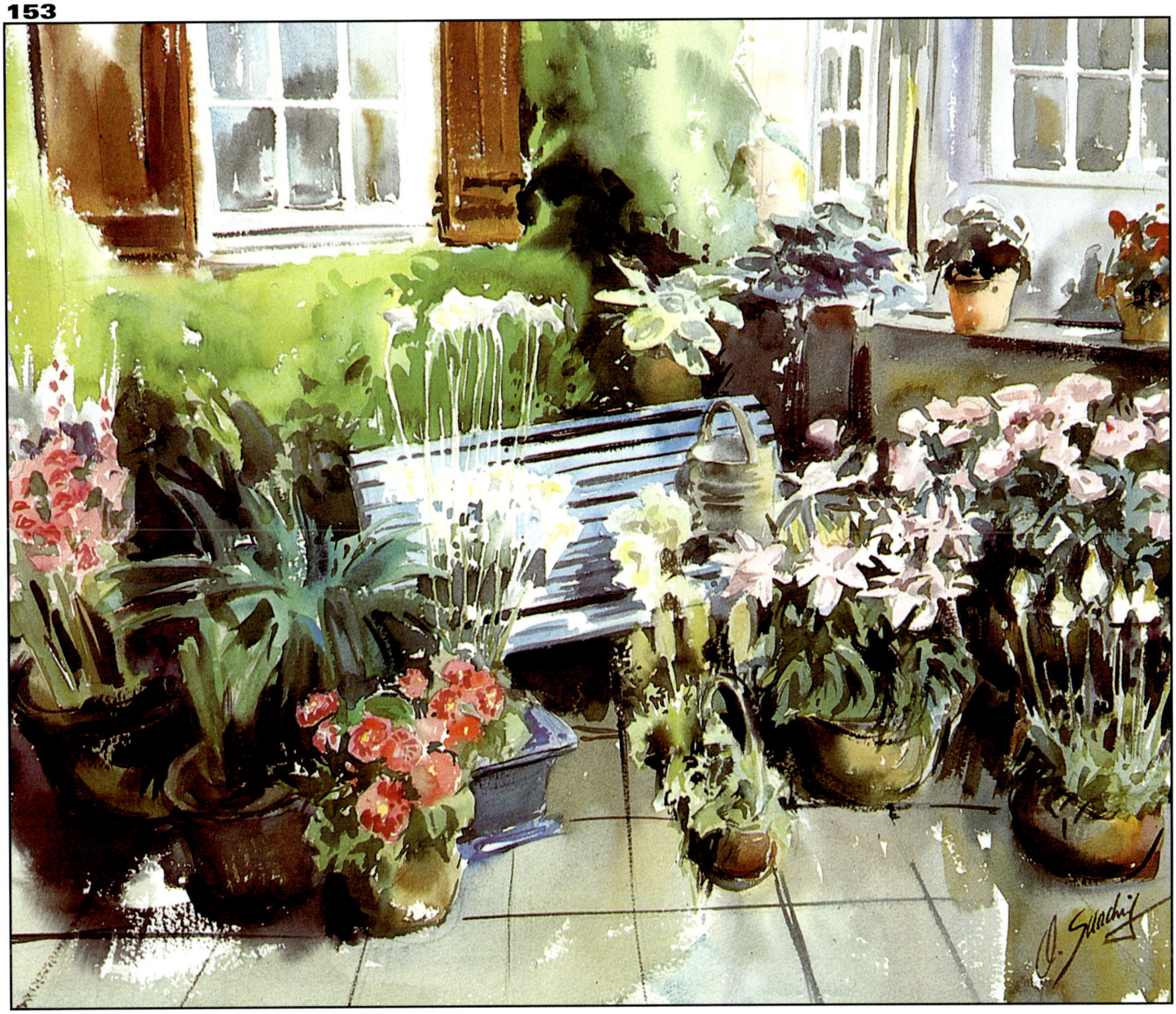

If you compare the final state with how it was just one step before you will see that the watercolor has changed. The foreground now offers us more detail, the result of more attention going into the form and texture of the plants and flowers. As a result the center of the painting has gained more light and emphasis.

Possibly, you have made the mistake of working with colors which are excessively dense. Imitate Oscar Sanchís who, like the majority of watercolor artists, leaves small holes (such as those in the floor tiles in the foreground) when painting large areas with blends of similar colors. Through these small, unpainted holes it is possible to see the previous layer or the white of the paper. As such, avoid as much as possible covering all of the watercolor with uniform and flat washes. The different gaps left in the pictorial layers give a more spontaneous quality and offer some variation in the textures obtained. In addition it is a mistake to put too much detail into the doors and windows of the house because this brings the background much closer. Representing three dimensions in this type of work is managed thanks to the accentuated contrast in shade and colors of the vegetation in the foreground with respect to the more uniform colors and less detailed forms in the background.

Fig. 153. This is the final result which is shown with a general retouching of the vegetation and the center bench, now painted. As you can see the visual result of the combination of elements is splendid.

Flowers Using the Technique of Painting on Dry

Going through the two following exercises you are going to paint the same motif with different techniques : with the technique of painting on dry and with that of painting wet into wet. The first of these exercises (on pages 68 and 69) presents a more colorful tendency. I would ask you to pay a lot of attention to the two step by step exercises about to be explained because I am sure that you will learn many advantageous things from them. These could then be later applied to your compositions. The model which we are going to use for these two exercises is a basket with a well-lit, varied bouquet of flowers with the warm colors dominating it (fig. 154). The first exercise is going to be carried out by Ester Llaudet. I invite you to practice it with her.

First of all, begin drawing the model in detail (fig. 155). Work on the painting with a heavy brush and start concentrating on the basket. Use a diluted ochre and a combination of the same ochre with Payne gray for the darker base of the basket. Next paint the center of the sunflowers with burnt umber earth (fig. 156). Continue painting the rest of the flowers. With cadmium yellow and ochre paint the sunflowers' crown of petals and with a little diluted carmine do the group of pink flowers. With this same carmine mixed with a little ultra-marine blue paint the purplish flowers in the upper part (fig. 157). All of this is done on dry which means leaving the earlier wash to dry to then superimpose new washes and new colors. From this point change the heavy paintbrush which you have been using since the beginning (to work on large color areas) for a smaller one to allow you to carry out work on more detailed parts.

Paint the irregular branches sticking out between the flowers with permanent green and a little umber. It will be necessary to paint the leaves with two or three colors. Each one of the elements making up the still life are progressively enriched with new details, these giving the sensation of volume (fig. 158).

154

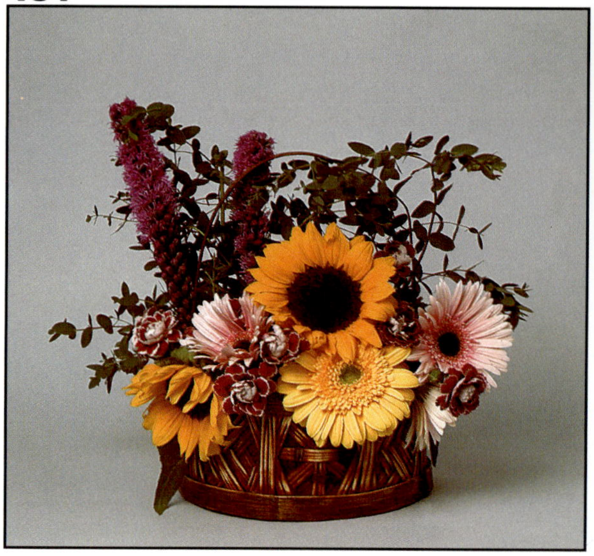

155

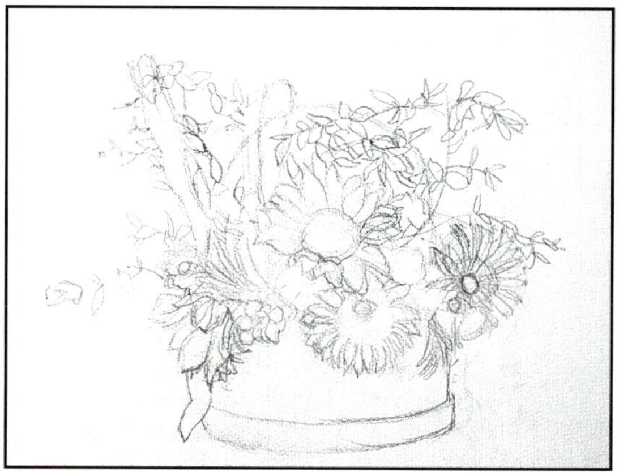

Fig. 154. This basket of flowers will be the model for carrying out the two following exercises.

Fig. 155. Painting in this style means that the drawing produced beforehand takes on special significance, given that it is an indispensable guide throughout the exercise.

156

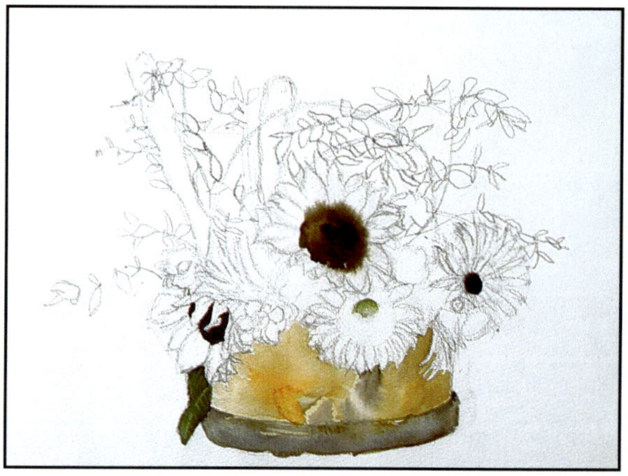

Fig. 156. The first objective is to pinpoint and highlight the darkest parts of the composition, which in this case is the basket wicker and the flower stamen.

Fig. 157. Draw and paint thoroughly, considering the small details and following the exact shapes of the petals.

157

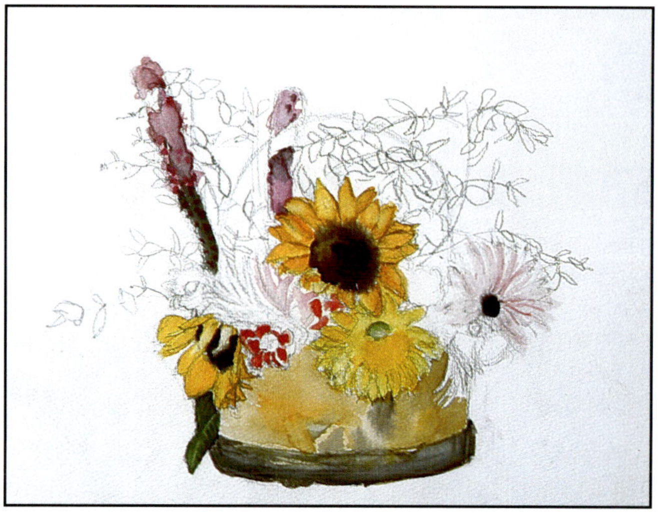

Now work on the background and make the mixture of colors colder by introducing a Payne gray wash. Concentrate on making sure the background is not uniform: it is a wash of gradated grays where the shadow from the model will be projected (fig. 159). Look for special qualities through small details here and there, layer after layer, image after image, until the painting acquires its definitive appearance. Strengthen and highlight the green of the leaves, and intensify the pinks of the flowers in such a way that the yellow flowers stand out better, as well as having areas of light and shade.

To finish, paint the structure or geometric fabric of the flower basket. For this take a small paintbrush, be patient and work on reproducing the shapes, the hollows and the wicker texture. Use two different browns, not only because one of these is lighter, but also for the composition- one with ochre and the other with more gray, doing so in such a way that they are in harmony with the tonal qualities of the painting and with the background color.

As you can see in the finished work, the artist has not taken a lot of liberty with respect to the final color. The painting has been dealt with in a realism style, meaning that it reflects the colors of the composition in a realistic way and without risking chromatic variations. Above all, the importance of the modelling must be pointed out, the result of which is the construction of shapes and the creation of volume (fig. 160).

Fig. 158. The watercolor is transparent and allows the mixture of colors or the superimposing of one color onto another, as in this case, where the different flowers of the bouquet are painted one by one.
Fig. 159. In this state the drawing, color, contrast and harmonization are practically complete. The missing parts are the small details these being the last features to be worked on.
Fig. 160. Barely, four hours have been necessary for Llaudet to finish her flower painting. Painting on dry needs a lot more time than painting on wet, because it is necessary in this method to let previous washes dry out before continuing.

158

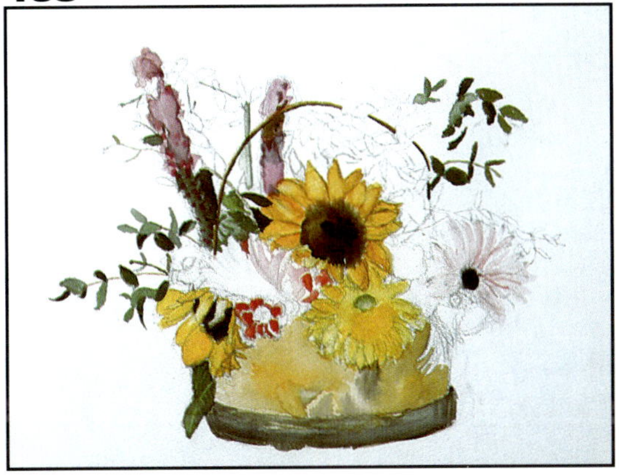

159

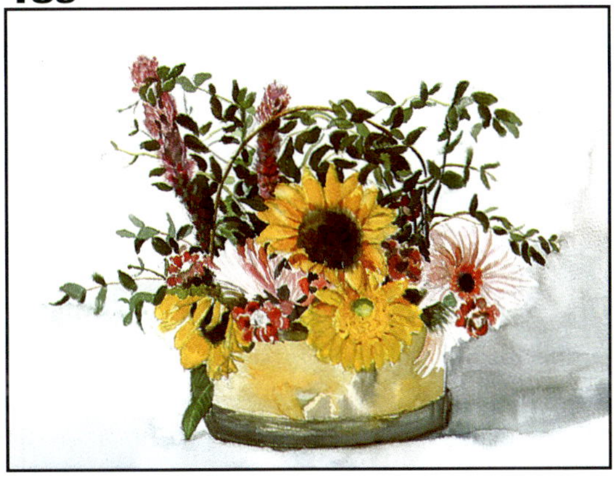

160

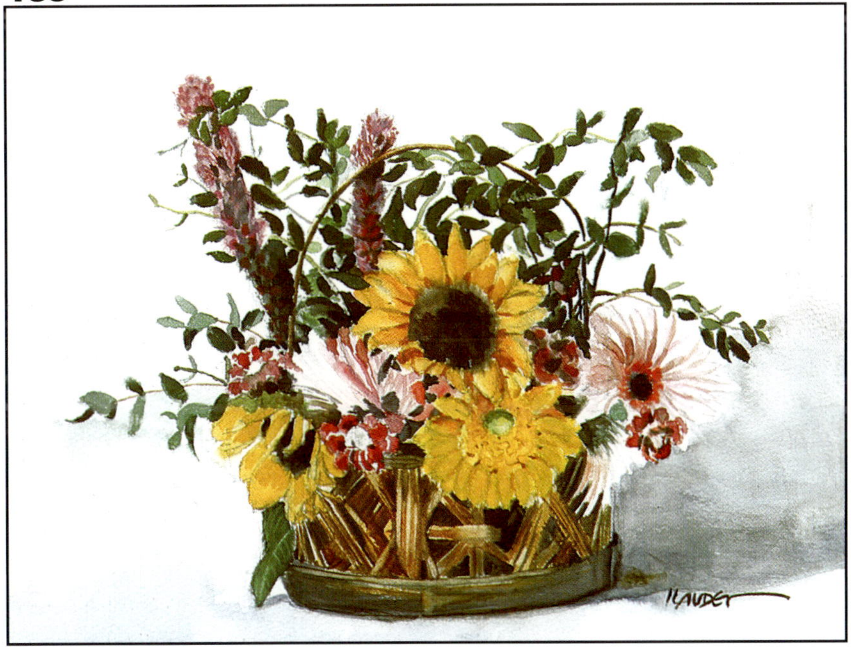

TIPS

- Do not confuse the technique of painting on dry with that of using a dry brush because the first of these consists of superimposing washes when the previous one has dried, therefore preventing the colors from blending together and becoming mixed. On the other hand, the technique of using a dry brush is one which means working with a brush loaded with paint and hardly any water, in such a way that rubbing the brush leaves a rough texture on the paper.

Flowers Using the Wet into Wet Technique

I would now like to invite you to paint the same motif as the earlier exercise, although this time it will involve using a different technique: that of painting on wet.

This concerns a treatment of the model which is more colorful, more lively, cleaner, and brighter. Painting on wet consists of painting on a area or layer recently moistened with water or recently painted and still wet, with the wetness being controlled depending on the effect that you want to create. In this way the mixture and fusion of the colors is carried out on the surface of the paper and not, as in the previous case, something which happens on the artist's palette. The author of this exercise will be the experimentational watercolor artist Oscar Sanchís.

Now you can begin . With a medium paintbrush dipped into cadmium yellow paint the sunflower's petals. Without hardly a rest and using an ochre colour wash, highlight the effects of light and shade. With umber and sienna paint the center part of the flower. As you can see working on wet allows the edges of the colors to merge together at the same time as giving the painting a more spontaneous effect (fig. 161).

The painting on wet technique does not allow for working on the whole model at the same time, going from less to more. Instead it should be worked on in parts, in fragments, and painted from the beginning while the watercolor is wet (fig. 162). This said, paint the two purplish flowers in the upper part in such a way that the green, to be blended with thc pink, forms free-flowing washes with irregular shapes and profiles.

Now paint the pink flowers in the center of the basket, first concentrating on the center of the flower and spreading the wash radially until completing the shape of each one of them (fig. 163). Next paint the stems for the leaves which have been added to complement the bouquet. If you look closely you will see that the green used to paint these contains a multitude of different colors which have merged together in a graded way (violet, green, yellow and orange– fig. 164 of the following page). Having reached this point the still life has taken on a lot of volume. Notice how, having always worked with light colors, the still life has gained a visual center and brightness in comparison with the previous exercise, where the grays and earth colors were present more. However, also notice how the shades have been accentuated by using purples, yellows and oranges, all of which mean that the painting has taken

161

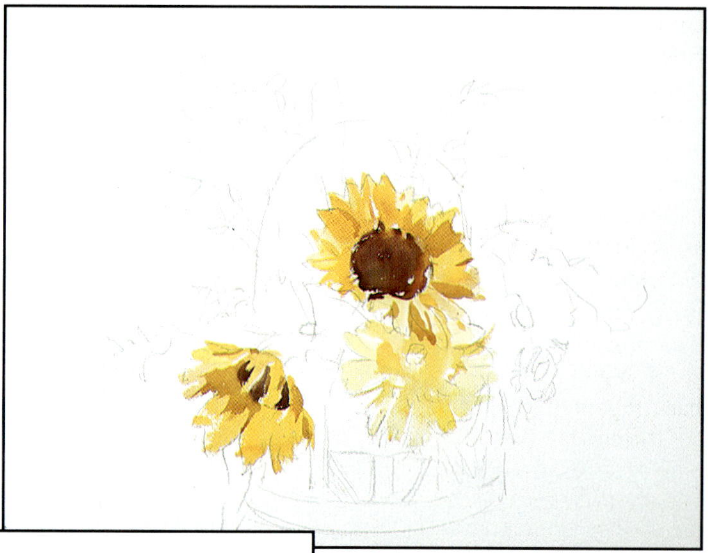

Fig. 161. This time begin by painting the brightest parts. Paint the yellow flowers, in only a few seconds filling out the shape and color, modelling by superimposing the colors on wet.

162

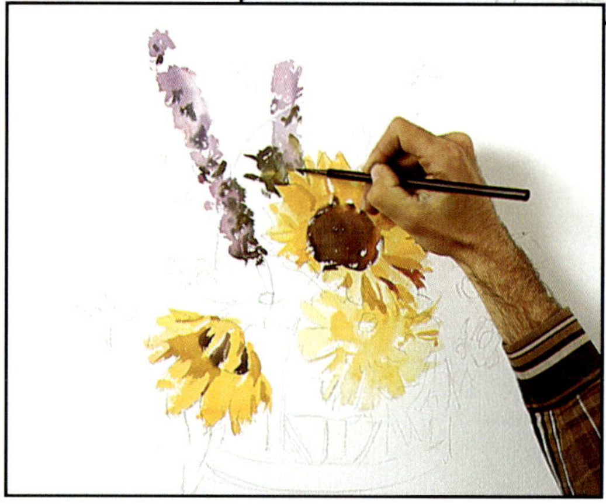

Fig. 162. Do the same with the purplish flowers, blending green and magenta colours in the same wash, this process being one which gives rich textures.

163

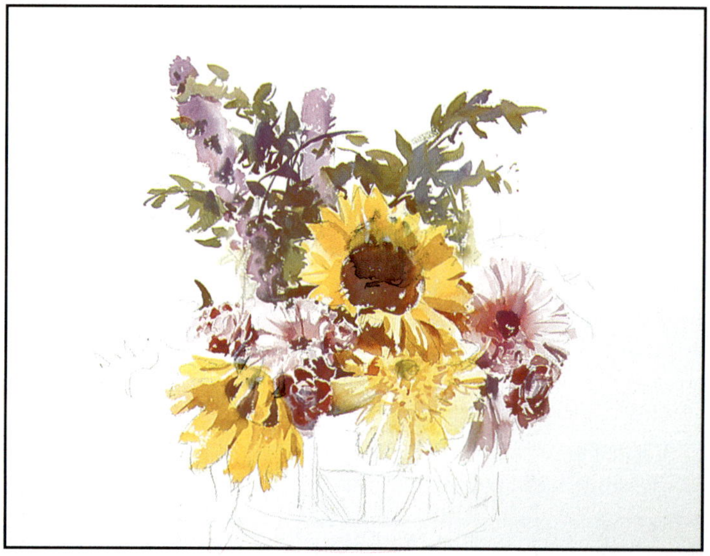

Fig. 163. In the third stage of the painting you can see that the center part of the composition is nearly complete. This is due to the fact that the technique of painting on wet allows work to be done at a faster pace.

on something of a more colorful tendency.
Now paint the basket's wickerwork and its characteristic texture with touches of ochre tinted with a little orange, burnt umber and little touches of ultramarine blue. Work on the wet colors giving them small straight strokes with blue and burnt umber in a way which makes the shadow vibrant. Given that this is not uniform the basket picks up a lot of emphasis (fig. 165). At this point the flower basket has such an intensity of color and texture that it has taken on an appearance which at many times is offered by oil paintings.
Take a medium brush and finish painting the background with purplish-greyish washes. If you want you can use the side of your hand to join or spread the still wet wash to achieve a sensation of translucence, taking advantage of the spontaneous fusion of the wet colors. Next paint with the same color, but somewhat more intense, the right side of the bunch to show the shadow and the contact of the model with the white surface.
As you can see in the already finished watercolor, Oscar Sanchís has produced the bouquet with some vibrancy, with great brightness and light in a way which creates a balance between color and volume (fig. 166). He has left a lot of white areas for the painting to breathe, while he has covered other parts with transparent colors. Note the background washes which smoothly blend into the paper, and the trimmed profiles of the flowers to the right which show us where the areas of light and shadow begin and end.

TIPS

- When you apply colors you must take into account the fact that a watercolor loses 10% of its intensity on drying.
- To control the spreading of the paint across the paper surface well, I recommend that you carry out this exercise on a board which is slightly angled. Do not work on a flat surface, because the excesses of water, instead of dripping down the paper will remain stuck and form small pools which on drying could badly effect the final result of the painting.

164

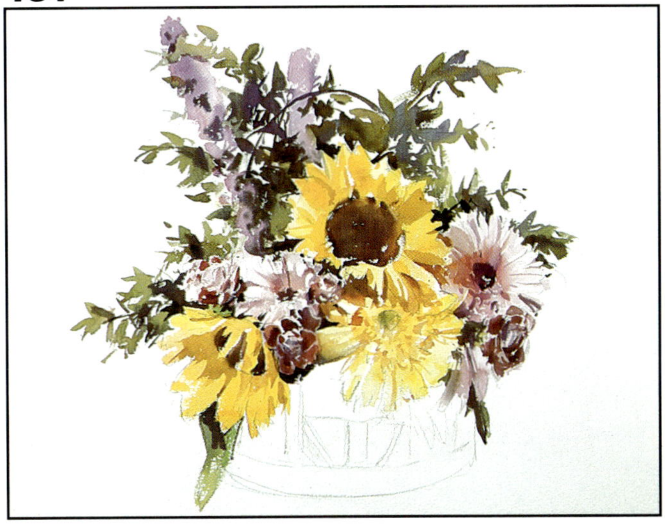

Fig. 164. Now paint the branches, complete with their irregular array of leaves, which complement the composition. To do this mix green-yellow, orange and blue or violet such that these washes do not appear uniform , but instead are gradated.

165

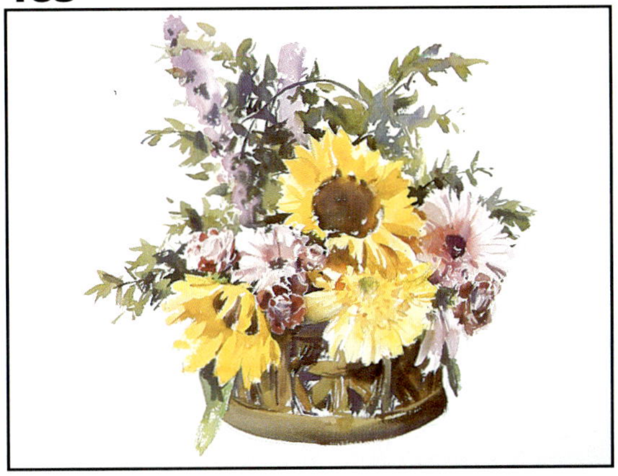

Fig. 165. With regards to the basket, not much time has been spent on either the details or how to manage the texture, in other words those parts, such as the interweaving of the wicker, which describe the material to perfection.

166

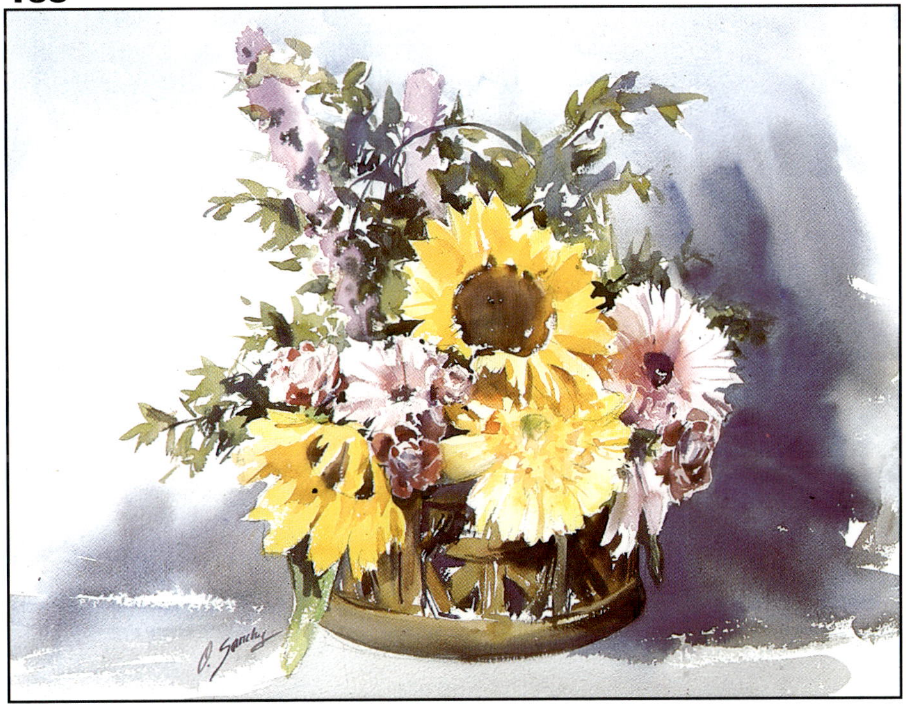

Fig. 166. Here we have the flowers of Oscar Sanchís in an original painting, with a particular conception and style, following the technique of painting on wet. As you can see the last step in finishing off the work has involved applying a very diluted grayto the background with the aim of spatially locating the bouquet.

Painting a Pond with Water Lilies

Bibiana Crespo is going to paint a pool of water lilies in a creative style. This will allow you to see the technique and resources used by the artist, the ease of making the brushstrokes, the flow of the paint and the fresh way of working with a watercolor. This will result in a simple painting which maintains a momentary impression and covers a wide range of methods which could be considered as semi-abstract. I invite you to join the artist in this work and to learn new systems of working.

This is the model chosen: it is basically made up of lilies, many of them in bloom (fig. 167). As you can see the model has a specific enough frame, given that it does not give a depth of field. In the picture only the motif appears, the lilies and the water, without sky, hills or trees which act as a backdrop, this therefore allowing us to deal with some parts of the painting in a semi-abstract way.

The drawing which you have to begin the exercise with corresponds to a line sketch, this only dealing with the location of the different elements in the painting and with a geometric design (fig. 168). There is no intention of detailing, profiling or evaluating the work.

Before you begin painting, do what the artist does, which is to wet the paper with clean water, using a wide deer-hair brush to remove grease and help the technique where the colors blend in the watercolor. With this same brush apply the first colors to the still wet surface, trying to create right from the beginning a more spontaneous finish. If you look closely at figure 169, you will see that the first washes are not uniform. In this first stage, the presence of emerald green, Prussian blue and Payne graycan be made out in the painting. The spaces corresponding to the leaves and flowers must be kept white in the meantime.

167

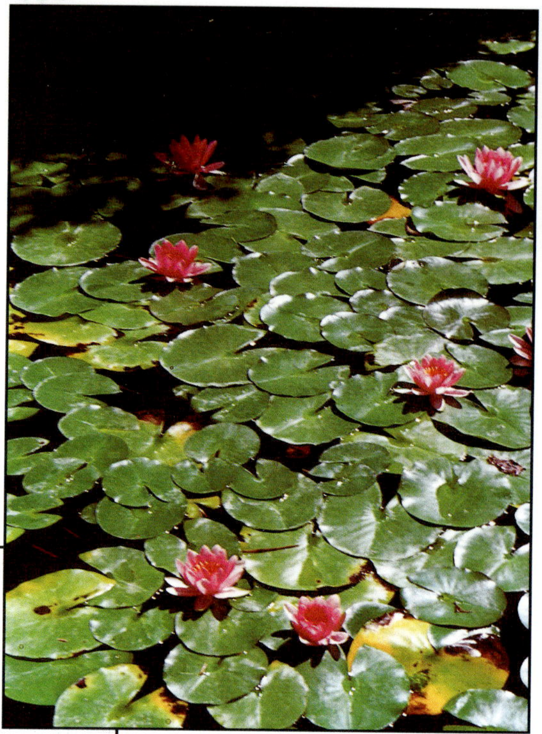

Fig. 167. This is the model: the sunny surface of a pool covered by lilies in bloom.

168

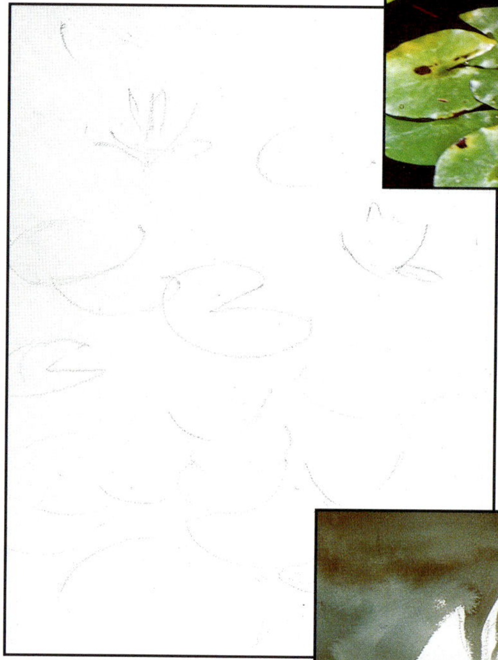

169

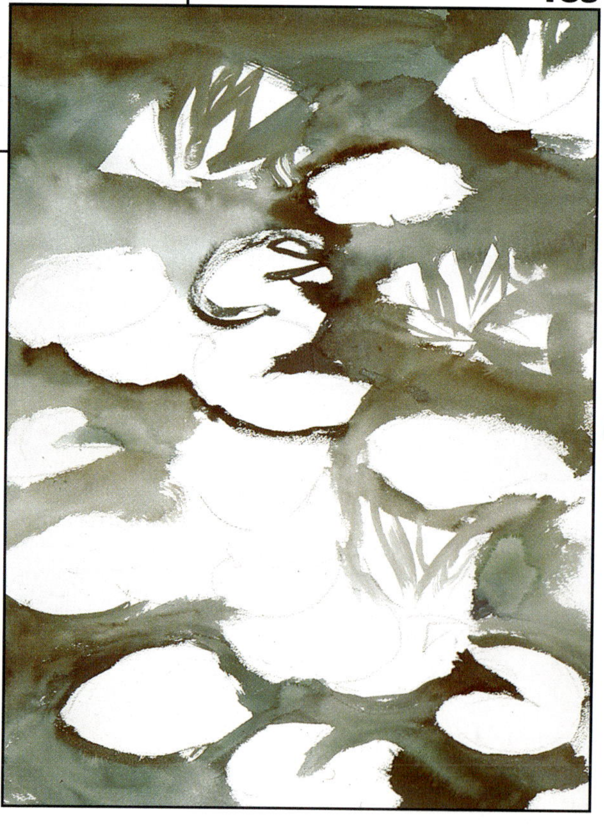

Fig. 168. Begin drawing with a graphite stick, for a few seconds, making some strokes to act as a reference for beginning the work, and also to later allow you to paint with greater ease and less concern.

Fig. 169. With a brush do the background wash, the space corresponding to the water, with small variations of green, blue and grey.

With the paintbrush loaded with color and using energetic brushstrokes, profile the lily leaves, leaving the painting so that the strokes spread and merge with the previous wash (fig. 170).

Continue with a flat brush loaded for a transparent wash and complete the color of the lily leaves in such a way that the white of the paper stops breathing. You will get the uneven green color, for painting the leaves, by mixing cadmium green, permanent green and a little burnt umber (fig. 171). The strokes should not be methodical, but instead have more expression. Learn to control the brushstrokes (fig. 172).

The use of expression, meaning the control of arm movement, can give the work an expressionist mood and a much more diffused treatment of colors. This needs an exercise in synthesis on the part of the artist, because it is necessary to sum up the shapes of the model in a number of strokes of color or in a large number of transparent brushstrokes. In this way the form of the painting is not constructed through a series of lines, but instead by applying strokes of color.

170

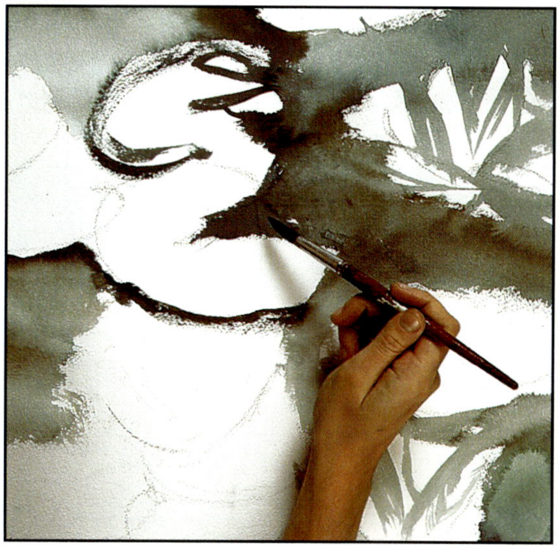

Fig. 170. The enhancement of the brushstrokes is clear at the beginning, but seconds later the color is stabilized, diluted and blended unevenly with the surrounding washes.

171

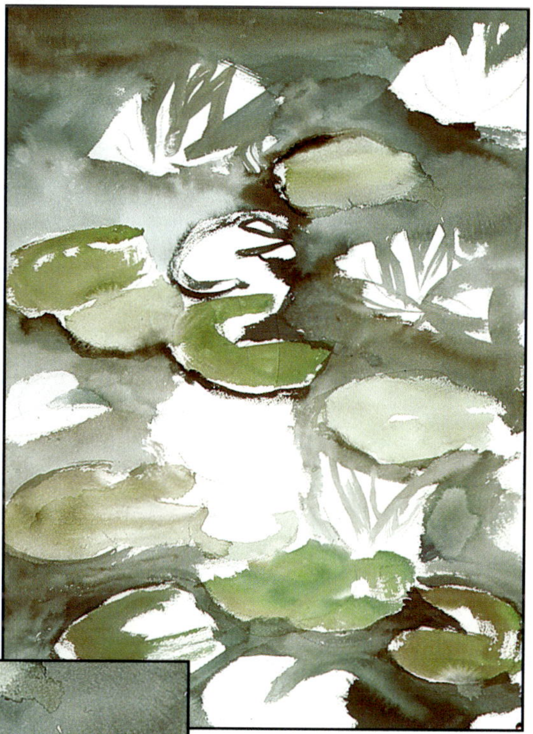

172

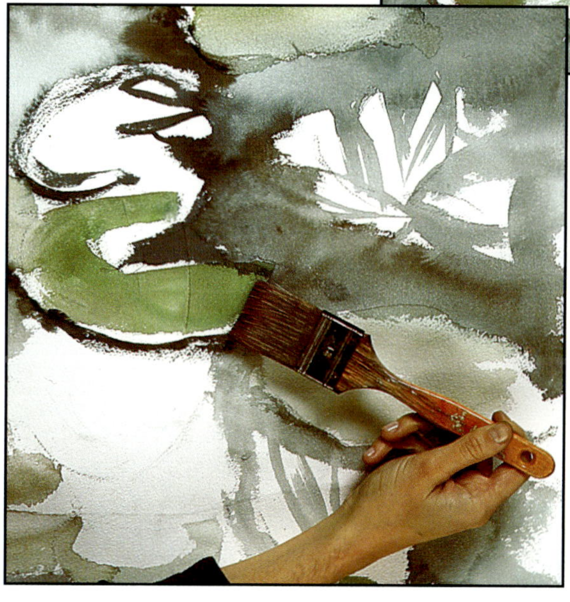

Fig. 171. Look at the synthesis of shapes and colors which make up the lilies in the composition. The transparency of the watercolor allows the mixture and composition of colors by superimposing some on top of others.

Fig. 172. In this image you are shown how the lily leaves are painted with a wide paintbrush. Look at how the wash applied is completely uniform and carried out in only one brushstroke.

From time to time rinse the paint from the brush and dry it with a cloth, which should always be at hand, and with the brush half dry, use it to absorb excesses of water in different places. After a few minutes finish the background, the leaves and the reflections, harmonizing them with some cold shading. As you can see the work has been carried out with excessive simplicity and a poor color appearance (fig. 173). As such we are now going to brighten it up by painting the flowers. Apply a magenta color to the wet surface, corresponding to the pink flowers of the lilies. Notice how the color is diluted as a result of the effects of the wet paper. With an oiled pastel stick of the same color define the shape of the flowers with quick and precise strokes. With a medium, paintbrush give the upper flower petals some touches of Prussian blue and paint some of the petals in the center an orange color, thereby giving greater variety and chromatic richness to each of the flowers. Again the colors on the surface of the paper are diluted because the paper is still slightly wet (figs. 174 and 175, the latter shown on the following page).

173

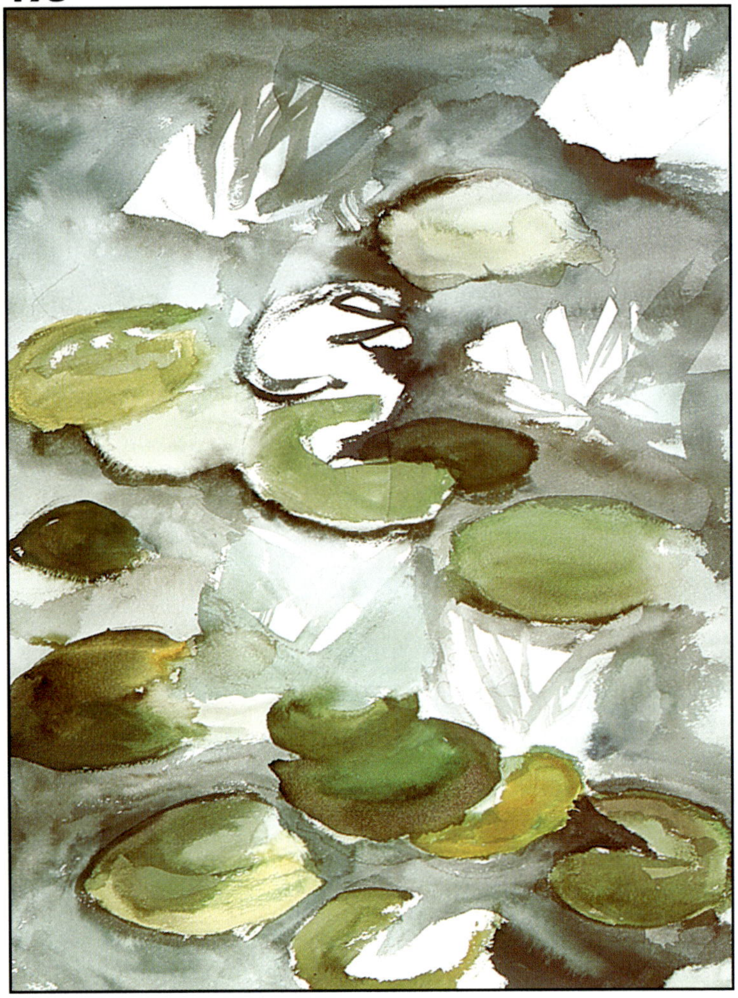

Fig. 173. The leaves and the reflections on the water surface have been succinctly painted in the stage shown here.

174

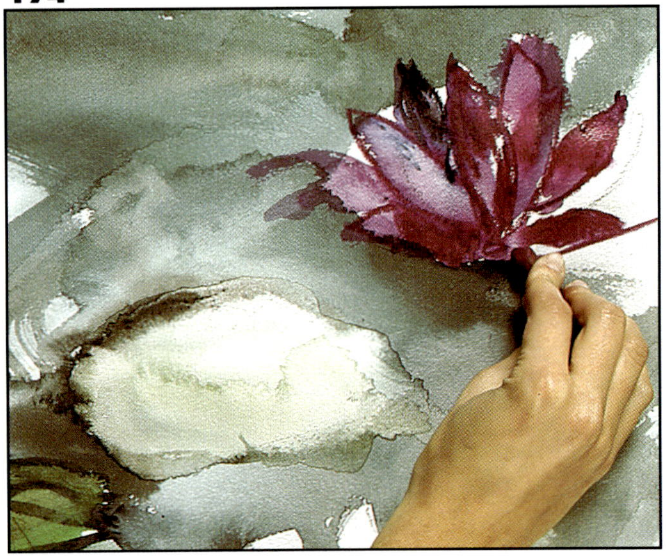

Fig. 174. With the aim of showing the well-defined outline of the flowers correct their appearance by modifying them with a watercolor pastel stick in the same color that was used in the watercolor.

TIPS

- Consider the risk of large drops as a result of an excess of water in the brush. In the case of working with an angled table you must be careful. Alternatively, if you are using a flat board you have to take care not to soak the painting too much. To get rid of excess water use a cloth or absorbent paper as much as possible.
- If you like , you can work as many professionals do by spreading, rubbing or painting with the fingers.
- Do not do this in a step by step manner, using small sheets of paper, because this type of exercise needs you to work on large sheets.

As you have seen, this exercise has been dominated by a sensation of freedom, something which every artist should experiment with. Without doubt, in subjects such as this, you should find the ideal framework to give free rein to your spontaneity (fig. 175). The greatest danger with this type of technique is that you are left feeling unsatisfied with the result and end up detailing the work too much, believing that it is the best option to sort it out. Don't do it. This technique relies on suggesting the shapes instead of defining them. Given the speed of carrying out this exercise I advise you that for whatever situation do various watercolors consecutively, in only one session, gradually entering this subject . Don't try to go over the mistakes and defects, but instead begin the painting another time, trying not to make more mistakes.

When establishing yourself in the work do not draw too much, in other words do not make a detailed drawing. Do not be carried along by the shapes, but instead deal with them in a way which is suggestive. A drawing which is too detailed could pre-condition the final result of the work.

Possibly, your rate of work will be slower than desired and the paper will dry out before finishing the wash. As a result the watercolor effects will not be the same as the painting obtained by Bibiana Crespo. The watercolor on wet demands a lot of attention on the part of the painter, before putting paint to paper. The execution as such must be fast to take advantage of the level of wetness desired. If you are working quickly and the paper is still drying out, make sure that where you painting is not in the sun, next to a heater or in the middle of a stream of air.

175

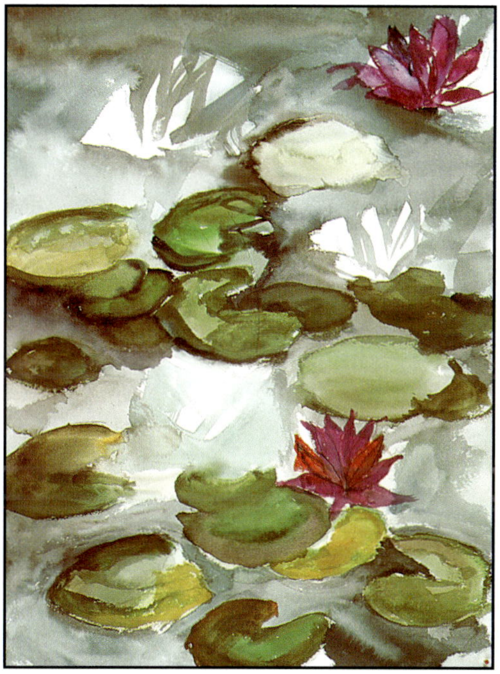

176

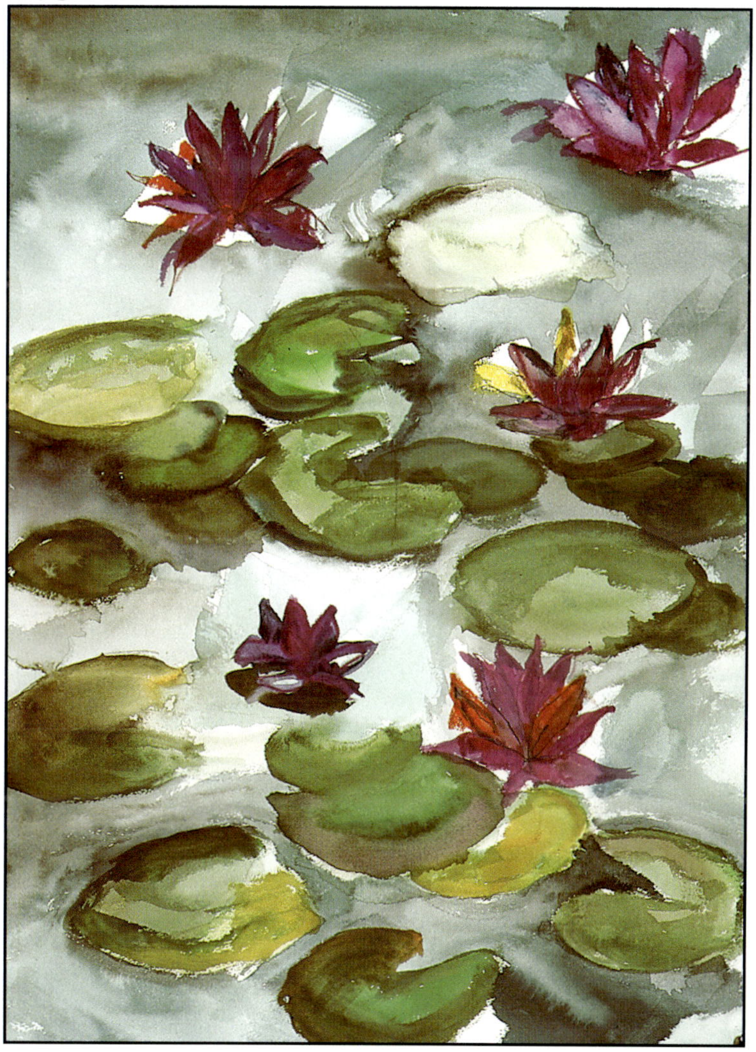

Fig. 175. With magenta colored washes mixed on wet with a drop of Prussian blue and orange, paint the flowers.

Fig. 176. Looking at the final state of the painting and comparing it the earlier condition, anyone would say that the artist has worked a lot more. However, in reality the most important work was carried out with the previously done washes. The only new features are the appearance of three more flowers and the profiling of some details.

Painting a Basket of Dried Flowers

If you try to paint a floral scene in various sessions it will be better if you choose dried flowers for this task, because these will not droop and the leaves will not fall after a few hours. It would be difficult to find dried flowers which could offer such bright colors as that of a still life of natural flowers, however, despite this, the challenge in painting them is interesting with the artist obliged to use a broken range of colors. The artistic range of such colors, as you should already know, comes from mixing in unequal parts, two complementary colors with white.

Look at the model (fig. 177): it is a basket of dried flowers containing muted greens and ochres with a tendency towards a grayish color. I have chosen this model because the whole gives off a certain warmth, an orange harmonization which will make the final result of the work more attractive. For this exercise we are relying on the collaboration of the artist Grau Carod. I would ask you to work along with him, paying attention to each one of the steps which are explained next.

To arrive at the expected sketch first draw a vertical line in the center, then approximate and mark out the space which is going to be taken up by the basket and begin detailing the motif. As you can appreciate by looking at the sketch made by the artist, it has been decided that the basket should be lengthened so that it appears more stretched and less wide (fig. 178). You can do the same if you like, but it is not necessary. This depends on each individual's own interpretation.

Paint the background with an ochre colored wash with a little sienna and vermilion. Use a no. 18 round paintbrush with marten hair. Do these washes in an uneven way, allowing the colors to mix on the surface of the paper (fig. 179).

177

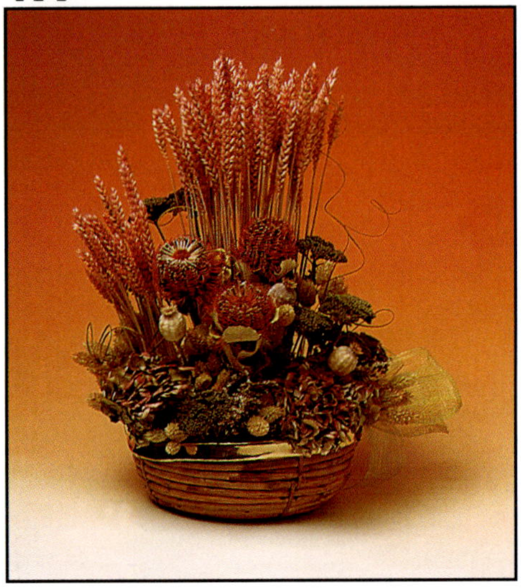

Fig. 177. The model is a luxuriant bouquet of dried flowers put together in a typical wicker basket.

178

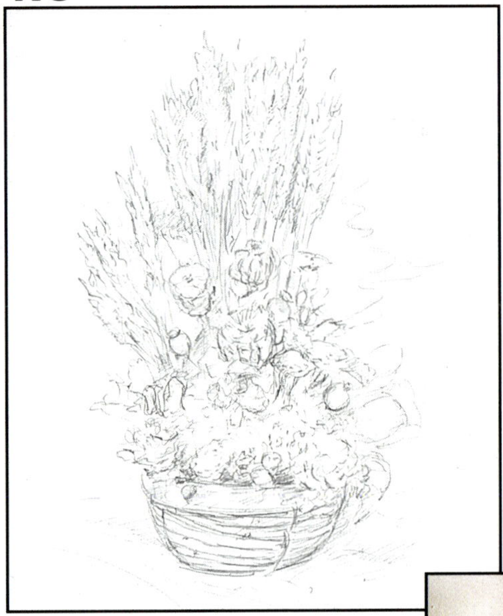

179

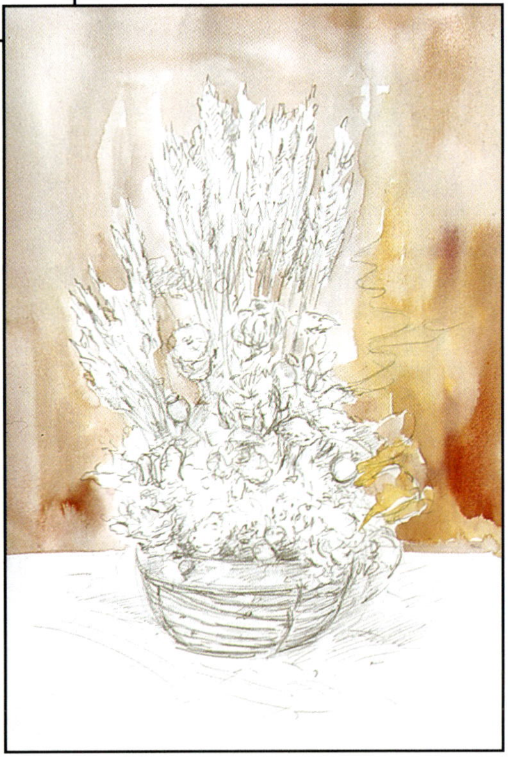

Fig. 178. First of all, make a really detailed drawing on paper. Indicate the position of each one of the flowers and detail the textures of the bouquet.

Fig. 179. With a thick paintbrush, spread a mixture of yellow ochre, earth sienna and vermilion.

When the background has been painted apply color to the base, table or support the basket is sitting on. For this mix yellow ochre with burnt umber and add the color with thick and uneven brushstrokes, without moving into the space being kept for the bouquet. However, shade off the background a little with the model boundaries so that these boundaries are not hard, to prevent them from looking trimmed(fig. 180). With a very diluted wash with ochre, give the basket its first coloring. Now take a medium paintbrush and begin working on the bouquet. Give the pink flowers in the center their first coloring, with a Naples yellow for the buds and pink for the colored spikes (fig. 181), doing so with light brushstrokes. Now take a small paintbrush and continue. Paint the wicker basket's framework and the most intense shadows at the base of the bouquet with Payne gray washes. With a semitransparent Payne gray wash and natural umber show the shadow projected by the model at the base of the basket (fig. 182). The darker, bottom part of the basket enhances the lower part of the bouquet and additionally, introduces new qualities to the dominating orange color of the model.

180

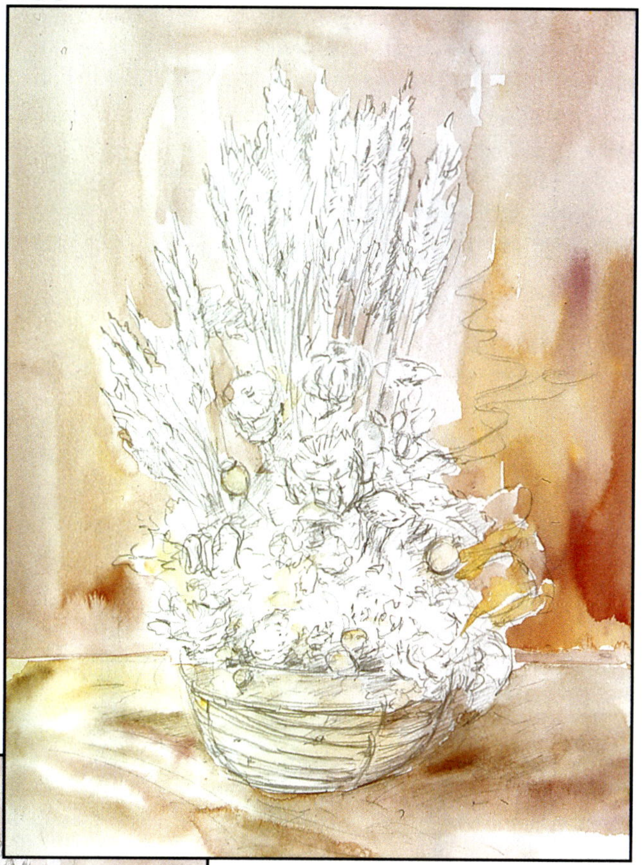

181

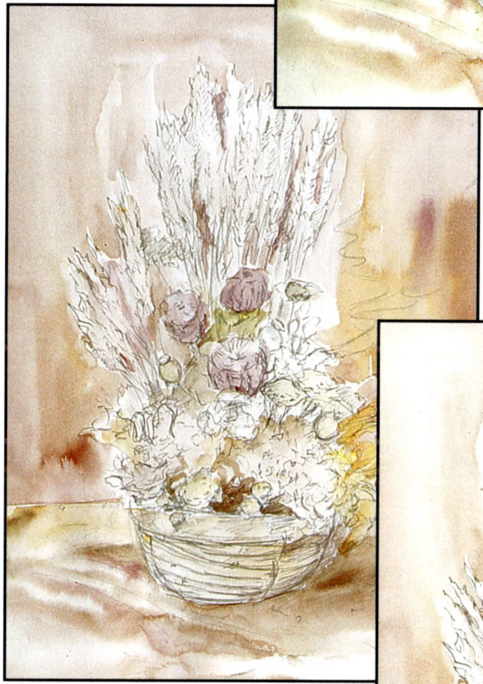

182

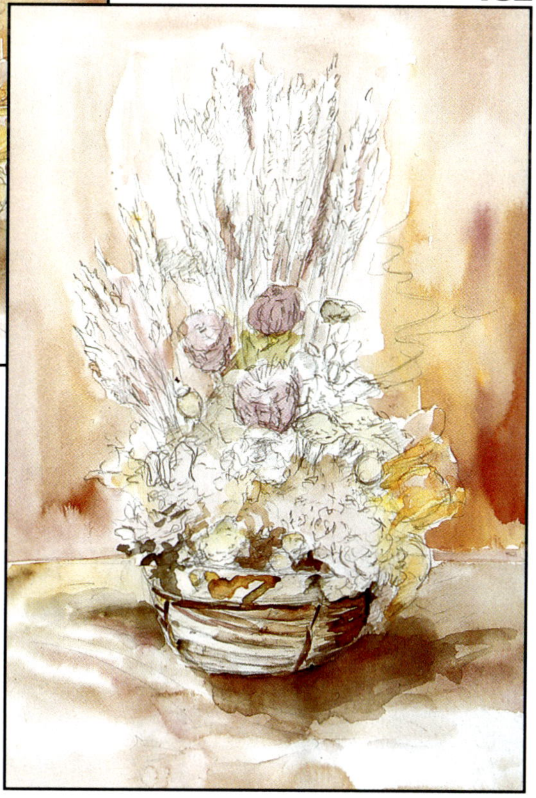

Fig. 180. Apply brushstrokes to the background in an uneven way, such that the different colors are mixed on the paper's surface, forming washes.
Fig. 181. Apply color to the center of the bouquet and begin painting some light and shadows.
Fig. 182. In this stage of the still life define the shapes using various paintbrushes which you will have to change continually, choosing them as a result of the desired brushstroke.

Endeavour to cover the whites of the flowers, adding shapes and colors, intensifying all the nuances, keeping some white areas, constructing, inventing or transforming flowers which do not exist in the model and which appear in the painting through as if by magic (fig. 183). With the aim of understanding better the progressive work involved in painting look at the process developed by Grau Carod through the pictures (Fig. 181, 182 and 183). On finishing this stage we can see that the center of the bouquet is well covered by different colors. The top third part, however, remains as it was at the beginning. The work for this part is done very quickly, although without any need for rushing it. Alternate the strokes on the painting in an almost automatic way, contemplating the motif quickly, which although it shouldn't be broadcast as such, does act as a constant stimulant.

With a small paintbrush detail the model even more and superimpose new strokes which enrich the earlier work, so that the flowers in the lower part of the bouquet take on more importance, this resulting in an amalgam of superimposed strokes which have also been worked with in an energetic and impulsive style (fig. 184).

With regards to this point the artist believes that it is opportune to leave the painting as it is, and if the work needs it, to add a few touches after a few days when it is dry. This is a practice which I recommend, because all recently painted work needs to be left for two or three days. After this period come back to it and if you believe it necessary, add some new touches. However, if you believe that it does not need any modifications sign it and consider it finished. It is worthwhile highlighting this fact, so that the still life does not loose the freshness and spontaneity derived from the earlier work.

183

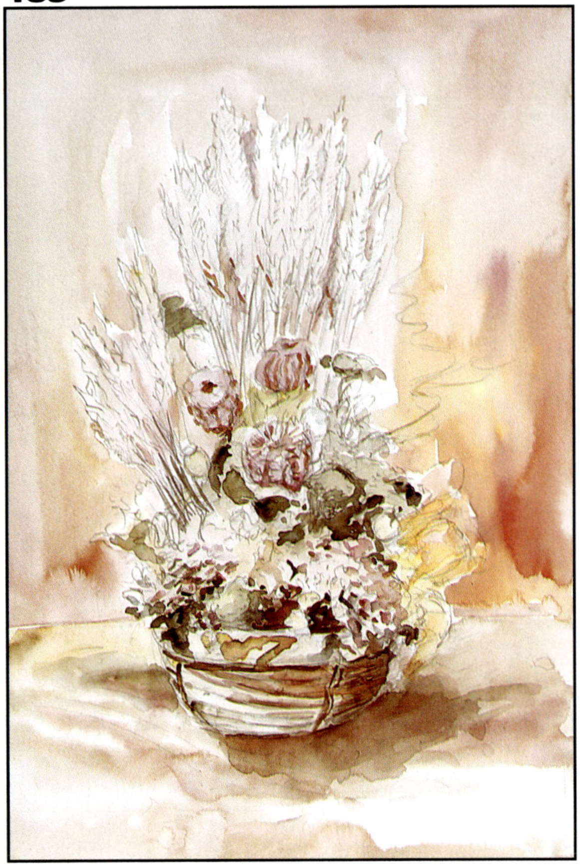

184

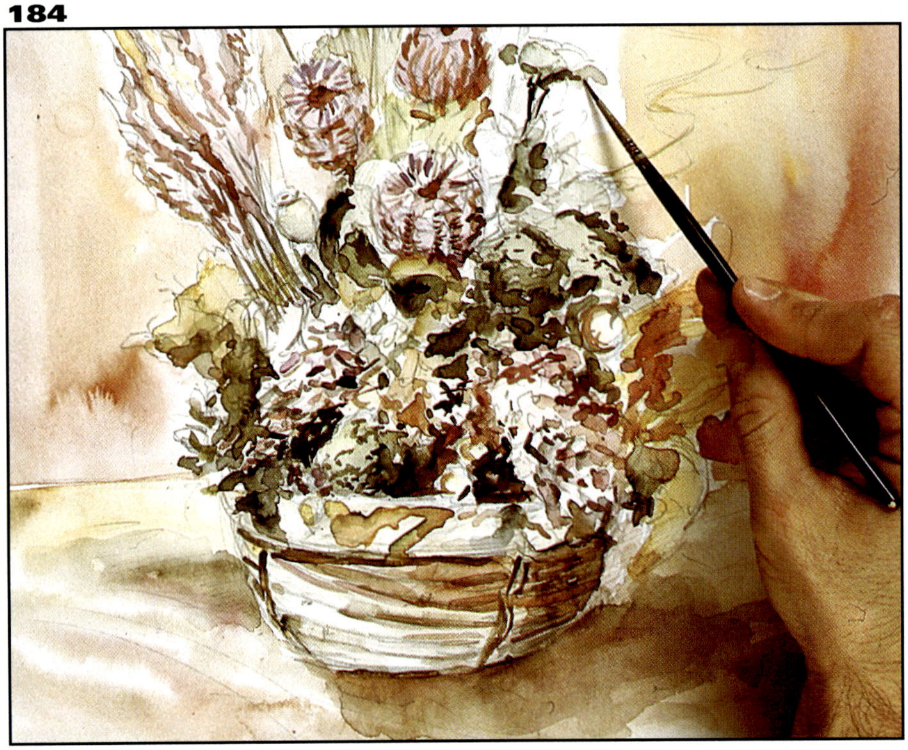

Fig. 183. Now the color has been added to nearly all of the paper's surface. Until this moment the artist has suggested working across all of the painting, leaving the shading work for a later stage when it will be worked on area by area.

Fig. 184. Continue painting with what appear to be loose, unworried strokes, which in addition to stressing the profiles, will also give volume to each of the elements in the bouquet.

TIPS

- All of the painting needs to be worked on at the same time, it is necessary to see the work as a whole, without concentrating on one small part. If the latter is done it can make us lose sight of the overall painting.
- The fact that you began to paint the background before the model will save you some worries. Establishing the tone for the larger areas of the painting right from the beginning means that you do not run the type of risks which exist when the individual elements of the still life are painted first. This is due to the fact that a color is lighter or darker as a result of the surrounding background color.

185

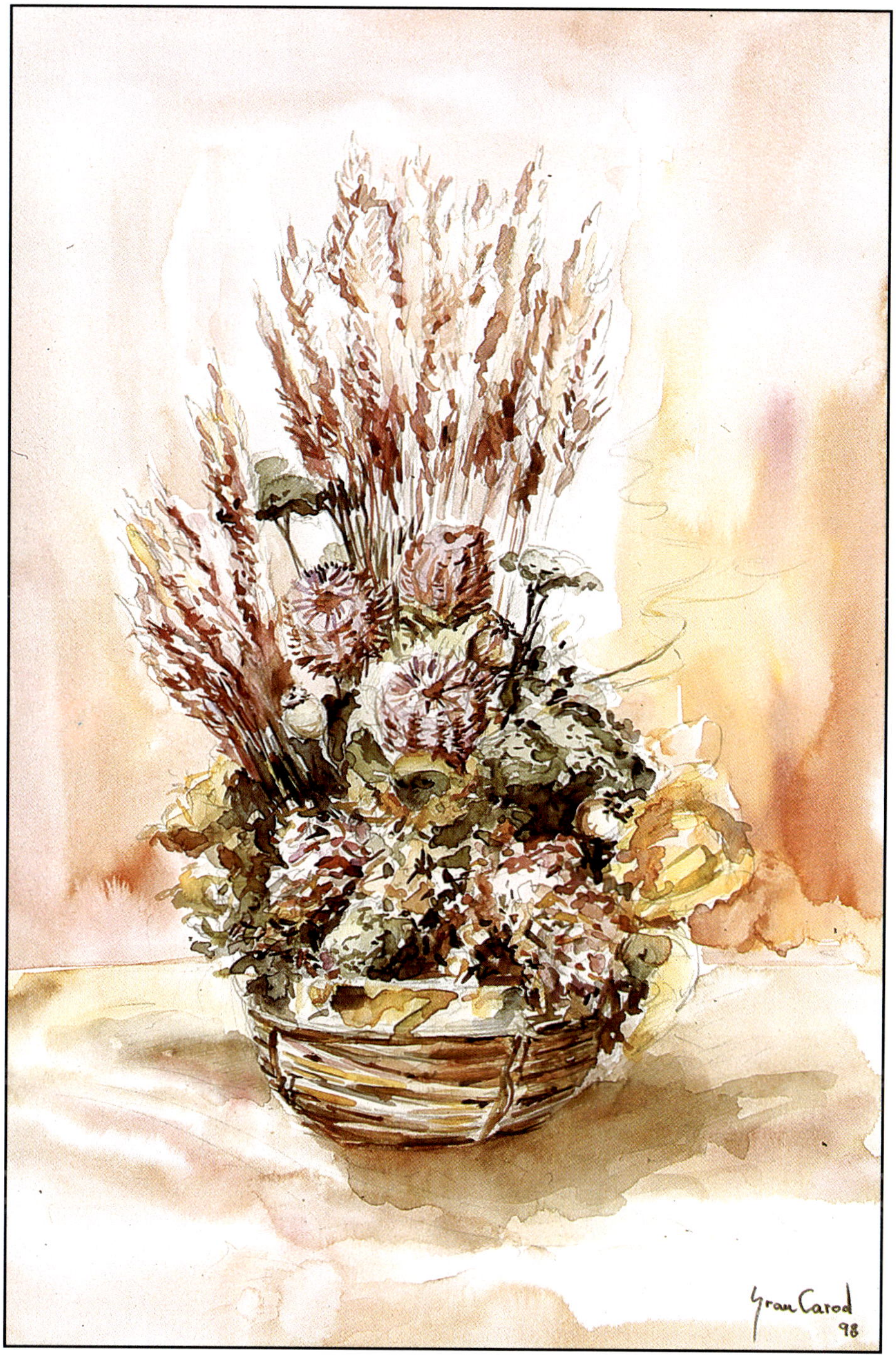

Studying the process and the final result, as shown in the finished painting in figure 185, will allow you to see that this work has been carried out by using somewhat specific brushstrokes. First of all, virtually right from the beginning you have been using a small paintbrush, this allowing the work on the painting to be more expressive, superimposing one stroke on top of the other. This has been done with the construction of small brushstrokes, in a broken up way, such that when the viewer contemplates the work from an adequate distance the colors come together, producing gradations and richness in texture. Secondly, at no time have you worked with pure colors and only a few times with clean colors, in other words with colors directly from the tablet . As a result of this the colors ended up being harmonized with something of an orange colored bias. Consider these two factors mentioned: the expression and control of the brushstrokes and the harmonic range of the colors.

Fig. 185. After some days you will have to confront the work with the aim of incorporating some new details and modifications.

Painting a Flowerpot of Oleanders

Josep Antoni Domingo is an artist well disposed to explain to us how interesting his creative process can be, based on the technique of painting with velaturas (glazes). I advise that to do this exercise you take the outline-guide no.4 and follow the instructions.

The subject you are going to paint has already been indicated in the title, this being a flowerpot of oleanders, a shrub which flowers in August and which is made up of small flowers. You are working with one of the most popular garden plants in the Mediterranean.

Josep Antoni does not normally work with a pencil sketch because it is enough for him to take a small brush and highlight some areas of interest which can be used as a reference for constructing the painting. If you like, you can do the same, but of course if you feel more confident working with a sketch do not hesitate to do so, and do not forget that you can also use the previously mentioned outline-guide no.4. Highlight the background with a little ultramarine blue; the flowerpot with sienna; the vegetation, or the plant leaves with cadmium & emerald green and finally working on the group of flowers with magenta diluted in water (fig. 186).

Continue defining the different areas with small strokes of different colors and with some life. Apply a second coat of pink color in the flower groups adorning the plant and with short brushstrokes paint the long leaves so characteristic of oleanders an emerald green color. With the sienna-ochre color you have used for the plantpot, although somewhat more intense, draw the horizontal lines adorning it (fig. 187).

Continue being careful with the paper surface. First of all, add another transparent ultra-marine blue & cadmium green wash to the background. With a somewhat more intense ultra-marine blue and a mixture of emerald green natural umber earth begin to darken the shadowy spaces between the leaves of the plant (fig. 188). As you can see you are using colors which are virtually the same as those recently taken from the tube, in a pure state, without any changes or mixtures. As you are going through the drawing, notice how the

186

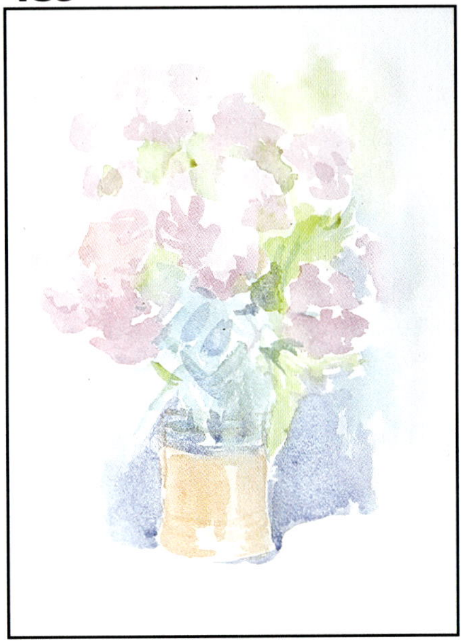

187

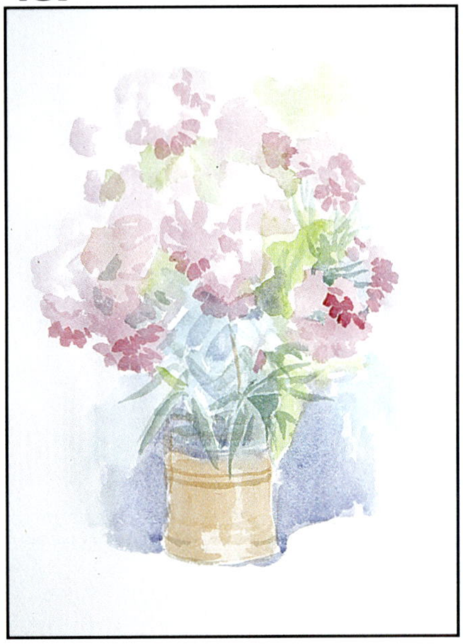

Fig.186. Josep Antoni Domingo does not use a pencil, but draws the first parts by painting with colors, using his paintbrush. You can do the same , make a sketch in pencil or use the outline-guide no. 4.
Fig. 187. The second wash complements the earlier one and gives more of a picture of what the final motif is going to be.
Fig. 188. Using emerald green with a little ultra-marine blue and natural umber gives the model more volume.

188

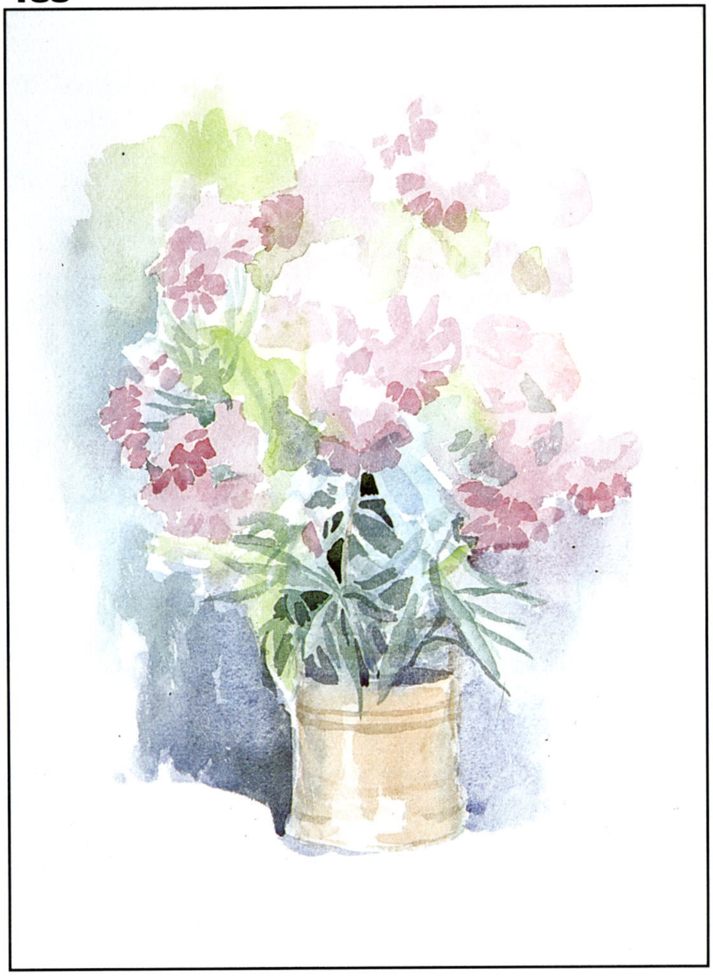

initial colors are being transformed by continually superimposing glazes, giving way to new colors and a rich harmonization of the work.

Gradually, the indeterminate paint-work done in the earlier stages is making more and more sense, this meaning that the harmonization of diluted washes, which produced a certain kind of abstract painting, are being transformed. It is becoming a work where you can begin to guess the shape of the flowers, the different textures, the shadows, and to a great extent the volume. Notice, for example, that the position of the fully composed flowers have now been set and that some areas now have two or three different features (fig. 189).

Now is the moment to detail the leaves, beginning with those to be found in the upper part of the plant. Apply cadmium green, ultra-marine blue and blister green brushstrokes to these and model them in such a way that the leaves are presented in an elongated style. Do not hesitate to work on the volume by adding two other different colors and paint the hollows with more intense colors so that the profile of the foliage stands out better. If you compare this with the earlier state you will see how the intensity of the background color has been progressively increased and darkened (fig. 190).

Now take a sponge and add the gre-enish paint which appears at the left side of the foreground. With a small paintbrush work on the colors and shapes of the flowers in more detail, in such a way that the bouquet has more contrast. If you look closely at the chromatic range of the flowers you will see that ultra-marine blue has been has been included in the most shaded areas and vermilion in the lightest, and in this way greater variation is achieved. To paint flowers which have a kind of monochrome appearance does not mean that other colors cannot be used in the mixture. A better way, which I recommend, would be to always use what you can, this often being necessary to prevent the painting from becoming monotonous, monochromatic and boring (fig. 191, on the next page).

189

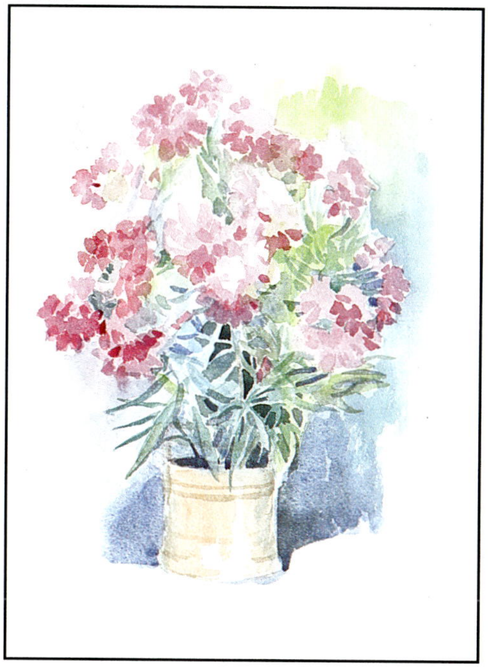

Fig. 189. Continue painting new glazes on top of the previous colors which have now dried, adding more substance to the initial flat wash.

Fig. 190. By showing the contrasts and painting with intense colors the spaces between the leaves take on a greater sensation of volume.

190

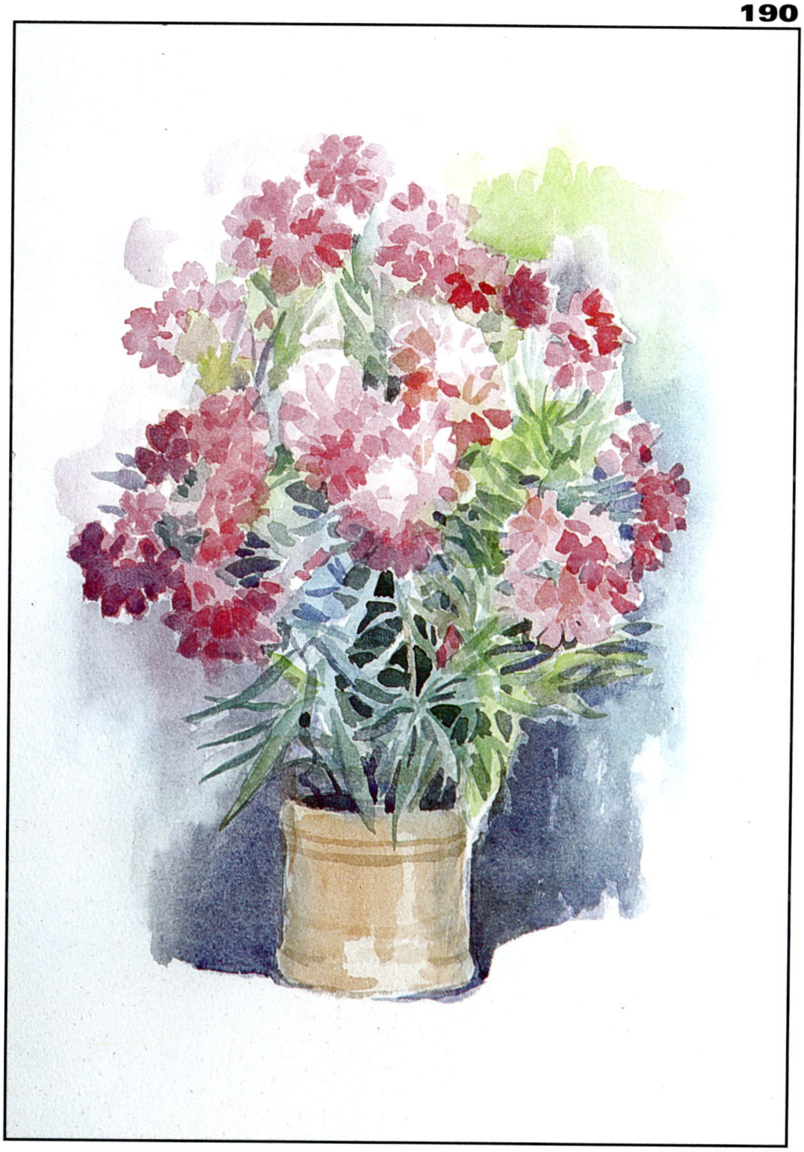

Continue detailing the grass on the left in the foreground and darken the flowerpot with ochre colored washes, leaving a small vertical band which will help us to represent the reflection and where the earlier wash can breathe. With a small paintbrush lightly bring out the lines of the floor tiles the flowerpot is sitting on. In this way you are introducing a spatial reference to the work, albeit it in a fairly minimum sense.

Now go back and work on the irregular forms of the plant. See how it is gradually gaining in intensity and contrast. Given that the colors have been intensified in the rest of the work, changes must also be made to the flowers (fig. 192). As you can see working with the velatura technique does not mean that we are dealing with the painting of fragments, or working *alla prima* with the vegetation, but instead means that we are doing it all at the same time and allowing the work to emerge in the same way as a photograph when it is being developed.

As you can see the technique used means taking full advantage of the transparency of the watercolor to put across the brightness of the subject. The details which are going to be added next are those which will finish off the work. Look at how the flowerpot has been given an effect, using a delicate Prussian blue wash, which increases the sense of volume. The floor has also had more work done to it, having been given different touches, but without the modification of any of the basic structures (fig. 193, next page). In this last stage alternate the washes with heavier colors, until the watercolor is left with a much heavier feel.

The work you have done possibly includes colors which are much dirtier and not as bright as the original painted by Josep Antoni Domingo. This may be due to not having let the previous washes dry properly before

191

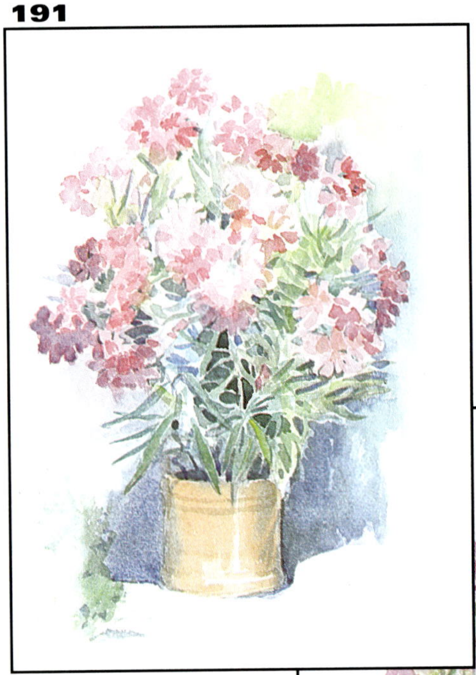

192

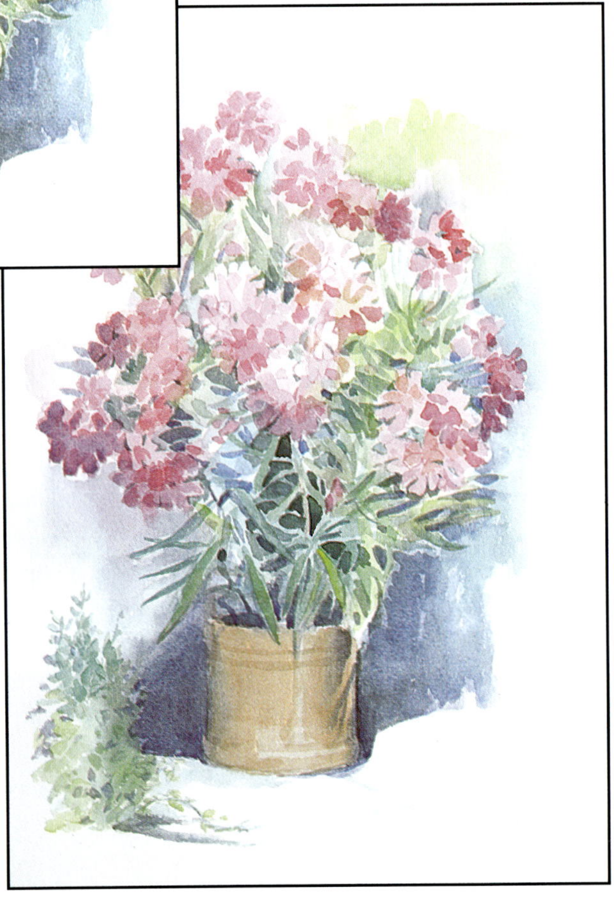

Fig. 191. Stain the area to the left with a sponge soaked in emerald green.

Fig. 192. Now is the moment to obtain textures, detailing the form of the vegetation with thicker paint and a small paintbrush.

TIPS

- Paint the branches of the shrub, preferably with a no.6 round paintbrush. This is a very flexible brush with very long strands and a fine point. It works very well because it allows fast hand movements.
- If you like you can paint false shadows and contrasts to enhance the shapes of the model.
- To accentuate textural effects open up white areas in the vegetation with a cutter.

193

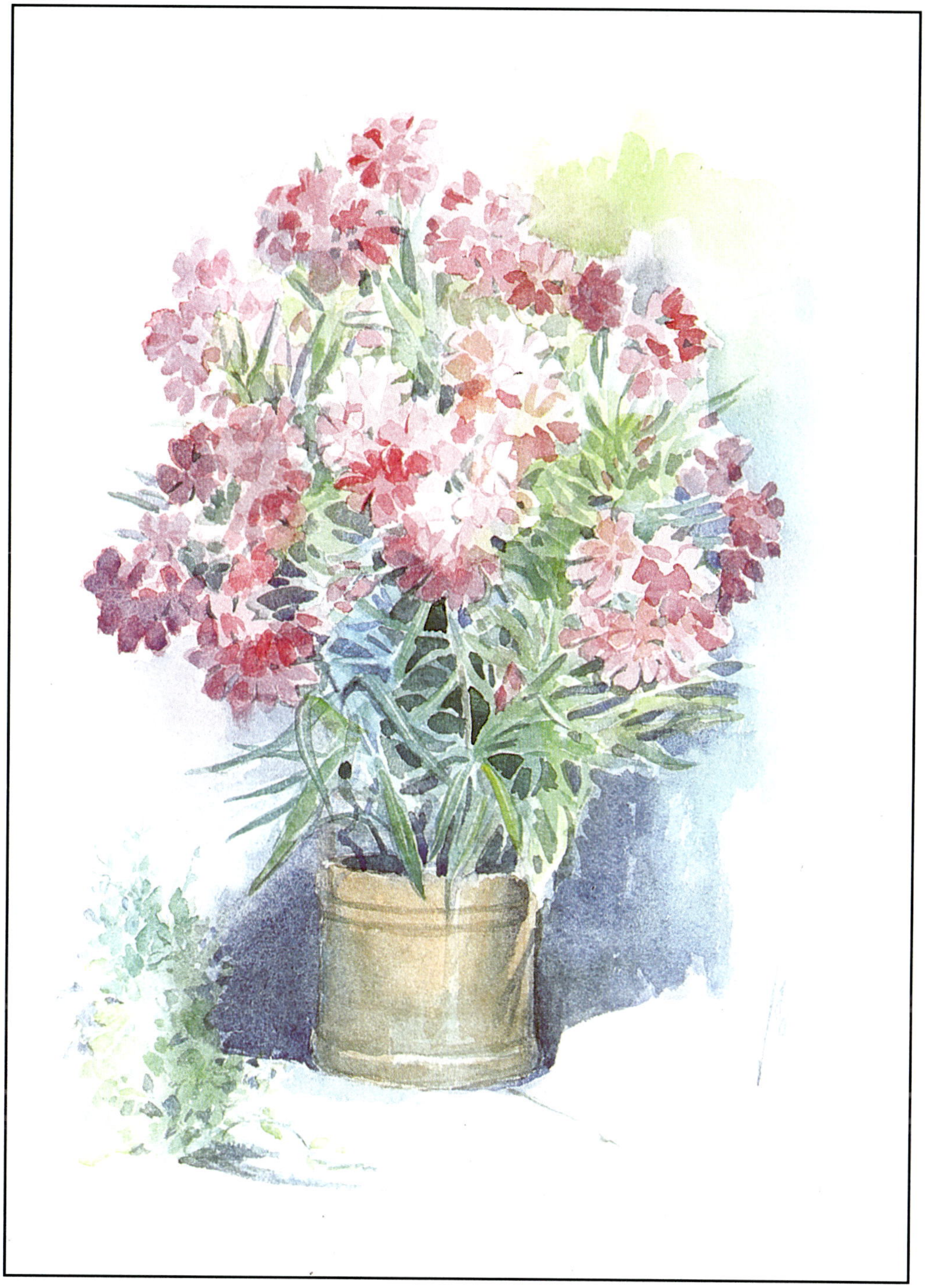

applying the next glaze and as a result the colors have mixed together. The painting must be worked on through a series of washes, and it is not until the end of the work that a heavier type of paint is used to define the textures and details. It is also probable that on examining the finished work you will realize that the subject looks as if it has taken on too much. This may be due to the fact that you have put too many details into the plant, the flowers and the floor tiles, or it may be that you have wanted to show too many things in the painting. The drawn, white floor is what we call a relief area, a space which every work needs for spectators to have a more relaxed view of the subject. Because of this, the way in which the artist has done the painting is worthy of respect. The painting should be worked on with washes without the introduction of an excessive number of brushstrokes, colors or textures.

Fig. 193. Here we have the finished painting. A complete lesson on watercolor painting using the technique of working with glazes and showing how to work with the painting as a whole.

Painting a Bunch of Roses with Only Two Colors

The artist and sculptor Francesc Mas is going to paint a bunch of roses with only two colors: permanent green and vermilion red. This is a good exercise to learn how to look closely at flowers, to understand their composition, their textures, as well as seeing the wide range of shades and colors which can be managed by mixing only the two colors mentioned. Look at the model. As you can see in figure 194, the subject being dealt with is a handful of roses with a neutral background.

Once the model has been carefully observed take a no. 2 pencil and begin outlining the motif in such a way that the slender form of the stems can be identified, as well as the concentric distribution of the petals (fig. 195). As you can see, the drawing is fairly precise and describes to perfection each one of the forms and profiles of the flowers, stems and leaves making up the bunch. But, if you prefer you can use the sketch which appears in the outline-guide no. 5.

After this initial setting up process, begin painting. With a pure vermilion red wash, very diluted in water, begin to highlight the flower petals. With regards to this point it is important to keep some white areas in the subject so that gradations can be painted later on, these giving the rose petals their shape. Do the same with the stems, but with permanent green. In this state the painting is reminiscent of Chinese watercolors, where the gestures of the brushstrokes and the spirit of the plant captured were more important than the fine details and realism (fig. 196).

Continue developing the initial sketched shapes with a tinted wash. With a second wash, somewhat more intense, represent the shapes of the petals in such a way that the contrasts between the parts which are lit and shaded can be distinguished. With a green transparent wash tint the background with the aim of highlighting the white parts more (fig. 197).

In this state the flowers and leaves

194

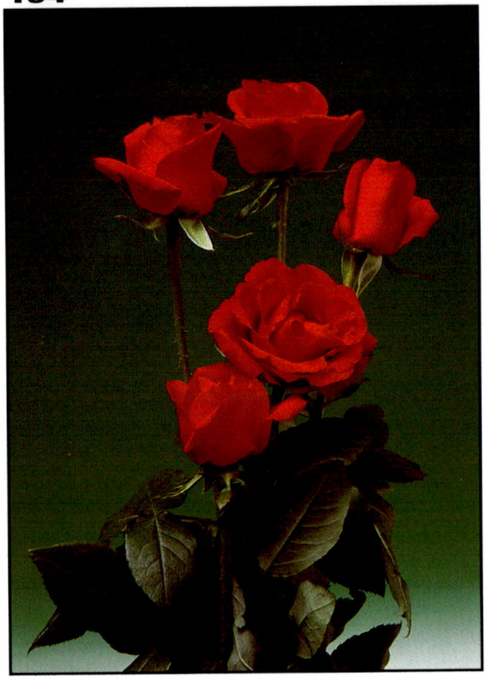

Fig. 194. Here we have the model which you are going to paint, a bunch of five garden roses with a neutral background.

195

Fig. 195. First of all, begin laying out the model with the aim of establishing the shapes and proportions.

196

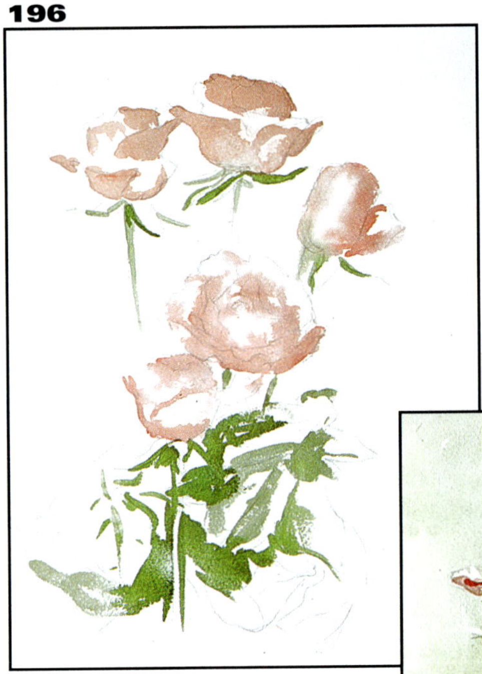

Fig. 196. Plants drawn in the studio do not give any problems with respect to movement, this being normally caused by the wind, but they do give problems of synthesis. When you are drawing a plant you must learn to see the structure at the expense of the details.

197

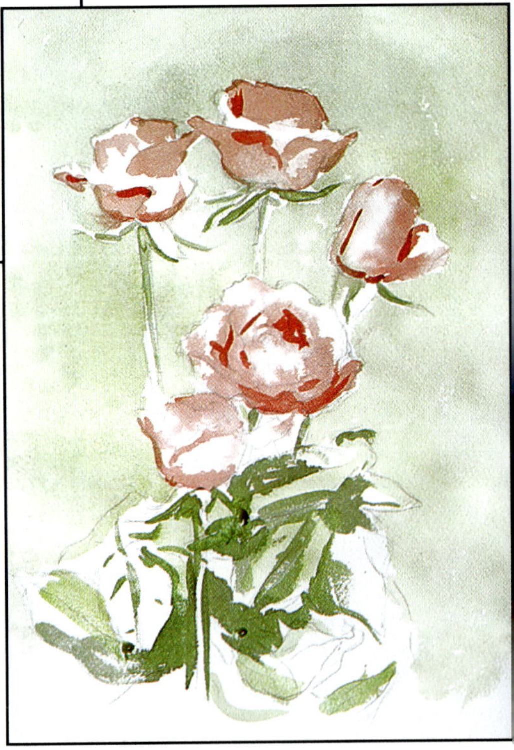

Fig. 197. Carry out a second wash as smoothly as possible, thinking carefully about each step and with the aim of not rushing or ruining the work.

present the first coating carried out with barely three tones. See how the flowers have been worked on a lot more than the rest of the painting. The greatest difficulties are with the roses because the contrasts are more marked in the shades of the leaves than in the flower petals. This means that they must be worked on with the greatest of care. You must think about each one of the steps you are going to take beforehand, because a mistake in the wash could mean ruining the work (fig. 198).

New transparent glazes have been carried out to cover the white of paper on the petals. This way of working with the painting makes it look similar to the developing of a photograph, with images gradually appearing stronger and stronger. With a somewhat more intense green now highlight the characteristic pointed form of the rose sepals (fig. 199).

Now work on the lower part of the leaves and each one of the stems. Model and intensify them through successive glazes, superimposing brushstrokes of the most intense green, obtained by adding a little red. At this point the group of leaves should now present darker shaded features than those of the flowers (fig. 200).

198

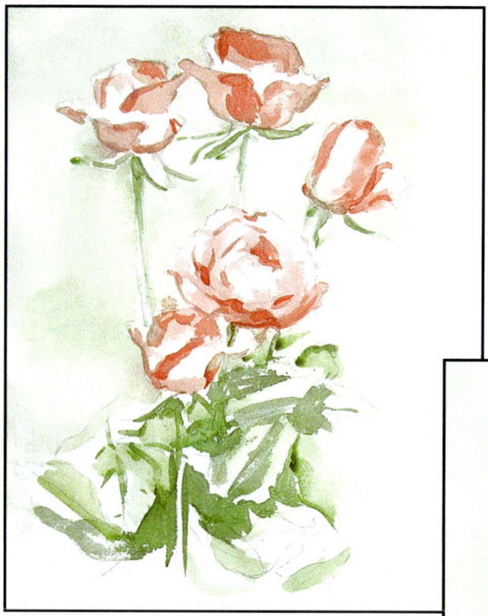

199

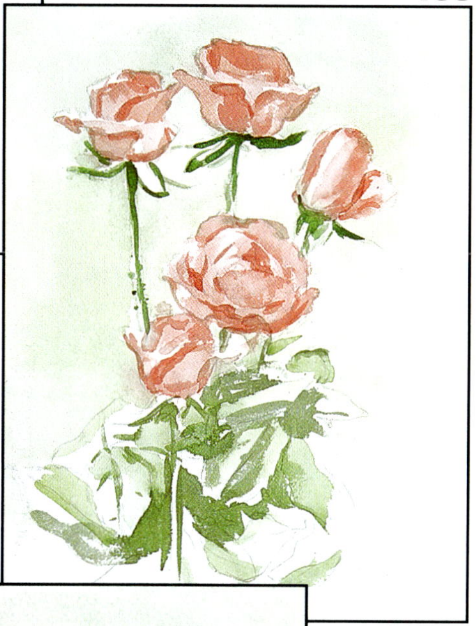

Fig. 198. Gradually, the successive application of glazes give the desired sensation of relief.
Fig. 199. Gradually, the white of the paper is giving way to the gradated shades which form the outline and volume of the bodies.

200

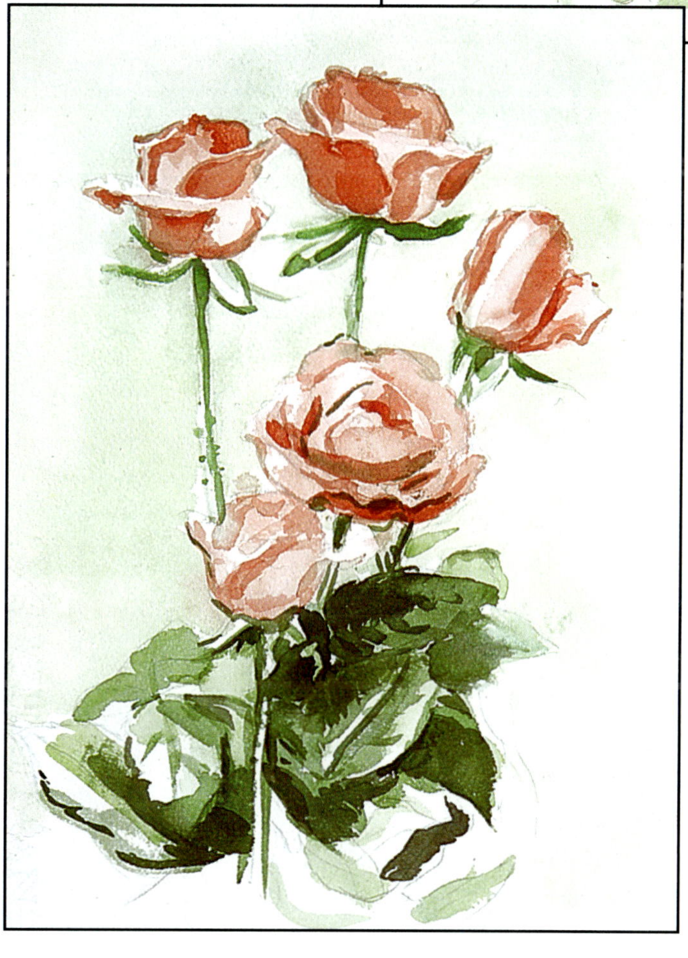

Fig. 200. Continue detailing more and more, above all intensifying the contrast between the light and darker parts of the flower petals.

Go back to the flowers, painting with short strokes, supporting the paint-brush and giving it small flicks. Use a fairly wide brush to paint the curved and gradated forms of each one of the rose petals (fig. 201). If you look at the flowers at some length, you will value the importance that gradation takes on to describe volumes. This means, the loss of color from a wash follows the direction of the strokes used in the body being represented. In other words, in the stem, the strokes appear to be longitudinal; in the flower petals the strokes show a concentric distribution; while in the sepals the direction of the strokes are more imprecise.
In some cases, owing to the greater intensity of the color vermilion in some parts of the petals, such as the rose in the center of the bunch, mix the vermilion red with a little permanent green to paint with a more intense and deeper color, in accordance with what you see in the model (fig. 202).

201

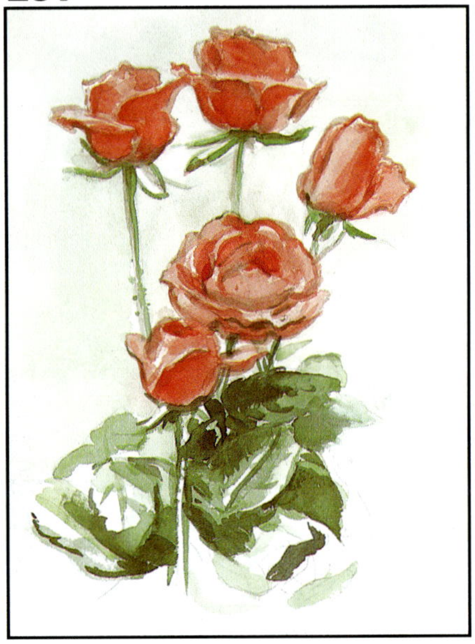

Fig. 201. If you compare this picture with the two previous ones you will see how the colors have gradually been added to and have grown, beginning weakly and progressively intensifying until reaching the stage of a well painted model.

TIPS

- If you are having difficulty in appreciating the contrasts between light and shadow, I advise that you half shut your eyes to greater appreciate the difference.
- In those areas where you want a more fluid outline or something more shaded off, use your finger to blend in the washes.
- Once in a while check the colors on a piece of paper kept at the side of the watercolor.

202

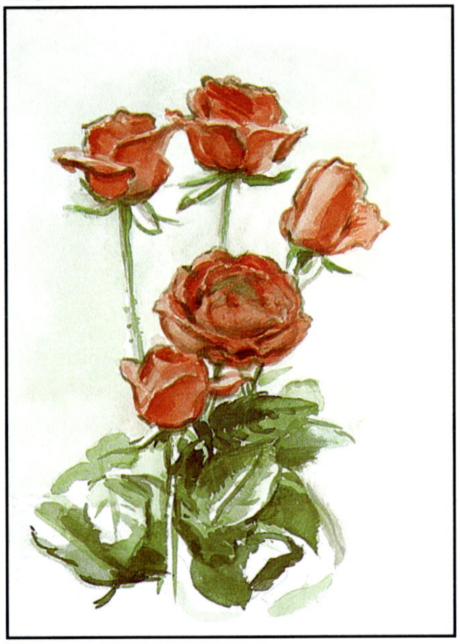

Fig. 202. As you can see considering the brush-strokes can also be a great help for modelling flowers. If you are capable of managing well painted strokes your painting will transmit a greater sense of volume.
Fig. 203. Darken the background with a more intense wash: the background incorporates washes to give greater textural variety to the subject.

203

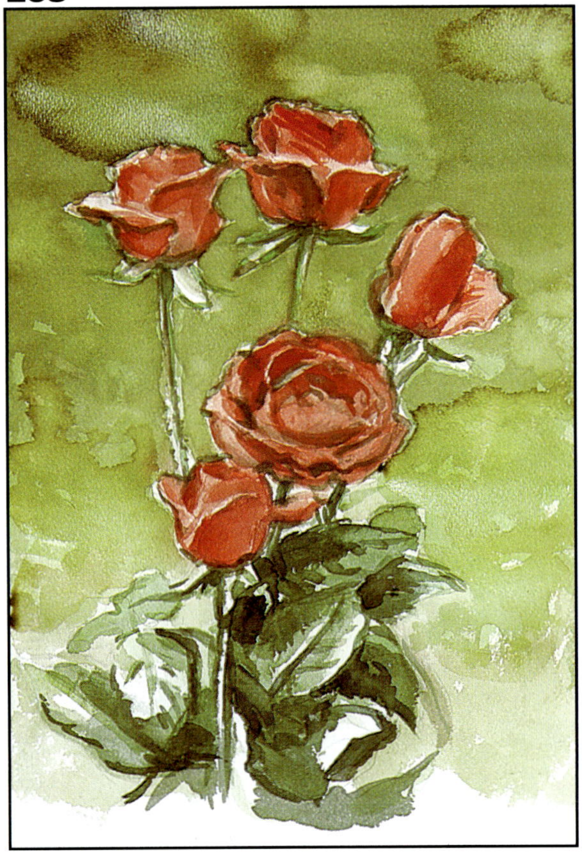

204

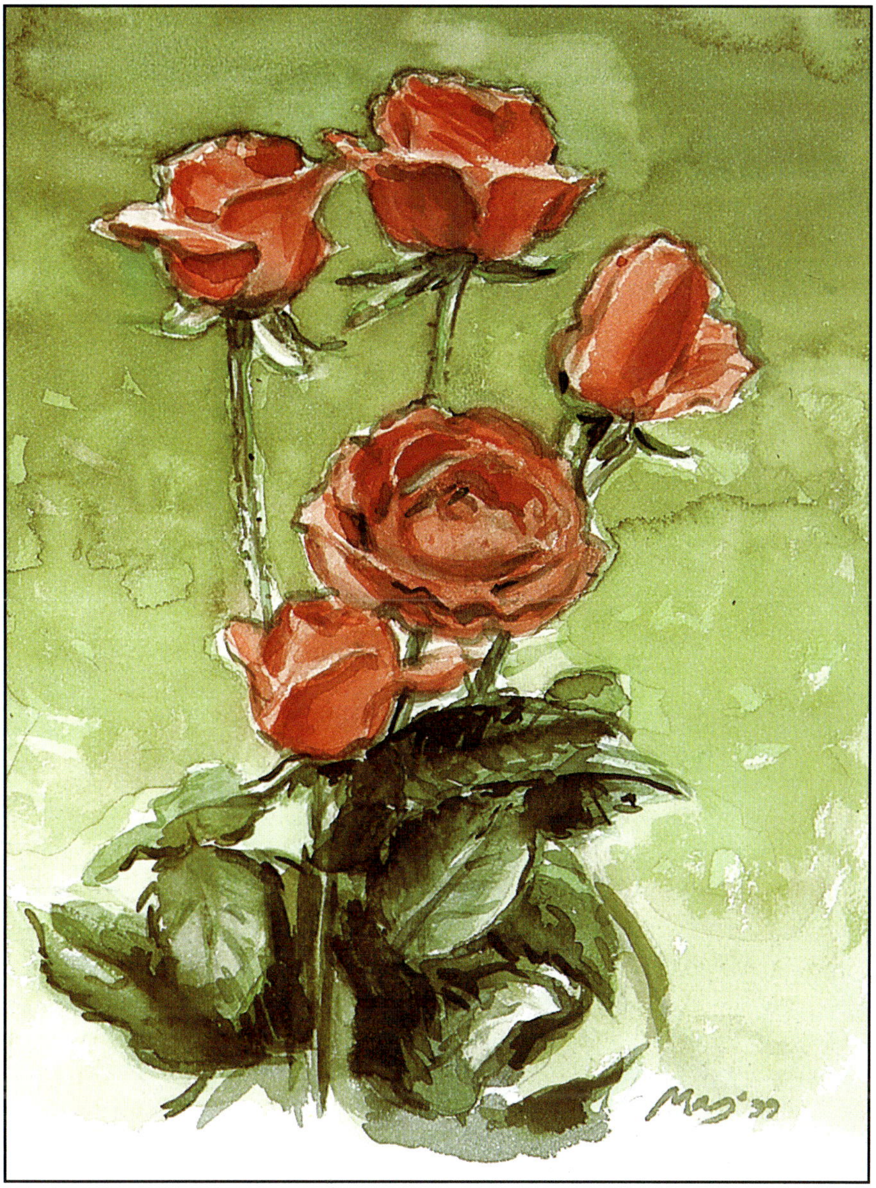

In this last stage first darken the background with a uniform wash, then allow small drops of water to fall onto the painting, these forming irregular stains which give the subject greater variety (fig. 203, previous page). Lightly darken the petals in some of the flowers gradate small parts in others.

Look at the final result with the addition of some details to the leaves and petals, where the dark color has been dampened, the color has been absorbed by a narrow paintbrush and the shades and colors of the roses in general have been intensified (fig. 204). The background color appears neutral, in other words monochrome. Do not try to detail it with a background made up of small cypress trees or garden plants which would appear blurred and vague behind the roses. It would be a mistake because in an analytical and precise piece of work such as this it is appropriate to have a neutral background. The great difficulty in doing this type of painting successfully comes from the fear of mixing colors in a way which might turn out to be inadequate. This can lead to the danger of leaving the stems and leaves too green and the rose petals too red, using shades that are too pure. The colors must be mixed without fear, they have to be deepened. In this case it is worth being mistaken for having done something to excess than to have fallen short, even though the colors may end up being darker than normal. Remember to treat this as an exercise and that we are trying to learn, and often learning means that it is necessary to make mistakes.

Fig. 204. The work is now finished and the result is this: a good watercolor painted with only two colors.

Painting a Recently Cut Bouquet

Now Josep Antoni Domingo is going to show us his technique for painting a beautiful floral composition consisting of a basket with a varied assortment of flowers, adorned with ferns and stalks of oats. The recently cut flowers are presented in a bouquet sitting on a chair, in a beautiful corner of a garden. The scene presents a complementary element which is very much a part of summer, a hat which has been hung from the trunk of one of the two trees appearing in the middle distance. For this exercise you should take the outline-guide no. 6.

Sketch without too many details, the shape of the chair and the tree trunks in the center with a sienna color and medium marten brush. Next extend a second application using burnt umber to the tree trunks and tint the position of the bouquet of flowers with cadmium green (fig. 205). As you can see the artist has done away with any references to pencils, but in any case if you believe it to be necessary make a sketch in pencil, although endeavouring not to press on it too much. It is important to try and make sure that the pencil line is not visible when the watercolor is finished. The outline-guide no. 6 can of course also be used. Continue filling out the spaces on the paper, always limiting the colors to flat tones. Paint the background with emerald green mixed with cadmium yellow and apply a transparent turquoise blue wash to the tree trunks. For the moment do not paint the area corresponding to the bouquet of flowers (fig. 206).

When the outline has been finished begin painting the different tonal areas and mix the colors according to what you see. Treat each tonal area as if it is an independent and flat figure. In this sense paint the hat hung to the right with a little cadmium yellow and ochre. Paint the shadow with a transparent ochre wash tinted with violet and project it in a descending direction, as if the sun is in a high position. With a medium paintbrush paint the flowers in a somewhat disordered way, without going into details on the flowers' forms. Use enough paint with successive colors: violets, Sienas, cadmium green and carmine (fig. 207).

205

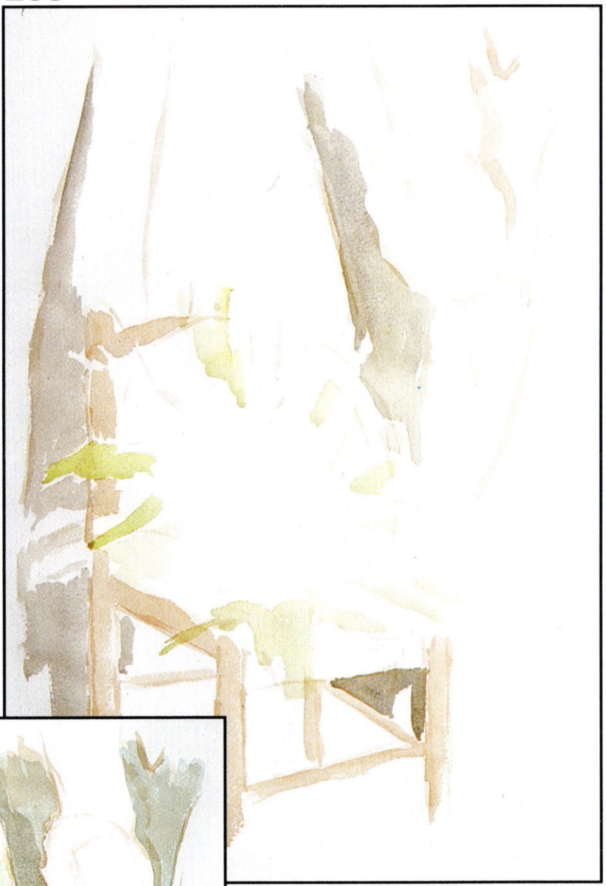

206

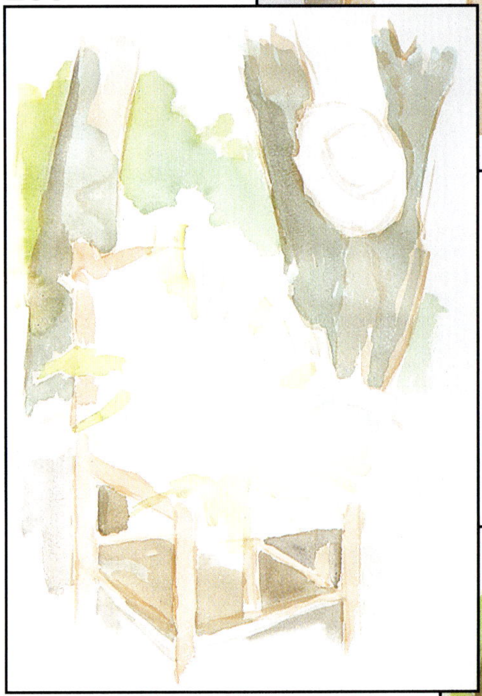

207

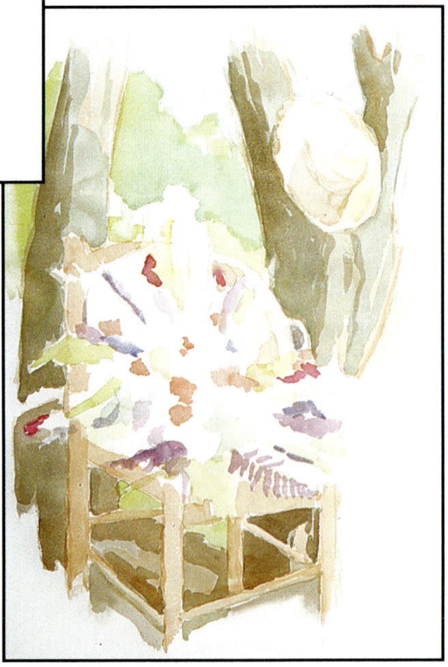

Fig. 205. Begin sketching with a paintbrush, or if you prefer, use the pencil sketch which can be found in the outline-guide no. 6.
Fig. 206. In the initial stages the motif is reduced to a few basic washes, although each one of these is divided into various shades and tones.

Fig. 207. In principle, if it is possible, you should endeavour to limit the colors that you are going to use on the flowers to only two or three different shades.

Through fine and transparent glazes, continue darkening the colors in the background and that of the chair. With diluted emerald green finish highlighting the vegetation in the background and using cadmium green with a little natural umber paint the darker upper part of the image (fig. 208).

Leave the earlier washes to dry and continue adding new glazes slowly and progressively darkening the subject. With an ultramarine blue wash paint the shadows of the tree trunks and the base of the chair. With cadmium green and a little lemon yellow add another wash to the vegetation in the background (fig. 209). Now take a small paintbrush and simulate the tree trunk texture with broken lines which should be applied longitudinally with ultramarine blue.

To make the work more attractive, concentrate on darkening and strengthening the overall painting. Intensify the background colors in a way which defines the foreground and continue adding more color to improve the flowers and leaves, adding stronger tones where it is necessary (fig. 210). Apply purplish and dark colors to the vegetation surrounding the trunks to give an effect of greater depth and to allow contrasts without which the well lit part of the trunk would not be emphasized.

208

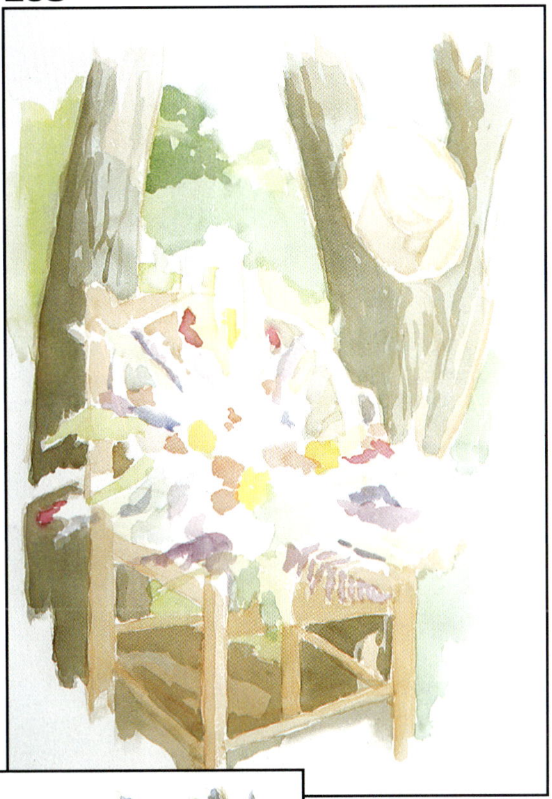

Fig. 208. When you are painting large areas with "flat" colors, dilute the paint before applying them, to give a fluid and transparent consistency.

209

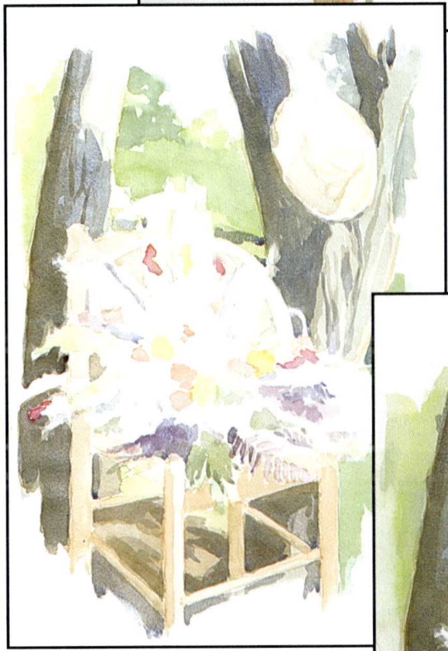

210

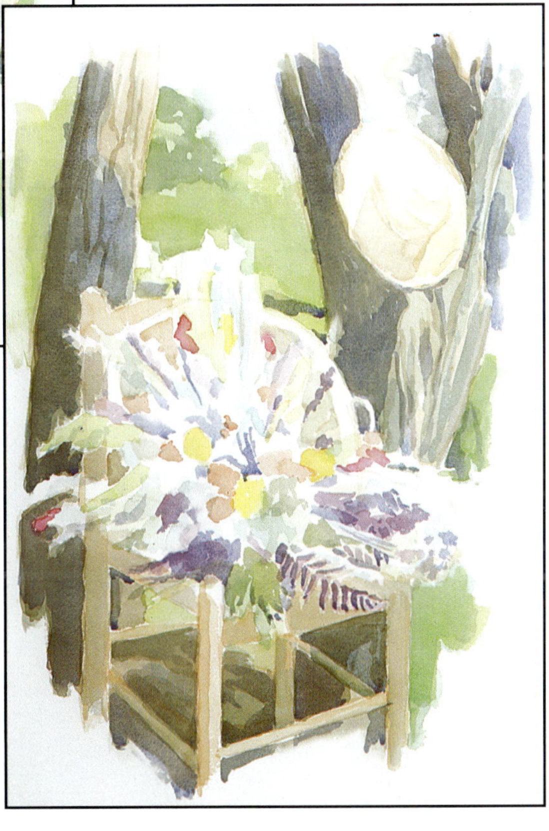

Fig. 209. Once the main areas have been painted, carefully work on the smallest and most textured areas such as the rough tree trunk surfaces.

Fig. 210. To cover all of the work finish painting the background, then any part of the paper where there are still white spaces, including that occupied by the flowers.

Now is the moment to work on the leaves and petals with greater detail. Apply the colors, one next to the another so that they create their own mutual influence on each other, then superimpose the washes to give the work some new qualities (fig. 211). Treat the greenery of the leaves in the same way, with the aim of capturing their characteristics of light and transparency. Now the moment has arrived to distinguish the different tonal areas of the flowers by means of color forms. For the darker areas use the same color, but more heavily filled. For areas with an intermediate tone add enough transparent glazes in the same color or another which is similar. Do the same with the green colored leaves (fig. 212). Use chrome green with a drop of red for the dark areas. If dark and clear tones are used for each color it can create the sensation of three dimensional space on a flat surface. With the whole of the painting showing more intense tones, you should also add new washes to the hat so that it appears more defined, painting the ribbon with a medium intensity purplish wash. The finished painting is an example of a determined pictorial focus, using small glazes and small semi-transparent additions of color to constitute a realist picture. This work is an example of the flexibility of the procedure of painting with glazes, and of the skill necessary to get as much out of it as possible. When you are

TIPS

- Work on mixing the appropriate tone for each area, comparing it with the other tones on the palette, before applying it to the canvas.
- Keep the forms as simple as possible and do not be tempted to create shadows by using the method of painting darker colors on wet.
- Work quickly, applying the paint with the greatest possible transparency.

211

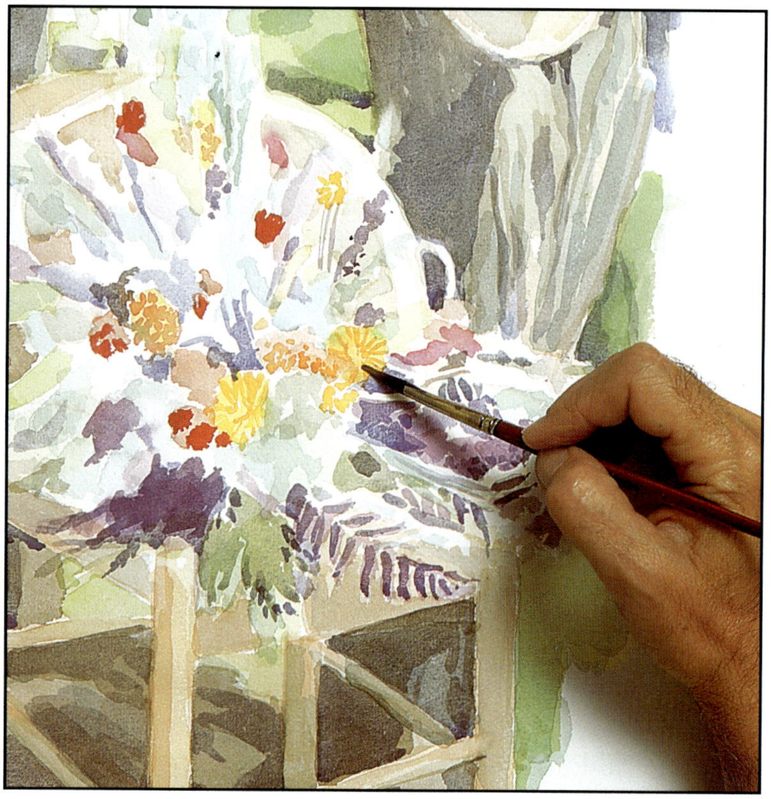

212

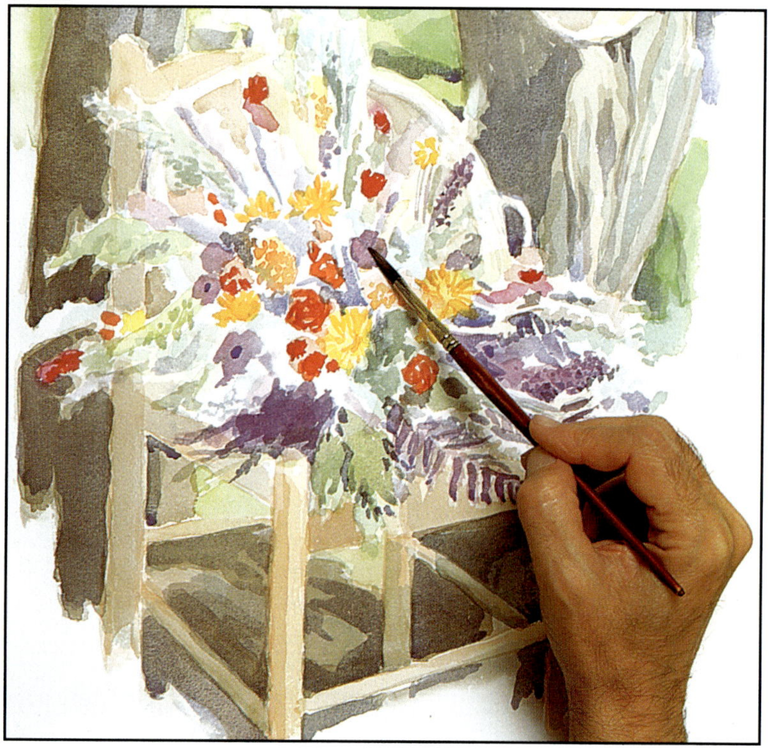

Fig. 211. Use a medium sized paintbrush to paint around the flowers and leaves and a small marten brush for the minuscule details.
Fig. 212. You should apply a combination of dark and light shades to both the flowers and leaves.

213

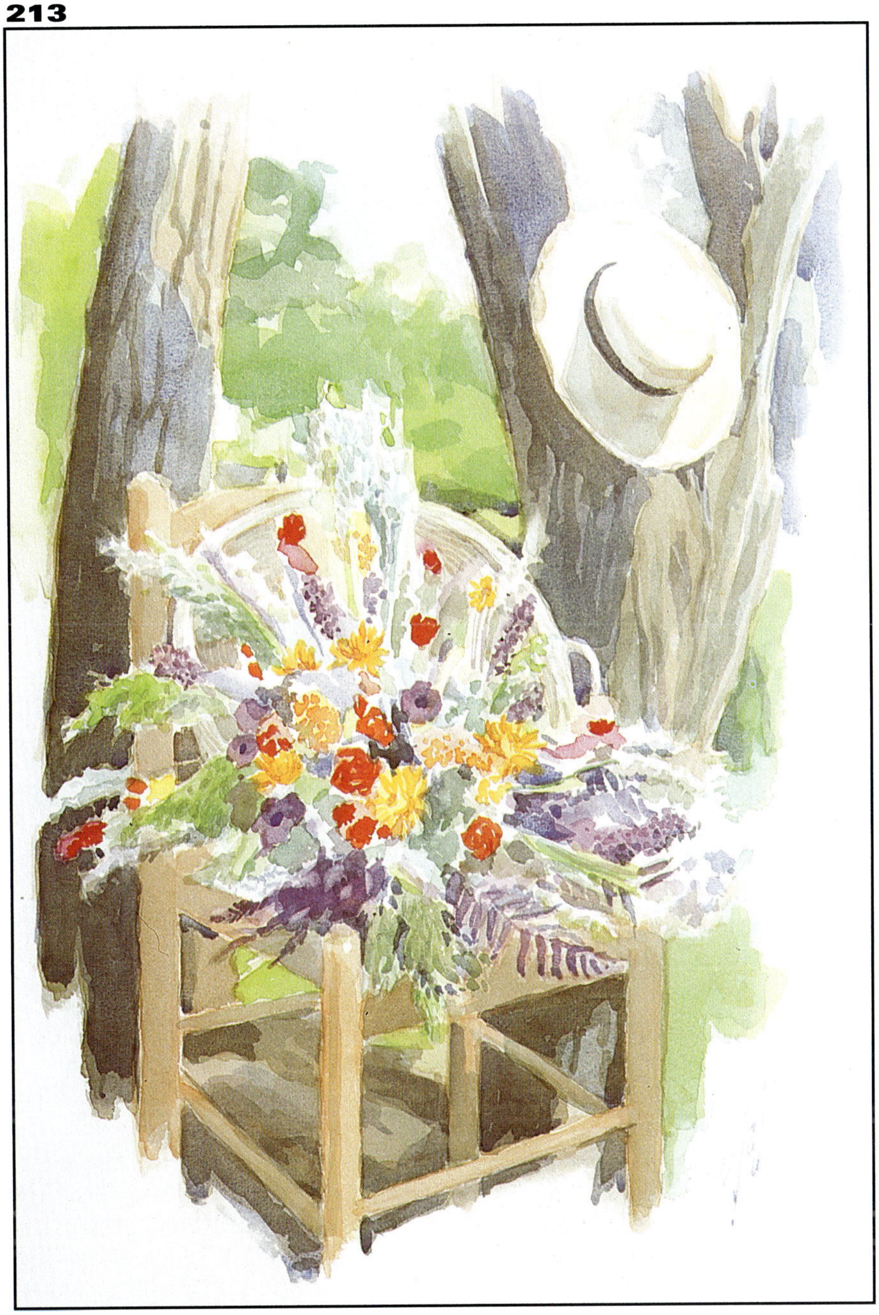

working with the glazing technique, you will surely be tempted to superimpose the colors and mix them. This will come from closely looking at the painting, with the lines between the different glazes appearing too well defined and the washes flat and monochrome. Do not be mistaken. Do not try to blend colors to make the work more realistic. Let the process follow its course and paint according to what has been indicated. You will see that as you move away from the painting the colors come together and achieve the desired effect (fig. 213). You will possibly have noticed that the washes you have done give a different watercolor in appearance to that painted by the artist. The appearance is the result of the type of paper used and the quality of the watercolors themselves. As such, for example, painting on paper with little substance means that the washes extend with great speed and little control, while those carried out on absorbent paper, with more substance, take on a smooth and mixed aspect when dry. Always leave earlier washes to dry and do not work on wet, because working on dry paper gives a sharper and fresher effect. There are also some artists who consider this to be a very safe method.

Fig. 213. This is the finished painting. To achieve a good reproduction it is necessary to study the existing relationships between colors, because shades and tones are altered by what surrounds them.

Painting Flowers in a Creative Style

You are going to finish the book with a more imaginative painting. Miguel Olivares is going to paint flowers creatively because once in a while it can be useful to try out other painting styles. In this way the workings and different characteristics of various methods and techniques can be learned, and if you decide that this way is not the one which could be most adapted to your style of painting, you will discover that you have acquired some techniques and that you have incorporated then in your normal style. If you never change the system you run the risk of becoming monotonous and boring. This time the artist has used a tempera, a painting which is derived from watercolors, offering a more opaque and dense appearance.

As is normal to see in the paintings of Miguel Olivares he begins with the background color, which in this case is an irregular ochre wash. You should do the same.

Take a pencil and begin drawing the composition. Here the artist has used his imagination to develop the drawing (fig. 214). As you can see, this early drawing of the bunch of flowers has little to do with an academic governed representation, being much more inspired by the naivety and purity of children's drawings. Take some time to bring out the forms of the flowers, the leaves and the vase, although in a way which is more synthetic (fig. 215).

Take a medium paintbrush and apply the first washes. Paint the leaves hanging from the lower part of the bunch with a fluid Payne gray and emerald green wash and the center of the flowers with burnt umber (fig. 216). A *gouache* is equally valid to carry out diluted and semi-transparent washes, these having a smooth and velvety texture when dry. Take a decorative piece of paper, like the kind used for wrapping presents, and after cutting it into a rectangular shape, stick it over the space destined for the vase in the *collage* style (fig. 217, next page). This will give the work a more colorful finish and introduce graphic variety to the mixture decorated with pieces and touches of opaque color. Continue sticking new pieces on the canvas. Cut pieces of yellow paper from a magazine to represent the petal corolla of the sunflowers.

214

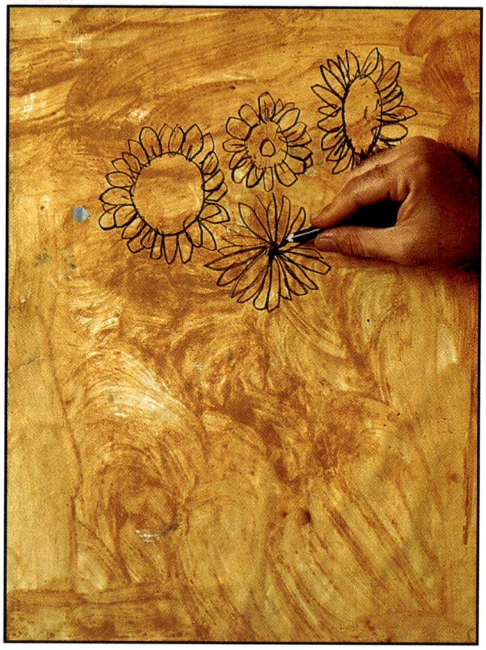

Fig. 214. With a pencil draw the model with linear strokes and with a resolution which is not too detailed. It should have a naive appearance, reminding us of children's drawings.

215

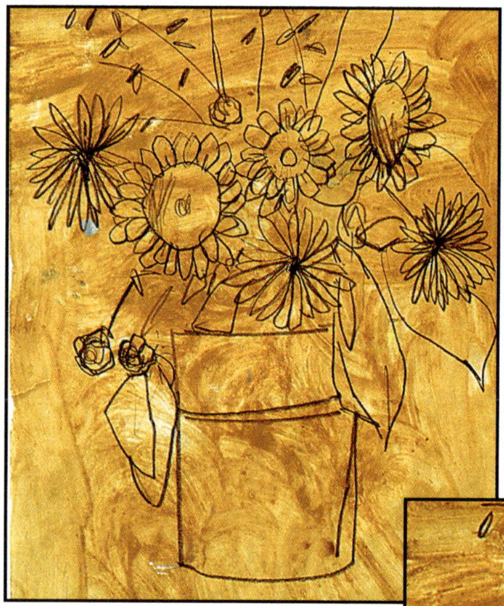

Fig. 215. As you can see, the sketch shows a certain lack of concern in avoiding academic rules and is part of a style which is much more modern and creative.

216

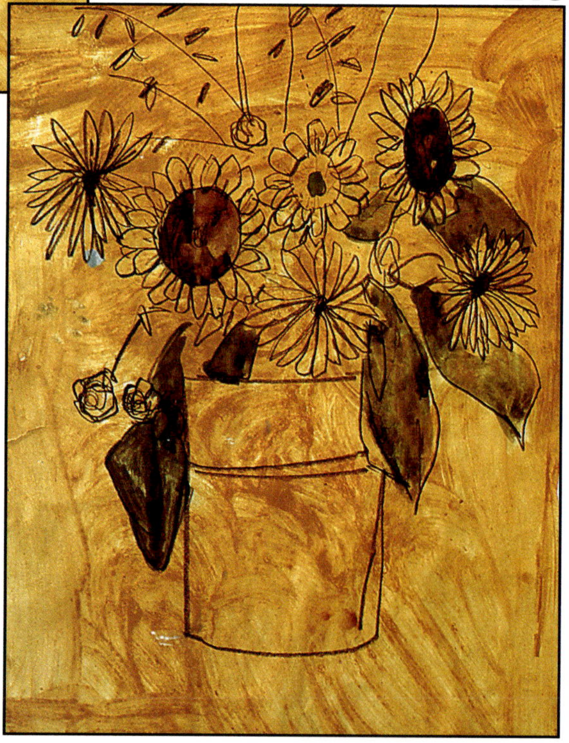

Fig. 216. Gouache colors can be modified by adding water, which creates similar washes to those created by watercolors.

Now, again take the medium sized paintbrush and paint the center of the anemones with pink colored opaque washes and the roses with an intense red color. *Gouache* is a type of opaque painting for which, in theory, clear colors can be applied on top of dark colors, including the covering of pencil marks (fig. 218).
Finish painting the clear colors for the anemones, which from the previous stage appear next to the sunflowers as visual and light centers of the still life. Also, accentuate the cadmium green leaves surrounding the flowers which, because of the contrast, will give the group of flowers greater relevance and volume. Miguel Olivares declares that eagerness for perfectionism can be extremely boring, not only for the person who is painting, but also for the viewer.
The shadow projected over the flat surface by the vase (fig. 219) finally gives the relief necessary for this composition. Having achieved the final result of this exercise, I would like to conclude the book by wishing that you too will be creative, and not be stuck in what can be strictly academic painting. Practice in the same way as Miguel Olivares has, trying to look for new points of view, new processes and new ways of representing the amazing world of flowers.

217

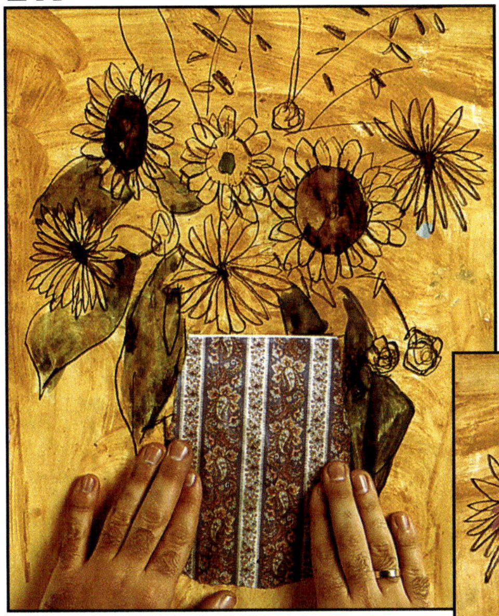

Fig. 217. Combine the tempera painting technique with a collage substituting the volume of the vase with a decorative paper.

218

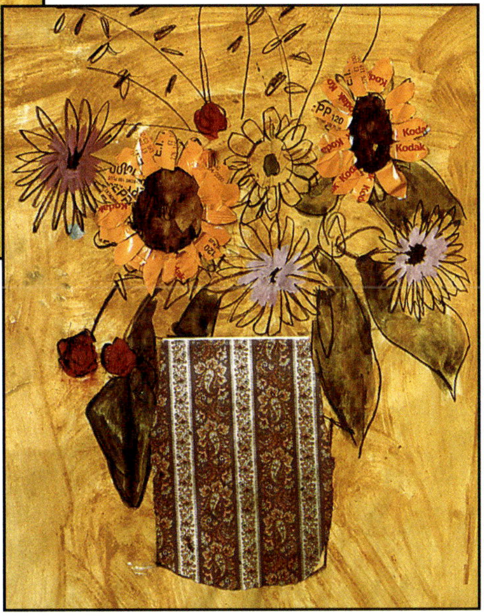

Fig. 218. Cut out yellow paper from different magazines, with the aim of these representing the sunflowers' petals.

219

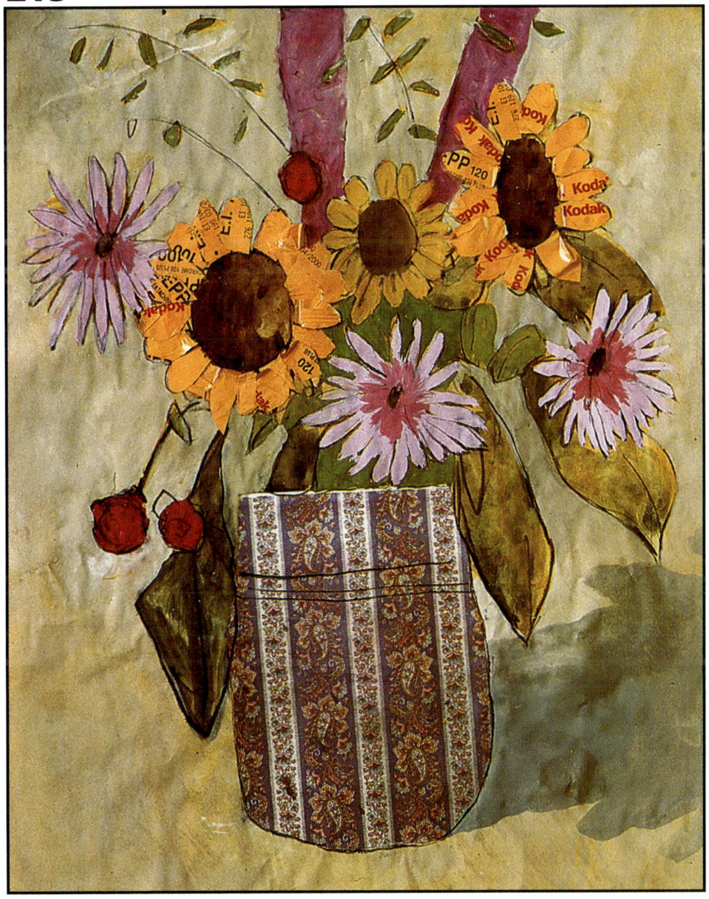

Fig. 219. This is the finished work of Miguel Olivares. He has not stopped to detail the forms of the still life, in fact he has done the complete opposite, creating a work with bright, attractive and decorative colors. It is a creative exercise which I recommend.

TIPS

- Avoid light paper because the film which makes up a gouache painting is thicker than that of a watercolor and can be broken if it is used on somewhat weak surfaces.
- If the *gouache* is applied when it is dry and thick it can completely cover a color, however this is not so recommendable, because it could consequently produce a broken picture surface .
- Leave previous layers to completely dry before applying the next one.

Glossary

A

Agglutinating agent. A substance which is mixed with powdered pigment to form a pictorial medium

Alla Prima. A technique of direct painting which can be summarized as painting in only one session. It means painting quickly and without going back over the paint.

Arabic gum. Acacia resin which is used to agglutinate watercolor and *gouache* paintings.

B

Blending. A procedure which consists of blending or smoothing the outlines or areas of contact between two colors so that they form a light gradation.

C

Chiaroscuro. Rembrandt is the great master of chiaroscuro. In his work the forms and colors of areas which are covered in the most intense of shadows are still visible. In his books on the teaching of drawing and painting J.M. Parramón has always defined this as "the art of painting light in shade".

Colour (local). A body's own color, when this is not altered by shadows and reflections.

Colour (tonal). The color offered by the shadow of bodies.

Composition. This describes the disposition of different elements to come together in a work in the most harmonious and balanced way possible. All in all , this involves composing and choosing the best conditions for the harmony and equilibrium needed in a drawing or painting.

Covering power. The power of a color with respect to dominating other colors in the mixture or glaze.

Cutter. A sharp knife for cutting paper, consisting of a blade kept in a plastic sleave.

D

Direct, painting. A painting technique called *alla prima* in Italian, *au premier coup* in French or *a la primera* in Spanish. It is a technique which can be summarized as painting in only one session, in working quickly and without going back over the paint.

Draft. This is the name given to the stage prior to the sketch or execution of a drawing or painting, from which a later work can then be derived. The draft allows many studies to be carried out before the artist develops his idea and how he is going to develop and work with it.

F

Fixative. An aerosol used for spraying over drawings done in charcoal, chalk or soft pastels to avoid the pigment being detached from the surface of the paper.

G

Genre. The classification of pictorial techniques according to still lives, landscapes, figures, interiors etc.

Gradating. Reducing the strength of a tone, gradually moving from an intense tone to an area with a smoother one, in such a way that there are no harsh transitions between the two.

I

Impasto. A technique which consists of applying thick layers of color with the aim of creating a textured surface.

Induction of complements. This concerns the phenomenon derived from simultaneous contrasts where the following norm is worked to: "When modifying a predetermined color it will be sufficient to only change the background which surrounds it."

M

Medium. This is the liquid which pigments are suspended in, for example linseed oil used in oil paintings, or acrylic resin as used in acrylic paintings.

Modelling. Despite being associated with sculptures this can also be applied to drawings and paintings to designate shades by the application of distinct tones. The aim being to create the illusion of three dimensions.

O

Opacity. The capacity of a wash to cover another color. The opacity varies from one pigment to another.

P

Palette-case. A metal, plastic or ceramic case used for keeping or mixing the colors. Opening the case, there are holes in the lid which allow the mixing of colors. Metal or porcelain palettes are the most appropriate for certain types of paintings; those made of wood are good for oil paintings, and plastic for watercolors and anilines.

Patina. This describes natural effects as a result of time or exposure, generally referring to metallic surfaces.

Proportion. The relationship of a part with the whole of the drawing.

S

Sketch. A preliminary drawing which tries to express the basic structure of bodies through simple geometric forms (cubes, rectangles, prisms....). They are called boxes, as a kind of analogy.

Style. In sculpture, drawing and painting, this designates the manner in which something is done. As such it can refer to: excited, brusque, delicate, slow, fast..... All in all, the style defines each artists own special way of working.

Surface. The material used for drawing or painting on, such as a wooden board, canvass or sheet of paper.

T

Techniques, mixed. This designates the use of different pictorial procedures in the same painting or for working on a combination of surfaces.

Texture. Tactile and visual quality presented by the surface of a drawing or painting. This can be smooth, dimpled, rough, cracked and for all of them they refer to visible and tactile qualities.

Tone. This terminology has a musical origin, but when applied to painting refers to the vigour and relief of all the different parts of the work with respect to color and light.

Transparency. The way of applying paint in such a way that the light or color from a previous layer is allowed to filter through.

V

Velatura. A layer of transparent color (glaze) superimposed on another color which intensifies or modifies it.

Volume. The three dimensional effect of a model in the two dimensional space of a painting.

W

Warping. An undulation which the surface of the drawing paper suffers from as a result of soaking or wetting. This phenomenon is particularly apparent when the paper used is thin.

Washing. A style of drawing-painting which has been used since the Renaissance. It consists of a painting done with a color, generally sepia, diluted in water, although it can also consist of Chinese ink or aniline watercolors.

Wet, painting on. A technique which consists of painting on an area or layer recently dampened with water or which has been painted on and is still wet. The artist controls the level of moisture on the paper according to the effect he or she wants to create.

Acknowledgements

The author of this book would like to thank the following companies and people for their collaboration in the publication of this volume in the series *Techniques & Exercises.*
To Gabriel Martín Roig for his collaboration with the texts and in the general coordination of this book. To Antonio Oromí for his photographic work. To Vincenç Piera of the company Piera for his advice and orientation,with regards to materials and utensils used for drawing and painting. To Manel Ubeda of the company Novasis for his help in the editing and production of the photocompositions and photomechanics, and a very big thank you to the artists: Carlant, Bibiana Crespo, Josep Antoni Domingo, Manel Grau Carod, Ester Llaudet, Francesc Mas, Miguel Olivares and Oscar Sanchís for the paintings and step by step development.

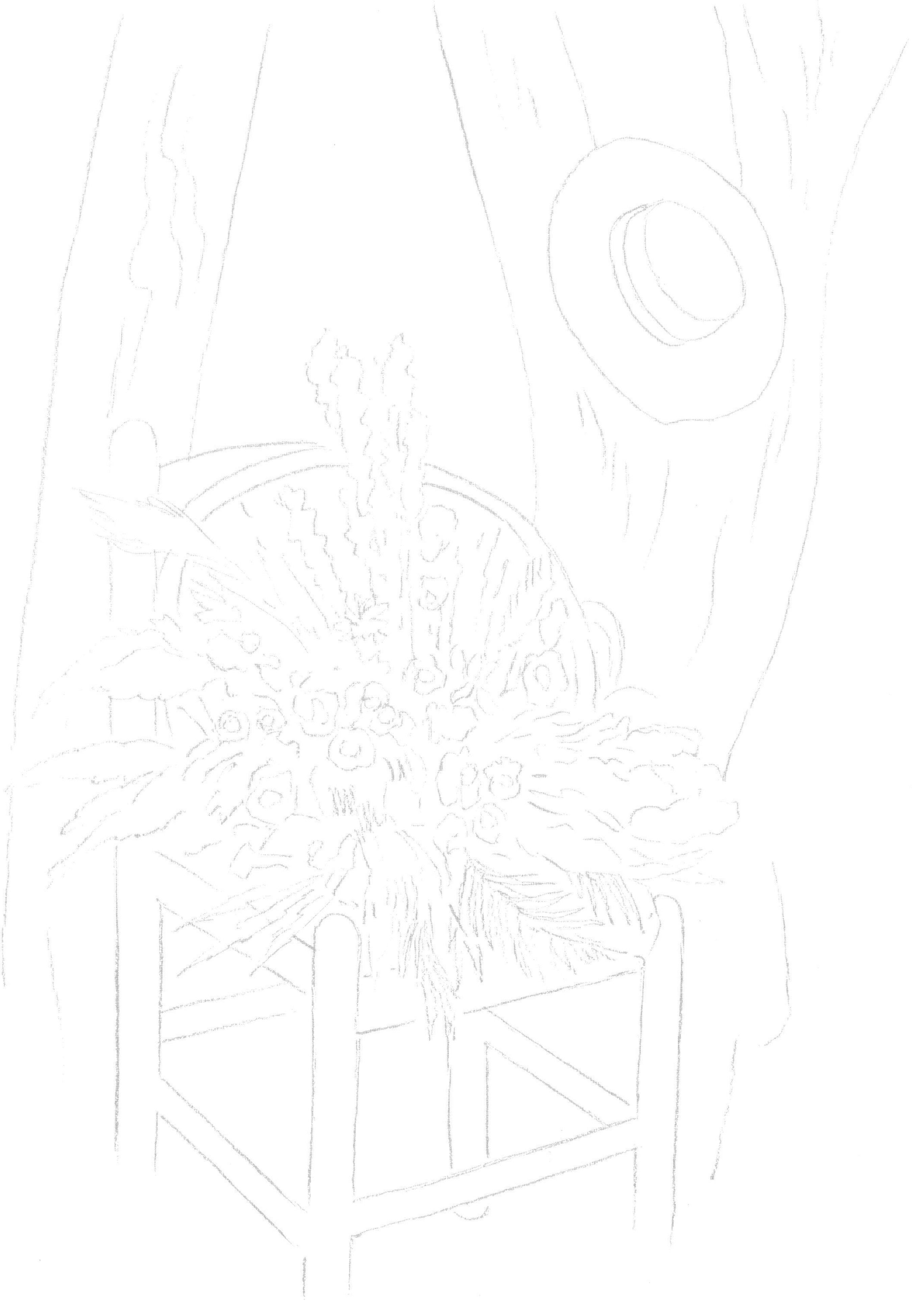